The Politics of U.S. Labor

D0869404

The Politics
of U.S. Labor

*From the Great Depression
to the New Deal*

David Milton

Monthly Review Press
New York and London

Library of Congress Cataloging in Publication Data

Milton, David, 1923–
   The politics of U.S. labor.
   Includes bibliographical references and index.
   1. Labor policy—United States—History—20th
century. 2. Trade-unions—United States—Political
activity—History—20th century. 3. United
States—Politics and government—1929–1933. 4. United
States—Politics and government—1933–1945. I. Title.
II. Title: Politics of US labor.
HD8072.M646   1982   322'.2'0973   80-8934
ISBN 0-85345-569-4
ISBN 0-85345-570-8 (pbk.)

Monthly Review Press
62 West 14th Street, New York, N.Y. 10011
47 The Cut, London SE1 8LL

Manufactured in the United States of America
10 9 8 7 6 5 4 3 2 1

In Memory of Frederick (Blackie) Myers
Soul of the National Maritime Union, CIO, 1936–1948
A true representative of the great American
revolt from below, he was that rare leader
who returned to the point of production.

Contents

Preface and Acknowledgments

There have been few who dared to predict the demise of that great stabilizer of capitalist society, the welfare state. Nevertheless, the Reagan counter-revolution of 1980 marks the end of the forty-year compromise between capital and labor in the United States; the welfare state is being reshaped into the warfare state. Military Keynesianism and a return to the business society of the 1920s is the proclaimed goal of the Republican administration in Washington. The repudiation of the great bargain that many scholars believed to have permanently ended class conflict in the United States is now taking place in today's headlines. For a generation of American workers who have never experienced the transforming thrust of a great social movement, it should prove useful to review the victories and limits of the great industrial class wars of the 1930s. The emergence of the Congress of Industrial Organizations (CIO) in the thirties marks the attempt by a generation of industrial workers to put their stamp on a whole society. The present generation of workers, in their own way and on their own terms, will have to fight that battle again.

I make no pretense that my research on the triangular struggle between capital, labor, and the state in the 1930s is based on startling new documentation for a new interpretation of a crucial epoch in the history of the United States. The field has been thoroughly covered by scholars of the New Deal and the labor movement. However, through the examination of the archives and extensive labor collections at Wayne State University, the Columbia University Oral History Collection, and the files of the Roosevelt administration at the Roosevelt Memorial Library at Hyde Park, I found corroboration of a thesis that

7

had been generated by my own fifteen years' experience, from 1942 to 1957, as a member and officer of the CIO unions, and from extensive reading of labor history. The record speaks for itself; the question is one of interpretation and analysis.

A great deal of American labor history is written from the standpoint of the winners. I have found the record of the losers more interesting. While the former consolidated alliances at the top, the latter built the CIO from the bottom up, only to be cast out of the house they had sacrificed so much to create. The half-century of struggle for industrial unionism in the United States constitutes a major contribution of radical social forces in checking the unrestrained prerogatives of corporate power.

I owe a great deal to the hundreds of industrial-union activists I knew during the years I worked in the maritime, steel, packing, and electrical industries. Many of the social actors described in this book I have known personally; others I came to know secondhand through co-workers and friends who knew them well.

Particular thanks are due to Franz Schurmann at the University of California, Berkeley, who consistently supported an ex-trade unionist and guided him through the academic maze. I am also grateful to Neil Smelser and Lawrence Levine at the same university for their constructive criticism of a project that was often at odds with their own skilled analyses of the U.S. historical process.

A close friend, Hugh Delacey, who was a left-wing member of the U.S. Congress at the end of World War II, lent me his extensive labor library and did not complain when I sat on it for a number of years. It has been gratifying to entrust the publication of my research to three active participants in the history it descibes—Jules Geller, Paul Sweezy, and Harry Magdoff. Susan Lowes and Karen Judd deserve the credit for taking a bulky and digressive manuscript and shaping it so that it might make sense to the general reader. Finally, I am indebted to the Louis M. Rabinowitz Foundation for the generous grant that made the research on this book possible.

—May 1, 1982

Introduction

The past thirty years have produced a voluminous and complex literature to explain the differences between the American and European labor movements. The ongoing debate centering on the question of "American exceptionalism" attempts to account for the fact that the United States as the most powerful capitalist nation in the world has never produced a permanent mass labor or socialist party. This book is designed to accomplish a much simpler task. It will sketch out the essence of the politics by which a great mass movement of industrial workers in the 1930s finally won recognition from the corporations and the state as an organized labor force. My purpose is both qualitatively different and more modest in scope than that of scholars who are devoting themselves to the complex task of uncovering the social consequences produced by the "cumulative impact of the series of historic [political] defeats suffered by the American working class."[1] I intend simply to widen the research on the actual politics pursued by radical labor during the New Deal years and lay the basis for further study of the implications and outcome of those politics.

In the final analysis, the industrial warfare of the thirties represented a process whereby legions of workers in the mass production industries won the right through coordinated struggle to bargain collectively and to form broad inclusive trade unions of their own choosing. The goal of independent organization for which the unskilled and semi-skilled workers of the United States had devoted more than half a century of sacrifice and bloodshed was finally achieved, but only by abandoning the historic and classic working-class objective of political and eco-

9

David Milton

nomic control over factories and the system of production. In other words, socialism and independent political action were traded off by the industrial working class for economic rights. This historical outcome was neither automatic nor inevitable; the outcome was decided by dispositions of power and the nature of specific political coalitions contending for supremacy.

Three characteristics distinguish the politics of American labor during the 1930s. The first is that the political coalition led by President Franklin Roosevelt, a coalition including organized labor, was successful in the effort to channel social revolt in one direction—legal recognition of the right to make economic demands. The second, supported by incontrovertible historical evidence, is that the industrial workers had to fight for everything they won; the mass struggle for industrial unionism in the 1930s represented a great deal more than a simple process of cooptation of the labor force by prescient corporate and political elites.

The third characteristic of the politics of the New Deal era was the emergence of a massive and predominantly Left-led social movement of the industrial working class, which resulted in the creation of the Congress of Industrial Organizations (CIO). The major thesis I will present in the chapters that follow is that unlike craft unionism, which represented the narrow guild interests of skilled workers, industrial unionism has always defined the Left in terms of working-class organization in the United States. The most radical leaders of the American working class, Eugene Debs, William Haywood, and William Z. Foster, for example, were as much identified with industrial unionism as they were with socialism. Given the extraordinary power of American capital, the most powerful corporate class in world history, industrial unionism has established the boundaries for class struggle in the United States.

In the 1930s, a rank-and-file social revolt of industrial workers, led by Communists, Trotskyists, Socialists, and Left-syndicalists, paved the way for the formation of independent industrial unions, which had been blocked by established political and economic forces of opposition for more than fifty years. Professional unionists identified with the old American Federation of Labor (AFL) structure, and even Roosevelt, had to move to the left before they were able to link up with the revolt from below. Once the minimum goals of this social uprising were achieved by the formal recognition of industrial unions and the fight for independent political organization had been relinquished, the stage was set for the purge of left-wing leaders who represented potential political as well as economic demands.

The great lacuna in the present upswing of historical analysis of the working class in the United States continues to be the pivotal epoch of the thirties. In the post-World War II era scholars of all persuasions came to believe that the American industrial system, buttressed by the welfare state, had resolved all or most of its economic and social problems. In particular, it was asserted that a combination of overseas expansion and Keynesian credit mechanisms had produced a passive and consumption-oriented working class, thus resolving the historic struggle between capital and labor. Reading the present back into the past, a number of revisionist historians advanced the novel thesis that U.S. corporate capital was itself the historical initiator and sponsor of the welfare state. According to this argument, the politics of the thirties could be ignored, since the New Deal was simply a continuation of the Progressive movement that flourished at the turn of the century and was fleshed out in the business society of the twenties. This thesis is not supported by the historical record.[2]

Robert Wiebe, in his extensive research on businessmen and the Progressive movement at the beginning of the century, argues that of the many programmatic reforms initiated by the Progressive movement, business supported only one—economic regulatory agencies: "In this area businessmen exercised their greatest influence on reform and laid their claim as progressive."[3] Even this reform was nullified during the twenties, when business captured control of the very agencies designed to regulate business. Moreover, as Wiebe states: "Progressive businessmen singularly lacked a grand social vision. Placing reform on a business basis, they represented—to borrow a phrase from Hofstadter—the hard side of progressivism."[4]

Business, both large and small, resolutely fought against all labor legislation, consistently took a stand against social insurance laws, opposed the formation of independent unions, and was generally against any measure to improve the lot of low-income Americans. From the dawn of the century until the present day, corporate power has not been in the forefront of the campaign for social welfare programs. Readers of *Fortune, Business Week,* and the *Wall Street Journal* are not inclined to respect social agencies of the state. Government regulation of business until the most recent times has constituted instead the promotion of business. In one recent study it was shown that 85 percent of corporate communications to government officials were in opposition to proposed legislation.[5] I will argue that business did indeed establish a society in its own image—the business society of the twenties. This was a society where business, rather than suffer regulation by the state, boasted of self-regulation; it is the social model corporations are attempting to reinstate in the 1980s.[6]

A central argument put forth in this book is that economism—the legitimate right to make material demands on the system—was firmly established in American society as the result of an intense and violent struggle by industrial workers against the largest corporations in the country. The settlement of the capital–labor struggle during the late thirties through mediation by the state, consolidated by a state-directed war economy, laid the foundations for a restructured capitalist system in the post-World War II era. While World War II and the rise of nationalism strengthened the central role of the state in American society, the value system or ideology of economism arising from the compromise of the capital–labor conflict provided the ground rules and social justification for the central role of the state in mediating social conflict. Economism was to become a universalized ethos, growing over time and putting its stamp on a whole society. It was an ethos that captured the public sector and its budget bureaucracies as well as the profit-propelled private sector of the economy. Collective bargaining and the cash nexus became the instruments for meting out shares of an ever increasing material product, a device seen as constantly guaranteeing new winners without producing new losers, since costs were passed on in an endless cycle.

The "great bargain" struck by capital, labor, and the state in the late thirties proved remarkably adaptable to the task of damping social conflict and was soon heralded as the stabilizer that would guarantee the balance of the American social order. Constant expansion of the economy in the postwar years was soon taken as a given by the architects of the new order of state-directed capitalism. The imperative of expansion could be met by a constant rise in productivity, the stimulus of war production, and the construction of empire. Since expansion had characterized every stage of capitalism it was assumed that when the system faltered in the 1930s all that was necessary was to implant the state as the new pacemaker to assure that the heart of the nation would beat in a measured, if ever faster, rhythm. By the 1950s growth was once more taken for granted and the newly proclaimed "postindustrial society" was viewed as self-perpetuating.

Economism was thus adopted as a worldview admirably suited to the incremental distribution of an ever expanding pie to social groups conditioned to substitute material demands for the right to power and decision-making. What was not seen until the decade of the 1970s was that a rampant materialism might itself undermine expansion and become a leading factor in the generation of new systemic crisis.

After forty years of consolidation, the New Deal solution to social conflict began to unravel under the relentless pressure of inflation and fiscal bankruptcy. The veil was lifted from a system that boasted all winners and no losers; social costs could no longer be passed on in an endless progression. It became evident that total demands on the system, particularly those by business and the military, exceeded the capacity to pay. The worldview of economism, its offspring consumerism, and its reinforcing network of values responsible for the socialization of the generation of the 1950s and 1960s faced a crisis of legitimacy. Social scientists warned of the new threat to the principles of authority, the end of the era of American exceptionalism and perhaps of the American dream of success as well.[7] However, having tamed labor, the corporate and political elites of the 1980s apparently believe that they can now repudiate the social bargain forged in the New Deal without re-creating the class conflict that bargain was designed to resolve. Only the future can reveal the social and political effects of the "great take-back" of the 1980s. What follows, then, is the retelling of the story of the industrial war of the 1930s, the politics among labor, capital, and the state to resolve that conflict, and the undoing of that social contract in our own time.

Without entering deeply into the thickets of the theoretical debate concerning the historical laws of capitalist development in the United States, I wish to remind the reader of the long-standing controversy concerning the nature of trade unions and to point out a few patterns characteristic of the trade union struggle in the United States.

Historically, social theorists have divided into two schools over the question of the revolutionary potential of trade unions. Marx and Engels were relatively optimistic about the role of trade unions as an integral part of the processes of social revolution. They saw trade unions as the basic primary class organization of workers and believed that when workers organize they are expressing themselves as a class. Once workers have formed their own organizations, Marx believed, they are revealing the first level of their own class consciousness. In the struggle to organize militant organizations of their own "a veritable civil war" develops—"all the elements necessary for a coming battle unite and develop. Once it has reached this point, association takes on a political character."[8] For both Marx and Engels, trade unions, particularly all-inclusive industrial unions of the unskilled, represented a school where the workers were trained in class struggle. Both Marx and Engels made a clear distinction between narrow craft unions of skilled workers, which fought for exclusive gains for small sections of the working class, and the industrial unions, which united the most oppressed unskilled workers into all-inclusive federations. Marx and Engels were the first socialists to understand and actively support the new trade unions. Marx criticized socialists in Europe who failed to support the real struggle carried on by workers themselves: "In order to rightly appreciate the value of strikes and combinations, we must not allow ourselves to be blinded by the apparent insignificance of their economical results, but hold, above all things, in view their moral and political consequences."[9]

Lenin, Trotsky, Robert Michels, and Max Weber laid the foundations for the pessimistic approach on the part of socialists and New Left
theorists concerning the potential of the trade union as a vehicle of the
transformation of capitalism. This view was that workers, primarily
because of a lack of education, could not develop socialist consciousness on their own and that trade unions were simply economic organizations with little or no potential for revolutionary ideology or
action. American academic specialists on American labor unions, such
as John Commons, Selig Perlman, and Clark Kerr, all supported the
pessimistic approach that trade unions do not facilitate the revolutionary transformation of capitalism and, in fact, are more likely to
inhibit that transformation.

My own view is that although it is clear that trade union demands
"can normally be accommodated within the framework of capitalism,
this is not universally the case," as Richard Hyman asserts.[10] The
potential always exists that trade unions might become political. The
present rulers of Poland understand precisely the significance of this
truth as they attempt to keep the Solidarity trade union movement from
transforming itself into a political movement. In the half-century of
violent action that culminated in the great industrial-union movement
of the 1930s, American workers were unable to pass beyond the first
stage of working-class consciousness. My research attempts to explain
the actual politics involved in the subordination of the CIO to the
Democratic Party. I wish to explain what actually happened rather than
what might have happened or should have happened.

Workers who have achieved a high degree of self-organization through
strong unions might either ally themselves with a labor party, as they
have done in Sweden, Great Britain, England, Italy, and France, or they
might become instrumental under certain conditions in forming the
base of a political party of their own. As Hyman argues, "In a pure form
. . . business unionism is inconceivable; not merely because it seems
improbable that workers' deprivations are ever experienced as exclusively economic, but also because the 'effort bargain' implicit in every
employment relationship is a persistent source of political conflict."[11]

Naturally, if an organized workers' revolt can be channeled within
the limits of pure economism, the revolt can be accommodated by the
system, and this is what happened in the United States during the 1930s.
However, it took an astute politician like Roosevelt to accomplish that
task, and this is why historians like Arthur Schlesinger, Jr., argue,
rightly or wrongly, that Roosevelt saved the system from revolution.
Trade unions, then, are nonrevolutionary organizations of the working
class that may or may not transcend their functional design. In the
1930s the great fear of corporate capital was that the CIO might give

birth to an independent political party. The outcome calmed the fear, but the fear was justified.

The political and economic results of the industrial warfare of the Great Depression and New Deal years were incorporated in a national social settlement whereby a number of material demands of the new industrial unions were legitimated in exchange for the renunciation by labor of its independent political power. In short, the crisis was resolved in a classic trade-off: the exchange of power for money.[12] It was a bargain granting the political sphere, then represented by the Roosevelt administration, the right to determine the policies and interests of the society as a whole. The separation of the polity and the economy was once more assured and the boundaries of labor action once more narrowed, but the specter of labor revolt and what it might accomplish still haunts a business society that has never given up its fear of an organized labor force.

The competition between craft unionism, representing the native-born and skilled workers, and industrial unionism, representing the interests of the great mass of unskilled workers in basic industry, in essence shaped the history of the labor movement in the United States. Engels was the first to note the differences in organization and ideology of these two categories of workers in England. Writing to his friend Sorge in New York, Engels stated that the movement of the unskilled workers to build their own type of economic organization was under way, but that it was "not directly socialist." He argued that "formally, the movement is first of all a trade-union movement, but utterly different from that of the *old* trade union; the skilled laborers, the labor aristocracy." The demands advanced by the unskilled workers were more far-reaching: "The eight-hour day, a general federation of all organizations, and complete solidarity." These immediate demands, Engels asserted, were "only provisional," and even though the workers "did not yet know toward what final goal they were working," they elected "as leaders only openly declared socialists."[13] This was a pattern of behavior and action to be followed by industrial workers in the United States for the next half-century. Unionized workers in the 1890s, during the great 1919 Steel Strike, and throughout the 1930s, although not ready to replace the system, did not want leaders who were excessively loyal to it.

Given the segmented character of the American workforce, noted by every serious commentator on the working class in the United States, solidarity was fully realized only during the periodic outbursts of collective action called forth by nationwide strikes and organizing drives. During these periods the heterogeneous workforce often transcended the divisions caused by ethnic, racial, religious, sexual, and occupational differences. When collective action subsided, the working class fell apart once again into its component parts. It is in this context that active struggle in the United States became the prerequisite for the realization of class unity. The greatest unity was achieved by the unskilled industrial workers when they repeatedly attempted to form industrial unions and, in Engels' words, raised the "general cry for the organization of all trade-unions into one brotherhood and for a direct struggle against capital."[14]

Class struggle in the United States took the form of a social movement led by unskilled labor in the struggle for an all-inclusive form of trade union organization. Despite all the forces acting against working-class solidarity, the future of labor lay in the hands of the American unskilled native and immigrant workers in the basic industries. When necessary, American workers have shown a consistent willingness to resort to what Hobsbawm has defined as "collective bargaining by riot."

In the American political context, it was the iron unity of business, the judiciary, and government that blocked the road to industrial unionism. Business hired strikebreakers, courts issued injunctions, and the federal government called out the troops to break the major strikes for recognition of workers' rights in the basic industries. Only in 1935 was the trinity broken, when first Roosevelt and then the Supreme Court broke with business and supported labor.

Corporation and financial elites always perceived the inherent threat to their own interests in a social movement involving hundreds of thousands, perhaps millions, of the unorganized workers in the basic industries. There was no guarantee that these new mass organizations could be contained within "job conscious" and "wage conscious" channels. Every such movement included the possibility that the workers might raise the issue of control and management of industry. This fear, shared by both political and economic elites, generated the attempt to brand industrial unionism "un-American" and "communist."

1877: The First Industrial Revolt

The great confrontation between labor and capital in the United States emerged during the nationwide railroad strike of 1877, when rank-and-file workers protesting a wage cut organized mobs of the unemployed, tramps, and black laborers for an assault on the railroad corporations, the newspapers, and allies of capital. As riots broke out from Baltimore to St. Louis, federal and state officials began to warn of the danger of revolution. The New York *Daily Mail,* in an editorial typical of the period, told its readers: "The evil tendencies and examples of European Communists are potential with tens of thousands of men in this city."[15] Working-class organization was denounced as a foreign ideology and the railroad rebellion was crushed with bayonets.

On May 1, 1886, 350,000 American workers in every industrial center of the country shut down 11,652 factories, shops, and businesses as a part of the worldwide struggle for the eight-hour day led by the International Workingmen's Association under the guidance of Karl Marx.[16] The consolidation and survival of the craft-dominated American Federation of Labor represented more than a simple evolutionary adaptation of a functional and specialized working-class form of organization suitable to the American environment. Consolidated by Samuel Gompers, a cigar maker, around the demand for an eight-hour day, the AFL rose to power on the crest of the nationwide strike movement. While craft unionism proved to be completely unsuited to the representation of the majority of industrial workers, the superior power of the corporations and the state forced American labor within the bounds of craft unionism. Thus a cigar maker became the symbolic representative of the working class in a nation emerging as the most powerful industrial society in the world.

Business finally accepted the legitimacy of craft organization as the maximum permissible form of organization. *Business unionism* was invented as a suitable term for the association of small groups of skilled native-born craftsmen. *Industrial unions* meant a labor movement, and social or class movements were European by definition. Given the internal divisions among the U.S. working class, and the power and cohesion of the business class, what is remarkable is not that there was so little solidarity among American workers, but that there was so much.

Three major strikes of the 1890s—The Homestead Steel Strike, the historic Pullman Strike, and the fight for industrial unions by the western miners in the Coeur d'Alene district of Idaho—established the framework within which American workers would attempt to move beyond the confines of craft unionism to industry-wide union organizations. The strike at Homestead showed that the AFL was incapable of leading the struggle for industrial organization within its own federation; Pullman proved that when forced to choose between the mass movements identified with industrial unionism and the exclusive principle of craft organization, the AFL would choose the latter; and the Coeur d'Alene struggle for the broad organization of all-inclusive unions demonstrated that American workers, given favorable circumstances, community support, and freely chosen leaders, were capable of building effective militant and class-oriented economic organizations. This pattern of interaction between the established American Federation of Labor and mass movements embracing the unskilled labor force in the basic industries continued up through the 1930s.[17]

The specter of labor revolt helped to shape the thought and action of corporations, government, and the new middle professional classes. Without the great American strikes and labor revolts, American history would, no doubt, look entirely different to contemporary generations. Yet, during the first quarter of the new century the American Federation of Labor, while benefiting from the general upsurge of worker demands for rights and recognition, served to contain the organizational form of the labor revolt. At a time when there was a continuous expansion of the population, of which immigrants formed a substantial part, the AFL tripled its membership. From 1900 to 1920 the U.S. population rose from 76 million to 106 million. During the same period, AFL membership increased from 548,000 to 1,676,200, about 80 percent of the total national trade union membership of 2 million. The greatest strength of the federation lay in the construction trades, where the contractors, hoping to crush their competitors, signed a closed-shop agreement with the building trades. These unions agreed in turn that none of their members would work for any company not a member of the General Contractors Association.[18] Despite such gains, there was a general decline in the labor movement after 1904, when American business launched its nationwide drive for the open shop. From 1904 to 1911 the AFL increased its membership by only some 85,000 new members.[19]

After the turn of the century, Samuel Gompers and other craft union leaders feared a movement from below that might sweep them out of office. At the 1903 AFL national convention, Gompers strongly supported a report condemning the movement from within the AFL for industrial unionism. Speaking on the report, Gompers stated: "It is time for our fellow unionists . . . to help stem the tide of expansion madness lest either by their indifference or encouragement their organizations will be drawn into the vortex that will engulf them to their possible dismemberment and destruction."[20]

Both sides involved in the struggle over forms of organization were quite clear about the issues involved. Philip Foner, who has researched the history of the conflict between craft and industrial unionism more thoroughly than any other labor historian, quotes the letter of a craft union leader to Gompers:

> On the whole, the skilled craftsmen, being better paid, are apt to be ultra-conservative. The unskilled, on the other hand, being poorly paid are the hardest fighters. But they are also the most troublesome, and I fear that this is the element we will have to cope with if the Socialists behind the industrial union scheme have their way.[21]

The secretary of the Brotherhood of Painters warned Gompers in another letter that if the concept of industrial unionism were adopted by the AFL, the leaders would lose their positions: "Some fine morning you will wake up with a revolution on your hands."[22]

What was at stake was also clear to at least one section of the corporate leadership. If it was impossible to maintain the open shop, then the line of retreat must be to contain labor within the confines of the craft-oriented American Federation of Labor. The overwhelming majority of basic industries in the United States thus remained unorganized until labor had broken with the AFL. Violent labor struggles continued to punctuate the steady industrial advance of a nation that doubled its Gross National Product in the years from 1900 up to World War I. The 1901 Steel Strike; the Anthracite Coal Strike of 1902; the strike battles in the New York City garment industry, and the dynamiting of the *Los Angeles Times* building in 1910; Industrial Workers of the World (IWW) strikes at Lawrence, Massachusetts, in 1912 and Patterson, New Jersey, in 1913; the Ludlow (Colorado) Massacre of 1914; and the railroad workers' campaigns for the eight-hour day in 1915–1916 were only the largest labor conflicts of the period.

A clear pattern of oscillation between political and economic action characterized the efforts of the class-conscious elements of the American labor movement during this period. The growing socialist political movement attempted to break the bonds of working-class organization on both fronts, while the leaders of the AFL fought to contain American workers in the straitjacket of nonpolitical unionism. This struggle was finally decided by power variables, not by processes of historical adaptation. Two taboos were set by corporate and financial capital to restrict labor action. The first was that there must be no political challenge to the system as a whole by working-class political parties; the second was that there must be no assault on the prerogatives of management in the basic industries by the unskilled labor force.

American labor made some gains during World War I, when the state made concessions to labor for its support of the war. Left leaders who opposed the war, on the other hand, were summarily jailed. Within months of the 1918 Armistice, the major wartime agencies were dissolved. Labor-management agreements enforced by Wilson's War Labor Board were viewed by corporation officials simply as temporary expedients required by the necessities of patriotism and national emergency. Welfare-capitalism of the twenties as an antidote to worker unrest was sponsored by the corporations, not the state, and had little in common with the welfare-state model adopted by advanced capitalist nations in the second half of the twentieth century. With the emergence of the Harding administration business had won its test of strength with both labor and the state. As historians Nevins and Commager put it, "Government withdrew from business, but business moved in and took over government."[23]

However, during the great 1919 Steel Strike industrial unionism and the specter of communism that had characterized the 1877 national working-class rebellion raised its head once more. The new rebellion in steel had to be crushed and its symbols exorcised before business hegemony could be proclaimed as the basic value of a mature American social order. The immigrant working class in the steel towns of the nation made up the armies that engaged the strongest industrial corporations in an economic civil war.

The first great breakthrough for industrial unionism in the early decades of the twentieth century was led by a former IWW syndicalist who had rejected the concept of dual unionism and returned to the AFL to organize the unskilled workers in the mass production industries. William Z. Foster, soon to organize the Communist Party of the United States, was instrumental in organizing the packinghouse workers in the Chicago stockyards. As secretary of the Stockyards Labor Council, Foster, together with John Fitzpatrick, president of the Chicago Federation of Labor, constructed an organizing drive that succeeded in unionizing the unskilled workers in the open-shop fortresses of Swift, Armour, and the lesser packers. A 1918 arbitration award issued by a Chicago judge gave the packinghouse workers the eight-hour day with ten hours pay, overtime rates, and other path-breaking concessions on working conditions.

Foster moved quickly to win the AFL leaders' approval for an organizing drive in steel. He skillfully couched his proposal in conservative terms by suggesting that the organization of the steelworkers should remain within the craft union framework so that no national union should have to give up its jurisdiction over the crafts in the steel industry. Fifteen national unions with Gompers as chairman set up the National Committee for Organizing Iron and Steel Workers. The radical western Mine, Mill, and Smelter Workers and the old craft association of Iron, Steel, and Tin Workers agreed to divide the jurisdiction covering the mass of unskilled workers.

David Brody estimates that approximately 250,000 strikers, or about half the workforce in the industry, took part in the 1919 Steel Strike. "A quarter of a million or more steelworkers across the country simultaneously on strike: America had never seen the like of this."[24] The steel companies, alarmed by the Russian Revolution of 1917, responded by turning an economic conflict into a political one. The corporations, the press, and congressmen all focused on William Z. Foster, the "anarchist" who "recognizes no rights of the capitalists to their property, and is going to strip them of it, law or no law."[25] Foster became the symbol of the strike. John Fitzpatrick, the other radical AFL strike leader, asserted: "We are going to socialize the basic industries of the United States. . . . We are going to have representatives on the board of directors of the steel corporation."[26] Eugene Debs, the Socialist leader, declared from his jail cell in the federal prison at Atlanta, where he had been sent for violation of the Sedition Act for opposing the war: "Anything is possible as the outcome of the present situation."[27] And Gompers warned the steel owners that if they did not settle the strike on AFL terms, the Left would win over the working class: "You will either come to agreement with us or you will destroy the ability of the men in our movement to stand up for right. We will be discarded as impotent or unfaithful; and . . . you will have somebody to deal with (the IWW and the Bolshevists of America), and you will not find them arguing and appealing to you."[28]

The government stood aside as the steel corporations mobilized to crush the strike. Thirty thousand black southern migrants were brought in as strikebreakers, armed vigilantes were organized in the steel towns, and picketing was prohibited. Craft union officials abandoned the unskilled workers in favor of the skilled and the strike was broken. With government deportation of radical immigrants, the Palmer raids, and a nationwide red witch hunt, the task of cleansing the nation of the virus of industrial unionism was completed.

Thus the era of industrialization ended as it had begun: the unskilled armies of labor, who had stood up to match the corporate organization of capital with organizational forms of their own, went down to defeat. Industrial peace was proclaimed and an integrated American business order was heralded as the most advanced society on earth. Labor, except for the remnants of the business-craft unions, was excluded from the business society of the twenties as un-American. Victory over the unskilled and semi-skilled workers in the basic industries was soon translated by politicians and scholars into the social conquest of all forms of political and economic class conflict.

Alfred Chandler, in the most recent volume of his history of the managerial revolution in the largest American corporations, does not feel it necessary to include labor until the end of the book, in his treatment of the formation of the CIO in 1935. Before that, labor was simply a raw material, the cost of which was to be kept at a minimum. At the end of his study Chandler succinctly characterizes the role of the American Federation of Labor in terms of its relation to the basic structure of American industry:

> The craft unions, however, made little effort to unionize those industries where administrative coordination paid off. Workers in the mass production industries, where the large modern industrial enterprises clustered, were primarily semi-skilled and unskilled workers. . . . And until the 1930s, these middle managers were rarely forced to consider seriously the demands of labor unions in making such decisions [hiring, firing, promotion, wages, hours, and conditions of work].[29]

The myth of the prosperous twenties, still perpetuated a half-century later by President Reagan, was not shared by the workers at the bottom of the economic ladder. Even during the 1920s union membership declined by an estimated 1.7 million from a peak of about 3.4 million during the war.

While profits soared by 62 percent during the "prosperous twenties," wages crept up by only 7 percent. The top 5 percent of the nation controlled 26 percent of the national wealth during the heyday of the business society. By the end of the era 65 percent of American families lived barely above the poverty line; most of the rest lived below it. "Republican ideology precluded government assistance for job creation, income security, or worker protection, and the opposition Democrats offered only a weak version of me-too-politics. Labor unions were in retreat, radical organizations had been crushed during the patriotic outbursts of World War I, and attempts to form a third party had ended with the losing candidacy of Robert M. LaFollette in 1924."[30]

However, the euphoria of a business society that boasted it had attained the apex of human potential soon turned to despair. The forces that had sustained the boom, the war-generated backlog of consumer demand together with large-scale investments in the production of consumer goods, petered out. The depressed state of agriculture, a great increase in consumer credit, and rapid decline in capital investment combined to bring about the collapse of the business society.

The extensive economic disaster in the United States was followed by a world economic crisis. The disintegration of the world economic and state political system has been described by Karl Polanyi as the collapse of nineteenth-century civilization. According to Polanyi, the failure of laissez-faire capitalism resulted in three important historical changes: (1) the generation of alternate social, political, and economic systems (state-directed capitalism, fascism, and state socialism) to cope with the chaos brought about by the destruction of the self-regulating market; (2) the emergence of a new center of world power, coordination, and leadership, as the United States replaced Britain following World War II; and (3) the rise of the state as the dominant institution in American society.[31]

Since the U.S. business order had been created through the denial of power to all other social interests, once the economy collapsed, the managers of great corporations and the financiers became a discredited elite. Frederick Lewis Allen described the bewilderment of the men on Wall Street in 1932: "Fear was everywhere; once there had been no more rapturous optimist in the business world than Charles M. Schwab, but now—in April 1932—he was quoted as saying, 'I'm afraid, every man is afraid, we don't know, whether values we have are going to be real next month or not.'"[32]

If the corporate business sector had no coherent policy to meet the national collapse, neither did the organized craft unions represented by the American Federation of Labor. A confused and fearful nation placed its hopes in the 1932 presidential elections. No sectoral interest— business, labor, agriculture, or the professions—was united behind any coherent program as the way out of the crisis, either for its own sector or for the nation as a whole. The historical challenge for labor in the thirties thus remained the same as it had been for the past fifty years—to organize industrial unions in the mass production industries and, once this was accomplished, transcend that economic organization by creating a viable working-class political party. A half-century later, in the decade of the 1980s, despite the enormous victories wrested from capital by American labor, the challenge has yet to be met.

1

Revolt from Below

From the great stock market crash in the late fall of 1929 to the inauguration of Franklin Roosevelt in 1933, the mood of the nation was one of despair. Roosevelt's campaign against Herbert Hoover took place in a climate of intensifying economic crisis that had paralyzed both the international and U.S. economies. Stark statistics reveal the national malaise: unemployment, which registered 3.2 percent in 1929, had risen to an unprecedented 24.9 percent in 1933. Employment declined in every occupational category except government, and average hourly wages of production workers in manufacturing fell from 56.6¢ in 1929 to 44.2¢ in 1933.

The collapse of agriculture pushed the price of many basic farm products below the cost of production. Index levels for the Gross National Product (1913=110) had declined from 163.4 in 1929 to 117.7 in 1933, while the Federal Reserve Board index of production for manufacturing (1935–1939=100) fell from 110 in 1929 to 57 in 1932. Never before had the United States experienced such a depth of economic ruin. It was under these historical conditions that national power began to be consolidated in the state.[1]

By now the United States was a world power. Yet before it could effectively exercise its world role, it had to reorder its own society. Roosevelt especially perceived that a strong hegemonic state was necessary to generate a unified national policy and to speak to the world with one voice.

Hoover, by contrast, considered external factors paramount in leading to the crisis. He argued: "Our major difficulties during the past two years find their origins in the shock from economic collapses abroad which in turn are the aftermath of the Great War."[2]

Roosevelt insisted it was necessary to look to internal causes—and internal solutions. In his first inaugural address, he stated: "I shall spare no effort to restore world trade by international economic adjustment; but the emergency at home cannot wait on that accomplishment." Later he commented, "The bubble burst first in the United States," and more precisely, "When the whole machinery needed overhauling I felt it to be insufficient to repair one or two minor parts."[3] Hoover favored the "incorporation of individual initiative within a framework of voluntary economic cooperation by groups of like interests."[4] His was a sophisticated twentieth-century version of the laissez-faire society, and he held unswervingly to his belief in voluntarism and individualism. Roosevelt, although lacking a clear program, was determined to seek a national solution to internal economic breakdown, apart from the world economy. Thus, a political evaluation of the causes of the economic crisis determined the policy orientation of each candidate toward its solution.

Roosevelt and Hoover carried out their electoral struggle within the parameters set by the two-party system. The workers of 1932 had not deviated from the political behavior noted by Engels in 1890; they had no intention of throwing their votes away. Hoover was perceived clearly as the candidate of Big Business, the very force that had shipwrecked the country. Roosevelt was the only sensible choice.

Once elected, the new chief executive heard constant reports from his administration aides about the deterioration and collapse of many of the formerly stable ramparts of the society. Frances Perkins described bank shutdowns, relief stations closing for lack of funds, hunger marches, food riots, "terror in the agricultural regions where sober farm people forcibly prevented sheriff's sales on foreclosed mortgages," and the increase in crime as the poor stole in order to survive.[5] Tugwell described the winter of 1933 as "the most distressful the nation had ever known."[6] Hoovervilles, as the cardboard shacks of the homeless were called, were spreading, soup lines extended around whole blocks in the major cities, and major industry was all but shut down. Sporadic and isolated revolt might be managed; the fear was that revolts from below might become linked and thus threaten the system. Roosevelt, however, temporized while listening to many voices. The "Brain Trust" that had planned his campaign dissolved, never to meet again as a coordinated team of policymakers.[7]

As Irving Bernstein makes clear, Roosevelt had no labor program when he came into office. Trade unions were not mentioned in his campaign speeches, and "at no time did he talk about governmental protection of the right to organize and bargain collectively."[8] Once in office, neither he nor his secretary of labor, Frances Perkins, showed any interest in establishing labor's rights. At the same time, U.S. trade unions were weaker than at any time since 1900. *Fortune* Magazine declared that the American Federation of Labor (AFL) suffered from "pernicious anaemia, sociological myopia, and hardening of the arteries."[9]

The United Mine Workers (UMW), historically the strongest union within the AFL, was in a state of collapse. The cause of the industrial workers would imprint itself on the consciousness of Roosevelt and the nation only by a radical rank-and-file movement from below.

The Radical Spark

With the shattering of the American dream, radical ideas began to spread among the farmers, unemployed, industrial workers, and middle-class intellectuals. To be sure, as Karsh and Garman state: "The radicalism which existed was in the main homespun and indigenous, a diffused mixture of organized and unorganized sentiment, generally devoid of any specific programmatic doctrine."[10] However, the workers and unemployed were receptive to class-conscious leadership, which they either produced out of their own ranks or discovered among the remnants of the communist and socialist Left that had survived the bleak twenties.

In Bernstein's view, "the reluctance of established trade-unions to assume responsibility for desperation strikes gave the Communists—and to a lesser extent the Industrial Workers of the World—an opportunity to exert leadership."[11] The radical class character of the fierce and bloody struggle for industrial unionism was, in fact, the product of suffering and desperation. But the only radical leadership capable of responding to and directing the upheaval produced by the Great Depression came from left-wing rank-and-file activists.

In 1930, 1931, and 1932, during that period when the established trade union movement was at its lowest ebb and union membership had declined drastically, unemployment, wage cuts, and bitter working conditions radicalized tens of thousands of workers consigned to the bottom of the occupational structure.

During the early years of the Depression, the forefront of the struggle against starvation and economic disaster was filled by the organizations of the unemployed. In a period when organized looting of food surfaced throughout the country, radicals of every stripe came into their own. Communist Party members and unemployed workers stormed city halls and fought with police in front of the municipal seats of government in Cleveland, Chicago, Philadelphia, and Los Angeles. On March 6, 1930, William Z. Foster spoke to a crowd estimated at anywhere from 35,000 to 100,000 in New York City. The meeting was brutally assaulted by police, resulting in hundreds of casualties.

Communist Party militants went on to organize historic councils of the unemployed, march on Washington, and unite black and white unemployed workers to resist evictions for nonpayment of rent. They led the Ford Hunger March in Detroit on March 7, 1932, which was one of the first attempts to link up the struggle between industrial workers and the unemployed in a major unorganized industry. During an ugly confrontation between more than 3,000 demonstrators and the Dearborn police, four workers were killed and more than fifty wounded. The Unemployment Council of Detroit, the Trade Union Unity League, the Communist Party, and the AFL Auto Workers' Union then led a massive demonstration and funeral cortege down Woodward Avenue to Grand Circus Park, where another 30,000 workers had gathered in class solidarity. In the ranks that day were many of the future organizers of the United Automobile Workers, CIO.[12]

The Communists' ability to shape this struggle resulted not only from the vacuum left by the trade union movement, however. Bert Cochran, a socialist scholar with years in the labor movement, argues that despite Comintern misdirection, errors of leadership, and occasional sectarian policy, the Communist Party maintained its hegemony within the ranks of the Left. "They had this unique hold on radicals so that they could harness their energies—in opposition to, or in alliance with liberals. A chain reaction had been set off: the Russian Revolution ignited militant youth; the militant youth were in the forefront of social battles, which reinforced the conviction in the radical world that only Communists stood ready to fight the system while others merely talked about it."[13]

Robert Wohlforth, a New Deal lawyer, recalls the first day he saw a hunger march—in New York City: "And the only people here in New York, and I'll say this for the commies; they had the guts to organize and lead these marches."[14] In fact, the anticommunism of the period in some ways strengthened the ability of the Communist Party to organize this movement. This was a time when every strike, every effort of the unskilled industrial workers to create forms of organization to match the power of American corporate capital, was red-baited, whether it was led by class-conscious socialists or not. As a result, as Cochran makes clear, workers were less vulnerable, they were "impervious to the usual anti-communist tirades."[15]

This was a period when the workers and the unemployed conceived of their organizations as a "social and moral force."[16] Thus anticommunist trade union leaders like John L. Lewis would have to transform themselves and break with the ideology and style of what Engels had referred to as "the fossilized brothers of the old trade-unions," before they could lead what *Fortune* Magazine was to describe as "one of the greatest mass movements in our history."[17]

Lewis operated on the Gompers tactic of threatening that if employers refused to deal with unions, the workers would then certainly turn to communism in order to achieve a semblance of industrial democracy. However, in order to organize industrial workers in the 1930s Lewis would have to adopt a strategy of militant economic class conflict, make alliances with left-wing trade unionists, and stand up to red-baiting attacks against himself and the CIO by the press, politicians, and corporate elites.

Bert Cochran's ground-breaking study *Labor and Communism* makes this clear. Cochran lays to rest the charge by Perlman, Taft, and others that it was the Communists who must be held responsible for arresting "the natural process of replacement and development of the leadership in the American labor movement," by driving "the progressives" into the arms of the old AFL leadership. As Cochran points out, the "Gompers' Old Guard did not make finespun distinctions" between Communists and non-Communists, between Foster's Trade Union Educational League and the socialist-oriented Brookwood Labor College. "The entrenched AFL bureaucrats of this period would not permit 'the natural processes of replacement to occur.'"[18] Industrial-union forces within the AFL had to move to the left before they could link up with the new great wave of industrial unionism.

The historic Passaic Textile Strike, the bloody battles fought in Gastonia, North Carolina, and the armed revolt against industrial peonage in Harlan County, while bringing publicity to the Communist Party, served the more important purpose of bringing national recognition to the cause of industrial unionism. Rank-and-file textile workers and miners put their lives on the line against national guard and corporate troops. Militant fur workers under the Communist leadership of Ben Gold linked Jewish workers of New York with Irish coal miners in West Virginia in a common cause. The fur workers won "the first 40-hour, five day week in the garment industry, a 10 cent hourly increase, 7 paid holidays, and other benefits."[19] The millions of unorganized workers in America's basic industries would have to fight before they could win the same kind of contract.

The New Deal and the Labor Revolt

While the radicals in the ranks of labor began to agitate their fellow workers for action, Roosevelt put together a labor policy. After consultation with business and labor leaders, he acted on the basis of an executive power that had previously been exercised only during times of war, introducing the program that would become known as the National Industrial Recovery Act (NIRA).

The National Recovery Administration (NRA) was forged out of materials left over from the previous decades; the model was the World War I War Industries Board and the trade associations of the 1920s that had attempted to limit competition through industrial self-regulation, price setting, and restricted production.

When it was introduced to Congress in the winter of 1933, the crisis legislation exempted industry from prosecution under the anti-trust statutes if companies eliminated competition by stabilizing prices and allocating markets. "In return for exemption from anti-trust legislation, businessmen had to adopt presidentially sanctioned codes that established minimum wages and maximum hours, eliminated child labor, and recognized the right of workers to organize unions and bargain collectively."[20]

The NRA was an American version of corporatism, a system designed in Europe to balance class interests in the management of the economy. The idea was carried out under the Italian fascist government of Mussolini. "The major interest groups are brought together and encouraged to conclude a series of bargains about their future behavior, which will have the effect of moving economic events along the desired path. The plan indicates the general direction in which the interest groups, including the state in its various economic guises, have agreed that they want to go."[21] This was the first attempt by the United States to introduce a form of social bargaining, as an answer to the dislocations produced by an unregulated and anarchic market system.

The congressional debate over the NIRA sparked an open struggle among corporate leaders, politicans, and labor representatives over the future of industrial relations in the United States. After heated debate before the Senate Finance Committee, John L. Lewis and other United Mine Workers (UMW) leaders won the struggle against Robert Lamont, representing the American Iron and Steel Institute, and a host of other corporation officials, to incorporate into the NIRA the famous Section 7a, the clause that guaranteed the right of workers to "organize unions of their own choosing" and the right to collective bargaining.

On June 16, 1933, Congress passed the National Industrial Recovery Act by overwhelming majorities, with Section 7a intact. John L. Lewis, the president of the United Mine Workers, hailed Section 7a of the NIRA as "the greatest single advance for human rights in the United States since Abraham Lincoln's Emancipation Proclamation."[22] While it is true that Section 7a was little more than a symbolic act, since no power of enforcement was written into the legislation, symbolic acts often serve to spark social revolutions. This symbolic recognition of the rights of the industrial working class in the United States was such a case. William Leuchtenburg, the historian, has noted: "When Franklin Roosevelt agreed to Section 7a of the National Industrial Recovery Act, he had little idea what he was letting himself in for."[23]

Once the armies of the unskilled and semi-skilled sensed a favorable climate for organization, they began to organize themselves. They wasted little time: in the two years between 1932 and 1934, the organized labor movement "recovered all the ground lost since about 1923."[24] In response to the signal flashed by Congress and the new administration in Washington, rubber workers, electrical workers, western copper and hard-rock miners, oil and gas workers, newspaper reporters, hotel and restaurant workers, and the unorganized in countless other industries began the search for an independent industrial organization that would allow them to conduct a united economic offensive against capital.

Workers throughout the country responded to the promulgation of Section 7a of the NIRA with the greatest strike wave since 1921. In 1933 more than 11,000 workers struck, most of them after passage of the labor clause. The employers, on the other hand, refused to recognize the right of workers to form their own independent organizations and those corporations that had not formed company unions rushed to do so. Workers' revolt in the United States was a struggle for dignity as much as it was for wages and working conditions. Nationwide strike struggles brought to the attention of the general public the conditions of industrial peonage suffered by hundreds of thousands of workers who produced the goods for the leading economic power in the world.

Auto

On January 24, 1933, 10,000 workers struck the Briggs Manufacturing Company in Detroit. Judge William F. Connally, who was also treasurer of the Briggs Company, declared in a public statement that "the strike is a clearcut issue between capital and communism." Walter C. Briggs, the president of the company, asserted that the strike at his plant constituted "the first step in a Communist plan to paralyze the nation's auto industry."[25] The rank-and-file negotiating committee elected by the workers at Briggs told the press: "We are asking for improved working conditions that are safe and sanitary, particularly for women workers."[26]

Most of the industrial towns in America in 1930 were virtually owned by the corporations. In Flint, Michigan, for example, six of the nine city commissioners were General Motors (GM) executives. The mayor was the former comptroller of General Motors and the police department was directly supervised by GM. A check list of all union sympathizers and strike leaders was kept by the chief of police. Strike leaders were automatically arrested and when released were picked up by company thugs, often through prearrangement with the police, taken out into the country, and brutally beaten. All "agitators," the police label for union organizers, were summarily expelled from town. Given these conditions of control and the cooperation of the AFL in keeping a lid on the new auto union, the corporations apparently were convinced that there was no reason they could not continue to control their workforce and maintain open-shop industrial towns.

It was the same in any major industrial center; as workers organized protests, public meetings, and strikes, they were met with unyielding force and violence. The wave of strikes in 1933 swept the whole country, from the auto workers in Detroit, to the textile workers in Philadelphia, through the coalfields of Pennsylvania, and on into the steel centers of the nation. Faced with the prospect of a society torn apart by class warfare, Roosevelt brought the power of the state to mediate the civil war between labor and capital.

Textile

On August 5, 1933, the president approved the formation of the National Labor Board (NLB), whose membership consisted of one public member, Senator Wagner; three members representing labor, Leo Wolman, John L. Lewis, and William Green; and three members representing industry, Walter Teague, Gerard Swope, and Louis Kirstein. Although the board had no legal power, it moved rapidly into the violent hosiery strike in Philadelphia, where 10,000 female and male workers were fighting the mill owners over the issue of union recognition.

On August 10 the NLB, after listening to arguments by representatives of the employers and the hosiery workers, mediated an agreement that came to be known as the Reading Formula. In return for calling off the strike, the NLB agreed to sponsor representative elections by secret ballot through which the workers might choose collective bargaining agents. Bernstein describes the results of this first mediation attempt by the state:

> The Board held elections in 45 mills in and about Reading in the week of August 15, 1933, with some 14,000 workers voting. The union carried majorities in 37 mills with 13,362 employees; nonunion representatives won out in 8 mills with 720 workers. But 36 of the employers, after meeting with the elected representatives, refused to sign written collective bargaining agreements and this issue was submitted to the Board. On September 27 NLB ruled that this was in defiance of "the intent of the agreement made with the National Labor Board by both parties on August 10, 1933." The Board, lacking the legal power to "order," declared that "it is incumbent on the respondents and the representatives of the employees to work out written agreements which shall deal with and define the relationship of the respondents and their employees for a stated period of time." The employers complied. Thus, NLB passed its first test brilliantly.[27]

Coal mining

The mine workers were in the first wave of the historic social movement that began to sweep the nation. Van Bitner, a United Mine Workers official, reported from West Virginia that "the current organizing campaign was like a dream, too good to be true. We expect to be practically through with every mine in the state and have every miner under jurisdiction of our union by the first of next week."[28] The pattern repeated itself in the other coalfields. And it was not John J. Lewis who was responsible for the organizational upsurge. Coal miners organized themselves.

Wildcat strikes erupted in the coalfields as UMW leaders attempted to negotiate a code for the coal industry under the NIRA. Lewis and the other UMW officials had little influence on the miners of western Pennsylvania, where a violent industrial war raged between the miners and the coal operators. "The miners, especially those who walked out of the captive pits, followed the leadership of such insurgents as Martin Ryan, an old line radical and Communist, and acted without orders from the UMW hierarchy."[29] Louis Stark, the *New York Times*'s labor reporter, wired Roosevelt on August 23 that unless a code was written for the coal industry, violent strikes would sweep the coalfields from Harlan Country to Alabama. He warned that "seething discontent in the fields may break out worse than ever. From coal it will spread to steel and autos" unless an agreement between the United Mine Workers and the southern coal operators was concluded.

Governor Pinchot of Pennsylvania advised Roosevelt that a general strike in the soft-coal industry might threaten national economic recovery. He reminded the president that the miners considered him a friend and expected him to help win recognition for their union. As a result of this pressure, Roosevelt attempted to intervene, calling a meeting between UMW officials and the leading coal operators at the White House. Despite his pleas, however, the mine owners refused to recognize the union. The Pennsylvania miners voted to call a general strike unless a code granting their demands was written. The president, fearful of what Governor Pinchot called the danger of "tumult and riot," forced a settlement on the reluctant coal operators. Dubofsky and Van Tine describe the historic settlement: "The bituminous coal code, as approved by President Roosevelt on September 21, granted the UMW what it had fruitlessly struggled for since its foundation in 1890: a contract that covered all the major soft-coal producing districts: Pennsylvania, Ohio, West Virginia, eastern Kentucky, and Tennessee—with supplemental agreements that covered Indiana and Illinois."[30]

In the low-wage districts, miners who had been earning as little as $1.50 a day were now guaranteed $3.40, and in most districts they were guaranteed $4.20. In addition, the UMW won an "eight-hour day, five-day week; the right to choose their own checkweighmen; and the abolition of wage payment in scrip and the requirement to trade in company stores and dwell in company houses."[31] Child labor was outlawed, the employers were compelled to check off union dues, and a grievance and arbitration procedure was established. Howard Brubaker in a contemporary *New Yorker* article wrote: "The defeated mine-owners agreed to all things that deputy sheriffs usually shoot people for demanding."[32]

The UMW next opened an assault on the captive mines run by the iron and steel producers. These captive mines, which produced coke for the steel mills, represented the gateway to the industrial organization of the basic industries of the country.

The whirlwind organizing campaign that had cracked the soft-coal industry was repeated in the captive mines. Again the rank and file led the way. But the steel companies knew what was at stake. Although they agreed to comply with the Bituminous Coal Code's terms on wages and conditions, they refused to recognize the union as such.

> They discharged union leaders, recruited strikebreakers, set black against white, exercised repressive local police power, and created company unions. Particularly in southwestern Pennsylvania, the captive coal com-panies refused to recognize the UMW or bargain with labor. To recognize trade unionism in the mines, they feared, would set a precedent that might open the iron and steel industry to organized labor.[33]

Once more the miners threatened to open up an industrial civil war in the coalfields. Once again Roosevelt intervened. He wrote to Myron Taylor, then representing the iron and steel industry, that the September 21 agreement included the dues checkoff and the right to collective bargaining.

The companies argued that the "checkoff" clause threatened to impose the union shop and that there was nothing to negotiate and nothing to propose except union recognition and the closed shop. Enclosed in the long memorandum was a copy of a letter dated August 31, 1919, from Myron Taylor to Woodrow Wilson, which stated the steel industry's classic open-shop policy: "The large majority of the men do not desire to become members of labor unions. They do not wish to pay the dues imposed. They object to being dominated by the labor leaders. They demand freedom from tyranny. And above everything else, our workmen generally are satisfied with their conditions and terms of employment."[34]

Roosevelt was not persuaded, however, and besieged by rank-and-file shutdowns of their mines and Roosevelt's refusal to submit to pressure, the captive mine owners accepted a compromise settlement on October 30. In return for an end to the strike, the companies pledged to implement the September 21 Coal Code, accepting checkoff union dues

for individual miners and agreeing that representative elections should
be conducted under the supervision of the National Labor Board. In
November the UMW won twenty out of thirty representative elections
in the captive mines.

But the steel companies still refused to concede the principle of
collective bargaining by signing the agreement with Lewis, Murray, and
Kennedy of the UMW as individuals. Dubofsky and Van Tine note: "It
was the militant behavior of coal miners, not the tough language and
sharp bargaining of John L. Lewis, that threatened Roosevelt's plans for
industrial recovery."[35]

Corporate Counterattack

Volcanic union organizing drives caught the corporate class by
surprise, but all they needed was time to organize their counterattack.
In 1932 and 1933 the largest corporations took over the National
Association of Manufacturers (NAM) in order to direct a national
counteroffensive against collective bargaining. By 1937 the NAM and
its allied network of industrial associations represented over 30,000
manufacturers with nearly 5 million employees. By October 1933,
companies were refusing to appear at National Labor Board hearings,
and on November 1 the NAM launched a massive open attack on the
National Labor Board. General Motors, the largest corporation in the
country, was soon chosen to hold the line against the rising tide of
industrial unionism. Roosevelt skillfully shaped his political response to
any shift in the balance of power between capital and labor.[36]

The showdown came in March 1934 in Detroit. Rank-and-file auto
workers who had organized an AFL auto workers' union at the Buick
and Fisher Body plants in Flint, Michigan, and the Hudson factory in
Detroit set up skeleton union organizations in a number of parts shops.
When a number of union members were discharged by the auto
companies for union activities, rank-and-file union leaders threatened
a strike unless the corporations agreed to recognize the union, reinstate the fired workers, and agree to a 20 percent wage increase.
Roosevelt quickly intervened and turned the case over to the National
Labor Board.

William Knudson, head of General Motors, appeared before the
board and stated that his company would not deal with any labor
organization or recognize the authority of the NLB to conduct elections
at any GM plant. A representative from the Hudson Motor Company
issued a similar statement. Under rank-and-file pressure, the passive
craft leaders of the AFL auto union announced that the union would
strike on March 21. Roosevelt then stepped into the dispute personally.

But as he had earlier responded to the organized weight of the miners, this time he responded to the newly organized power of the corporations.[37]

On March 25, Roosevelt handed down a decision that, in Bernstein's words, granted "the auto companies . . . a total victory on the application of Section 7a to their industry." The settlement provided that "the government favors no particular union or particular form of employee organization or representation." The labor clauses under the NIRA affirming the rights of workers to collective bargaining through unions of their own choosing were thus repudiated by the government.[38]

That repudiation, as Bernstein points out, showed labor leaders that they could not depend on the law, or the government, to win their struggles; to win bargaining rights they would have to show their strength. Thus, "the automobile settlement was to be a major cause of the great wave of strikes that engulfed the nation in the spring and summer of 1934."[39]

However, strikes alone could not guarantee legitimacy for the labor force in the basic industries. Union organization in the thirties is the history of strikes won and lost. What was required was power—as both capital and labor knew. The strength of the auto workers and the weakness of the textile workers was determined on the picket line. Collective-bargaining agreements in the thirties were thus the peace treaties of industrial warfare. In the early days many of these agreements turned out to be temporary truces between capital and labor while each side brought up its reserves for the next battle.

Steelworkers Pressure Business and Government

The intense triangular struggle for power between labor, capital, and the state burst into the open during the spring and summer of 1934. Workers fought employers and both fought for control over state labor policy. While Senator Wagner and representatives of the official labor movement tried to piece together a new labor law and the employers lobbied to retain the status quo, rank-and-file workers looked for allies.

A number of young, militant steelworkers, members of the Amalgamated Association of Iron, Steel, and Tin Workers, joined up with independent radicals in the steel towns. With Harvey O'Connor, a radical socialist writer and editor of labor publications, and Harold Ruttenberg, they outlined a strategy to reorganize the old craft union on industrial lines and to demand recognition. The radical caucus showed up at the Amalgamated convention at the end of March and put through a resolution calling on all lodges to present demands for recognition by the steel companies, threatening an industry-wide strike if the steel owners refused to bargain. The demands were rejected out of hand by the steel companies. An angry delegation of steelworkers descended on Washington to demand government intervention to force the steel corporations to bargain collectively with their employees. The steelworkers delegation pressured the NRA, the Labor Department, congressmen, and the White House. They had a run-in with Cyrus Johnson of the NRA, calling him a "windbag" and the NRA "the National Run-around."[40] The steel companies strung their plants with barbed wire, hired armed guards, and prepared for a bloody strike. Once more Roosevelt intervened.

Heber Blankenhorn, an assistant to Senator Wagner and prolabor newspaperman who had prepared the report on the 1919 Steel Strike as a co-director of the Bureau of Industrial Research, described the impact of the rank-and-file steelworkers' movement on the future organization of the CIO and its influence on the legislative process of the state:

> The "movement" was more than a precursor of the CIO. It was almost a little CIO in itself, a first experience of the fever. It demonstrated the underlying industrial union-mindedness, together with distrust to the point of hostility against traditional AF of L methods. . . . The 1934 movement demonstrated the limitations of a purely self-financed and self-led rank and file movement in a major industry. Those watching the movement in 1934 continually hunted around for the answers to two questions—money and experienced leadership. . . . The 1934 movement, moreover, demonstrates the importance of another factor—governmental protection. The climax of the movement was the attempt in Washington to disarm opposition within the Government (General Johnson) and to obtain active government aid; to keep government in the business of fostering and evolving a national labor policy.[41]

Blankenhorn's notes on the steel organizing movement of the summer of 1934 spell out the critical nature of that period. Labor policy was stagnant, sidetracked in congressional committees and in danger of expiring completely. "It was the scare thrown into the government by the rank and filers in these critical weeks that more than aything else resulted in the passage of the compromise Public Resolution No. 44 and the accompanying Steel Labor Board." He concludes that the failures of both boards "through 1934–1935 were a most important factor contributing to the passage of the Wagner Act in May 1935."[42]

It was during this same period that some of the greatest strikes in American history, all led by class-conscious leftists, swept the nation.

2

The General Strike Wave

The year 1934 ranks as one of the most decisive in U.S. labor history. Approximately 1.5 million workers struck some of the major industries in the country to win recognition for the industrial working class as an organized sector of society.[1] The four great strikes recognized by all labor historians as authentic social upheavals include the strike by auto-parts workers at the Electric Auto-Lite Company in Toledo; the historic San Francisco General Strike spearheaded by the longshoremen; the vast truckers strike in Minneapolis; and the massive and violent upheaval of the textile workers in New England and the South. The most significant and victorious struggles of 1934 were led by the political Left—Socialists in Toledo, Communists in San Francisco, Trotskyists in Minneapolis. In each case, American workers were extremely flexible in adapting either old or new forms of organization to their needs. All the great 1934 revolts from below took place within the AFL in the attempt to transform what had become a moribund institution.

Toledo: Strike at Auto-Lite

The great spring strike wave of 1934 began in Toledo, Ohio. A newly chartered AFL auto union struck the Electric Auto-Lite Company on February 28, demanding union recognition, a 10 percent wage increase, and seniority provisions; three other local auto-parts factories were struck at the same time. The NLB immediately entered the dispute, and the company offered a 5 percent wage increase but refused to recognize the union or guarantee seniority. This settlement was accepted by the union with the promise that the two key issues would be negotiated, and the strike was called off. Auto-Lite then refused to negotiate with the union and harassed its members, and the plant was shut down again on April 12. Only one-fourth of the union members went out on strike this time, however, and the company attempted to continue production with strikebreakers.

Support for the Auto-Lite strikers was mobilized by the American Workers' Party, headed by socialist A. J. Muste, who with a number of radical intellectuals had organized the Lucas County Unemployment League. They initiated mass picketing at the Auto-Lite plant with the aid of the league's unemployment members. The company soon won a court injunction to ban all picketing, but the injunction was repeatedly violated and the police carried out mass arrests. The company hired armed guards and special deputies to protect the strikebreakers. Production was resumed. This time, however, the story did not end with another crushed strike. Recognizing the strength of the city's unemployed workers, socialists rallied them by the thousands and placed the plant under siege.

The events that followed were to set a pattern for the general strike wave of 1934 and illustrate the way in which virtual class warfare again and again developed out of an industrial strike. Both sides mobilized support, along class lines, from the general population, until the society itself was divided into two warring factions. As striking workers rallied the unskilled and unemployed behind their strikes, political and corporate representatives closed ranks against them, drawing on the police to enforce their will.

On May 23 the "Battle of Toledo" broke out between a crowd of 10,000 workers outside the plant and the company police. Irving Bernstein describes the events:

> Auto-Lite barricaded its doors and turned off the lights. From the roof and upper-story windows deputies rained tear gas bombs on the people in the streets below. Their other weapons included bolts and iron bars, water hoses, and occasional gunfire. The crowd replied with a seven-hour barrage of stones and bricks, which were deposited in piles in the streets and then heaved through the factory windows. Fires broke out in the shipping room and the parking lot. In the latter, cars were overturned, saturated with gasoline, and set on fire. During the evening strikers broke into the factory at three points and there was hand to hand fighting before they were driven out ... The supply of gas bombs ran low during the evening and was replenished by airplane from a Cleveland munitions firm. While no one was reported killed on Wednesday, a number of persons were seriously wounded.[2]

On May 24, 900 National Guard troops arrived from out of town to lift the siege. In the afternoon a huge, taunting crowd appeared. They began throwing bricks at the soldiers, who responded with bayonet charges. Forced into retreat by the angry crowd, the troops opened fire directly on the strikers and their sympathizers. Two men were killed, at least fifteen wounded. The seesaw battle continued into the night when once more the troops opened fire, wounding two more workers. Four more National Guard companies were called out, "making this the largest peacetime display of military power in the history of Ohio."[3]

Adjutant General Henderson announced that the factory must stop work and the company agreed to shut the plant down. The same day Charles P. Taft, son of the former president, arrived as a special mediator from the Labor Department.

But the renewed struggle of the auto workers, backed by the city's unemployed, gained another crucial source of support—the rest of the city's unions. The Toledo Central Labor Union threatened to call a general strike in the city to support the Auto-Lite workers.

During the tense two weeks that followed, the strikers voted down company proposals for settlement and the International Brotherhood of Electrical Workers threatened to shut down Toledo Edison's power plants in a separate dispute. Soon Toledo was involved in a full-scale class war. On the side of capital stood the united employer associations of the city and the leaders of the national automobile industry, who publicly announced that they would back to the limit the decision of Auto-Lite management to defy labor unions. A number of socialist leaders of the American Workers' Party were jailed.

Finally on June 4, 1934, a settlement was reached. The union won a 35¢ an hour wage increase, an agreement to bargain with the union's negotiating committee, and the rehiring of all strikers. In return, the union leaders agreed to a preamble in the contract pledging union members "not to use the tactics of communists."[4] Thus management abandoned company unions, while the union agreed to sever its alliance with the socialists.

San Francisco: The Longshoremen Shut Down a City

Simultaneous with the great strike in Toledo, waterfront workers in San Francisco were preparing for an even larger battle with the united employers of the West Coast's largest port. With the passage of Section 7a of the NIRA, the process of rank-and-file organization erupted in San Francisco as it had in every other industrial center of the country. There, the employers had dominated the waterfront since 1919, and except for a small number of seamen who belonged to the International Seamen's Union, the seamen and longshoremen were unorganized. Although the rank-and-file revolt took encouragement from the passage of the NIRA and Section 7a, the workers did not rely on it. A radical faction of the International Longshoremen's Association (ILA) led by Harry Bridges and a number of Communist Party members met at Albion Hall regularly to determine a strategy of organization for waterfront workers. They agreed to build organizational strength through self-reliance: strikes, job actions, and slowdowns, rather than reliance on the NIRA.[5]

Harry Bridges, an Australian seaman who settled in San Francisco in 1922 and worked on the docks all through the 1920s, and Harry Hines, another Australian seaman, were among the first radicals who initiated the industrial union movement on the West Coast. In 1932 the Marine Workers Industrial Union (MWIU), organized by the Communist Party, began an industry-wide organizational drive among maritime workers on the West Coast. The MWIU published a mimeographed waterfront newspaper called the *Waterfront Worker,* which soon became popular among seamen for exposing working conditions on the Embarcadero, which longshoremen called "the slave market." Bridges became editor of the paper in 1933, the MWIU faded into the background, and the radical sheet then became the vehicle for organizing the San Francisco dockworkers, who began to join a newly chartered AFL longshoremen's association.

In September 1933 a protest strike against the Matson Navigation Company for firing members of the recently organized AFL International Longshoremen's Association brought the National Labor Board into the conflict. The board ruled that the fired union members must be reinstated, and, following the national pattern, waterfront workers swarmed into the union. When the employers refused to recognize the union, longshoremen in all Pacific Coast ports elected delegates to a coastwide convention. Meeting in San Francisco in February 1934, delegates representing 14,000 longshoremen drafted a uniform West Coast agreement. In this act they took over the power of their union—wresting it from the craft union officials of the AFL.

The longshoremen then elected a twenty-member delegation to present their demands to the shipowners and waterfront employers:

> The demands agreed upon were brief and to the point. They asked for an hourly wage of one dollar, a thirty-hour week, a six-hour day, and regulation of all hiring through the union hall. The hiring hall issue was regarded as the basic demand without which the other demands would be useless. The convention went resolutely on record against arbitration.[6]

The waterfront employers refused to see the delegation, called them "a bunch of communists," and instead opened negotiations with conservative officials of the AFL.

The employers argued that the rank and file were in effect demanding a closed shop, which was in violation of the NIRA, and that each port should negotiate separately. Ninety-nine percent of the 14,000 long-shoremen then voted to strike unless their demands were met by March 23. Roosevelt, who was busily attempting to ward off strikes in the rest of the country, intervened once more, appointing a mediation board headed by regional labor board heads on the West Coast—Charles Reynolds, Henry Grady, and J. L. Leonard. The mediation board held open hearings, but reached its final agreement behind closed doors with conservative AFL officials who claimed to represent the longshoremen through the ILA.

On April 3 the employers presented the proposed agreement and it was accepted by William Lewis, representing the AFL International Longshoremen's Association and other AFL officials. San Francisco newspapers called the agreement "satisfactory to the men." In fact, according to radical journalist Mike Quin, who chronicled the history of the strike, "the April 3 document recognized the ILA and agreed to enter into collective bargaining with it; in reality it was no agreement at all. It stated simply that both sides would enter into negotiations and outlined the objectives that the negotiations would try to achieve." Quin describes the rank-and-file reaction to the deal that was made behind their backs:

> By this time the longshoremen were so exasperated with negotiations that the mere mention of the word created resentment.
> When Lewis appeared before the union meeting with the agreement in his hand, he sensed the dissatisfaction of the men and tried to pass the whole thing off as a joke. He waved the paper at them and said: "Well, here's the damned thing I sold you out for." The men were in no mood for joking. Their attitude took his words literally and he was assailed with a rapid fire of questions from the floor. "Is the damned thing even in writing?" asked one longshoreman. "No," replied Lewis. "It is a gentle-men's agreement." A roar of ridicule shook the hall. Then a thin, sharp-featured longshoreman stood up and subjected the agreement to a scorch-ing analysis. This was Harry Bridges, an Australian-born dock worker who had been elected to the rank-and-file committee, and who was to become one of the outstanding labor leaders in America.[7]

Despite their distrust of the so-called agreement to negotiate by the waterfront employers and the AFL union officials, the longshoremen decided to wait out the results of the next round of negotiations. This disciplined and reasoned type of behavior on the part of the San Francisco longshoremen was characteristic of industrial workers in the 1934 labor wars. By and large, workers in the United States were very clear about their goals and organized deliberately, not impulsively, to achieve them. They understood clearly that socialism was not on the agenda, but that the right to collective economic organization was, because they had put it there. There were few unionists in the spring and summer of 1934 who did not recognize that the holders of power would never grant new rights without a struggle.

When no agreement had been reached after nearly another month of negotiations, the longshoremen, following the lead of Harry Bridges, on May 9, 1934, went out on strike in San Francisco, Seattle, Tacoma, Portland, San Pedro, Stockton, Bellingham, Aberdeen, Gray's Harbor, Astoria, and all other Pacific Coast ports. The strike was nearly 100 percent effective, despite pleas from the National Labor Board that it be called off in order to permit further government mediation.

The Waterfront Employers' Union immediately placed advertisements in all the San Francisco newspapers stating: "Longshoremen Wanted: Experience Desirable But Not Necessary." Strikebreakers were hired but proved to be of little use: more than 1,000 pickets sealed off the entrance to the docks. On May 13 the teamsters voted overwhelmingly to boycott the waterfront, and hundreds of teamsters marched down to join the longshoremen on the picket lines. During the next few days teamsters in Oakland and Seattle did the same. On May 14 the Boilermakers and Machinists Union declared a boycott against any ship worked by scabs and the Los Angeles teamsters voted support for the longshoremen. In Los Angeles, the police fired on longshore pickets, killing one longshoreman and injuring many more. On May 15 and 16 the Sailors' Union, the Marine Firemen, and the Marine Cooks and Stewards put forth their own demands for improved wages and conditions.

With some ninety-four ships tied up in San Francisco alone, the federal government showed its concern by dispatching Assistant Secretary of Labor Edward McGrady to San Francisco to mediate a settlement. On his arrival, McGrady sent telegrams to both employers and unions requesting that negotiating committees from both sides be empowered to reach a settlement. On May 19, at a general membership meeting of the longshoremen, Harry Bridges argued against "agreeing to any proposition sight unseen and against signing a separate agreement that would kick the props out from under the seamen." The rank-and-file longshoremen then voted unanimously that "any proposition arrived at through negotiations must be referred back to the rank and file for approval before it could be decided on."[8] Thus, the striking workers of San Francisco set down the principles on which the strike would be fought out: solidarity of all unions and all decision-making to rest in the hands of the workers themselves.

McGrady replied to the decision of the longshoremen by declaring: "Communists are throwing a monkey wrench into the situation. San Francisco ought to be informed of the growth of the Red element on the situation. There is an element among the longshoremen that lives on

strike and does not want a settlement."⁹ Later he issued a longer
statement on the same theme:

> A strong radical element within the ranks of the longshoremen seems to
> want no settlement of this strike. I have observed that Communists,
> through direct action and pleas made in the widely circulated Communist
> newspaper here, are trying to induce the strikers to remain out despite our
> efforts to arbitrate. . . . The Executive Committee appears to me to be
> helpless to do anything with the men they represent, or to combat the
> radical element in the Longshoremen's Union.¹⁰

J. W. Maillard, Jr., president of the San Francisco Chamber of
Commerce, took McGrady's statement as the principle under which the
united employers of the city would make war on rank-and-file industrial unionism. Maillard publicly issued an industrial manifesto.

> The San Francisco waterfront strike is out of hand. It is not a conflict
> between employer and employee—between capital and labor—it is a
> conflict which is rapidly spreading between American principles and
> un-American radicalism. As president of the San Francisco Chamber of
> Commerce, it is now my duty to warn every businessman in this commu-
> nity that the welfare of business and industry and the entire public is at
> stake in the outcome of this crisis.
>
> The so-called longshoremen's strike has spread since the morning of
> May 9 to include sympathetic walkouts by unions that presented no
> demands. On April 3, the workers and employers were in complete
> agreement on every point but wages and hours, and the President of the
> United States had set up machinery by which these differences would have
> been amicably and promptly settled through mediation.
>
> The longshoremen are now represented by spokesmen who are not
> representatives of American labor and who do not desire a settlement of
> their strike, but who desire a complete paralysis of shipping and industry
> and who are responsible for the violence and bloodshed which is typical of
> their tribe.
>
> The Assistant Secretary of Labor, sent here from Washington, in a last
> effort to terminate the strike, has indicated that the situation is hopeless
> and that all negotiations have failed.
>
> There can be no hope for industrial peace until communistic agitators
> are removed as the official spokesmen of labor and American leaders are
> chosen to settle their differences along American lines.¹¹

San Francisco newspapers translated the Maillard statement into time-
honored media slogans. Banner headlines proclaimed: "Strike Out
of Hand, Reds Lead Dock Strike, City Warned! Situation Hopeless
Says Mediator."

Waterfront workers, following the pattern of the times, proved their
immunity to red-baiting when a few days later the two remaining craft
unions—the Masters, Mates, and Pilots and the Marine Engineers

Beneficial Association—struck. All crafts in the maritime profession on the West Coast, as well as the longshoremen, now confronted an equally united coalition of employers.

Joseph Ryan, the crime-tarred president of the ILA who for years had maintained a connection with waterfront gangsters, arrived in San Francisco and immediately entered into secret negotiations with Maillard. On May 28 Ryan signed an agreement according to which the employers accepted the principle of collective bargaining but did not specifically recognize the ILA as sole bargaining agent, provided for an employer-controlled hiring hall, and established the employers' right to hire union or nonunion workers at their discretion. Ryan called in the press and boasted that the new agreement was a victory for the union; the newspapers announced that the strike was over. At that precise moment, mounted police and foot patrolmen suddenly attacked the mass picket line in front of Pier 18, which had been manned since the first day of the strike. The strikers fought back with fists and bricks; scores of strikers and police wee injured. Once again inflammatory headlines announced what was by then clearly industrial warfare. Lieutenant Mignola, the head of the waterfront police detail, told the press: "If the strikers come back for more, you'll find some of them in the morgue after the next time."[12]

On May 29 Ryan was roundly booed at a special membership meeting called by the San Francisco Strike Committee to consider the proposal signed by Ryan and the shipowners. Harry Bridges characterized the agreement as a "mere attempt of the employers to sound out the weak spots in the ILA organization." The agreement was unanimously rejected by the strikers. Ryan then flew up to the northwestern ports, hoping to find more support from the Portland and Seattle locals. Instead, both ports turned down the proposal, refusing even to submit it to secret ballot. San Francisco police launched another bloody attack on a large strike-support demonstration led by the Young Communist League on Memorial Day. Two teenagers were shot and another twenty or so were sent to the hospital. Two days later 5,000 people gathered on the Embarcadero to protest police brutality. The parade was led by a dozen small children of longshoremen, followed by a hundred women and long ranks of waterfront workers.

By the second week of June, the strike had taken on the character of a protracted showdown between the owners of capital and the ranks of labor. On June 12, Maillard released an open letter to John Forbes, president of the San Francisco Industrial Association, which represented most businesses in the city. The press played up the letter, which declared that the strike had been taken over by radicals, and urged the Industrial Association to "immediately assume responsibility for determining a method of ending this intolerable condition." The Industrial Association, acting out its rehearsed role, replied that it "accepts the responsibility which you ask it to assume."[13]

The method adopted by the propertied class in San Francisco for "ending this intolerable condition" was the same as that used by the employers at Homestead in 1892, Pullman in 1894, and by steel owners in 1919—force and violence. California Governor Merriam appended his own proclamation to the chorus calling for war on the striking maritime workers:

> Among us a horde of irresponsible, professional agitators, mostly aliens, are trafficking shamelessly in the agonies of these stressful times. They are seeking revolution, not reform; to make conditions worse, not better.
>
> These public enemies deliberately provoke demonstrations and incite alarms at a time when peace and civil tranquility are the supreme requisites in our battle for national recovery; a battle calling for all the energies of our people.[14]

The San Francisco business establishment, its political allies, and the Hearst newspapers now launched a step-by-step plan "to open the port." First, a settlement was reached among the waterfront employers, Joseph Ryan, and local teamster officials, and a prearranged press campaign then declared the strike over. When the plan was once again unanimously rejected by 3,000 longshoremen, and Ryan was once again hooted out of the meeting hall, he and representatives of the employers met in the office of Mayor Rossi, where it was announced to the press that the union had been captured by Communists and that the situation was completely out of control. The employers sent a telegram to Roosevelt saying, "Communists have captured control of the Longshoremen's union with no intention of strike settlement." They added that a crisis threatened "destruction of property and serious loss of life in various ports on the Pacific Coast unless you act to compel performance on the part of Longshoremen's unions of the agreement signed by their International President."[15]

Events moved rapidly. The striking maritime workers set up a joint strike committee consisting of five delegates from each of the ten striking unions, with Harry Bridges as chairman. The Industrial Association attempted to bribe Bridges by offering him $50,000 to sell out the strike. Bridges considered taking the money and donating it to the strike fund, but rejected the idea as too dangerous.[16] Angry workers demanded that all unions throughout the Bay Area begin to take general strike votes by their memberships and the process was begun.

On June 26 President Roosevelt utilized his new powers under the NIRA to establish the National Longshoremen's Labor Board. He appointed Archbishop Hanna of San Francisco, San Francisco attorney Oscar Cushing, and Edward McGrady to represent the NLB. McGrady immediately set up a meeting with Bridges and the rank-

and-file strike committee, but was told that the longshoremen did not trust the new commission.

Nor did the employers. They were determined, once bribery had failed, to resort to force. On Tuesday, July 2, they ran five empty trucks into Pier 38. Headlines in San Francisco papers announced the "opening of the port." Some 1,500 pickets converged on the pier in response to an emergency call from the strike committee to all unions in the city that city business interests were attempting to break the strike. On the afternoon of July 3, the five trucks, loaded with struck cargo and escorted by eight police cars, rolled out of Pier 38. Police Captain Thomas Hoertkorn, standing on the running board of the lead patrol car, waved his revolver in the air and shouted: "The port is open!"

After a tense period of watching the unloading of struck cargo at a nearby warehouse, thousands of longshoremen and their allies finally attacked the reinforced police ranks with bricks. The police responded with gunfire and tear gas. One strikebreaker was killed, thirteen policemen and twelve workers seriously wounded. The Industrial Association placed full-page proclamations in the newspapers announcing: "THE PORT IS OPEN."

Given the aroused consciousness of the industrial workers in the San Francisco Bay area, a general strike was now inevitable. On July 4, the Industrial Association called off its trucking operation in honor of the nation's holiday, but declared that it would continue again after midnight. Train crews walked off the Belt Line railroad in front of the docks, refusing to move struck cargo, and when the employers attempted to run the trains with scabs, a number of cars were derailed by the strikers. Governor Merriam notified the National Guard to be prepared to take over the waterfront. At this critical point, William Green, president of the American Federation of Labor, issued a statement supporting an anticommunist resolution passed by the reactionary craft-dominated San Francisco Labor Council. The alliance of U.S. capital and craft union elites, established at the turn of the century, continued to operate throughout the 1930s in the attempt to roll back the tide of industrial unionism.

Thursday, July 5, 1934, has gone down in the history of San Francisco as "Bloody Thursday," and is commemorated to the present day by San Francisco longshoremen as a stop-work memorial holiday for the workers killed in the struggle for industrial organization. A synopsis of the capital–labor wars of the thirties is captured by the headlines of the San Francisco press on July 5, 1934:

3 KILLED, 106 HURT AS TROOPS MOVE IN

S.F. Waterfront Rocked by Death, Bloodshed, Riots

BLOOD FLOODS THE GUTTERS AS POLICE BATTLE STRIKERS

Mike Quin reports a conversation he heard on the evening following the battle in the bar of the exclusive Union League Club: "'If I had my way,' said one [businessman], 'I'd end this strike in thirty minutes. I'd turn machine guns on those bastards and mow them down like wheat.' 'What ought to be done,' said the other, 'is to take that communist bastard Harry Bridges out and string him up to the nearest lamppost.'"

On the evening of July 5, 2,000 National Guard troops occupied the Embarcadero, mounted machine guns on the pier roofs, and cordoned off the entire waterfront. Harry Bridges told the longshoremen: "We cannot stand up against police, machine guns and National Guard bayonets."[17]

At midday on July 9 the historic funeral parade took place, in which 15,000 longshoremen carried their slain martyrs up Market Street to an undertakers' establishment in the Mission District two miles distant. Paul Eliel, research director of the Industrial Association, who understood the significance of the march, described it:

> The procession was orderly and quiet. Every marcher walked with bared head. Not a word was spoken. None smoked. The ranks were well formed and the cadence of the marchers' feet was set by the slow music of a Beethoven funeral march played by a single band. Tens of thousands of spectators lined the streets as the files of strikers, extending for more than a mile and a half down Market Street, swung slowly past. At each intersection volunteer traffic officers from the strikers' ranks controlled the crowds and the movement of the marchers through the intersection. Not a police officer nor a National Guard was in evidence from one end of the long line of march to the other.
>
> It was one of the strangest and most dramatic spectacles that had ever moved along Market Street. Its passage marked the high tide of united labor action in San Francisco. Its dramatic qualities moved the entire community without regard to individual points of view as to the justice of the strikers' cause. It created a temporary but tremendous wave of sympathy for the workers. Only after two or three days passed did San Francisco awaken to the fact that its sympathies had been aroused by a brilliant and theatric piece of propaganda. . . .
>
> As the last marcher broke ranks, the certainty of a general strike, which up to this time had appeared to many to be the visionary dream of a small group of the most radical workers, became for the first time a practical and realizable objective.[18]

Bridges and the rank-and-file strike committee met with the National Longshoremen's Labor Board after the funeral march and, according to Eliel, "made an extraordinary presentation before the Board. . . . Employers were able for the first time to understand something of the hold which he had been able to establish over the strikers both in his own union and in the other maritime crafts."[19] On July 7 delegates from nearly every union in San Francisco met in Eagles Hall and voted unanimously for a general strike. The old-line San Francisco labor leaders attempted by parliamentary maneuvers and subterfuges to sidetrack the strike but the revolt from below was too powerful to contain.

On July 8 rank-and-file teamsters packed Dreamland Auditorium and by secret ballot voted overwhelmingly, 1,220 to 271, for a general strike. Michael Casey and other conservative AFL leaders attempted to circumvent the vote by holding another meeting where AFL labor bosses urged that all action be postponed. The teamster rank and file booed their own leaders and shouted, "We want Bridges." Bridges was brought into the meeting, reviewed the history of the strike, and urged united labor action to defend the common interests of labor in the city. The teamsters voted unanimously to strike the next morning. One by one every union in San Francisco, often in opposition to their business agents and officials, voted to shut down the city.

The business community rallied its own considerable forces to counter the general strike offensive, coordinating action among employers, police, and the press. Governor Meier of Oregon telegraphed Roosevelt, who was vacationing in the Pacific aboard the cruiser U.S.S. *Houston,* that "we are now in a state of armed hostilities." The situation was "complicated by communistic interference" and out of control. The president was urged to return to the coast and take matters into his own hands. Roosevelt, irritated by the suggestion, cabled Presidential Assistant Louis Howe in the White House to reply to Meier, "I do not consider such action advisable. Communicate with me hereafter in the White House." He remarked after the strike that "a lot of people completely lost their heads and telegraphed me, 'For God's sake, turn the ship around.' . . . Everybody demanded that I sail into San Francisco Bay, all flags flying and guns double-shotted, and end the strike. They went completely off the handle."[20]

Roosevelt, an astute judge of power constellations, and facing a decline in the power of the National Recovery Administration machinery and its business leaders, had begun his search for new allies. In both the political and economic spheres, leaders of labor and government were becoming aware that the road to the consolidation of a new basis of power lay in the channeling of the revolt from below into organizational structures. A few months after the San Francisco General Strike, Roosevelt, in a private conversation with British and American newsmen, told them "off the record" that he had kept in close touch with the situation in San Francisco through his own agents:

> It appeared very clear to me, that just as soon as there was talk of a general strike, there were probably two elements bringing about the general strike. One was the hot-headed young leaders who had no experience in organized labor whatsoever and said that the only thing to do was to have a general strike.

On the other side was this combination out there of people like the editor of the *Los Angeles Times,* for instance, who was praying for a general strike. In other words, there was the old, conservative crowd just hoping that there would be a general strike, being clever enough to know that a general strike always fails. Hence there was a great deal of encouragement for a general strike.[21]

Franklin Roosevelt was not Grover Cleveland; he was beginning to understand that the industrial working class was a powerful emerging constituency that might be used to strengthen the power of the executive—a factor confirmed by the Left-Democratic sweep in Congress in the fall elections of 1934.

Unlike their fellow workers in the maritime trades, the rank-and-file members of the AFL crafts in San Francisco had not seized control over their own unions. They had simply forced the old-line leaders to call a general strike. The old craft union elite was thus able to dominate the General Strike Committee and pursue a strategy to stop the strike, and if that failed, to end it as rapidly as possible. However, for four days the working class, which many had argued did not exist in America, took over one of the country's major cities. Mike Quin best captured the spirit of 1934:

> The paralysis on the morning of July 16 was effective beyond all expectation. To all intents and purposes, industry was at a complete standstill. The great factories were empty and deserted. No streetcars were running. Virtually all stores were closed. The giant apparatus of commerce was a lifeless, helpless hulk.
>
> Labor had withdrawn its hand. The workers had drained out of the plants and shops like life-blood, leaving only a silent framework embodying millions of dollars worth of invested capital. In the absence of labor, giant machinery loomed as so much idle junk.
>
> Everything was there, all intact as the workers had left it—instruments, equipment, tools, machinery, raw materials, and the buildings themselves. When the men walked out they took only what belonged to them—their labor. And when they took that they might as well have taken everything, because all the elaborate apparatus they left behind was worthless and meaningless without their hand. The machinery was a mere extension of labor, created by and dependent upon labor.
>
> Labor held the life-blood and energy. The owners remained in possession of the corpse.[22]

Mayor Rossi proclaimed martial law: 3,000 additional troops with automatic rifles strengthened the National Guard, barricades were erected in the streets surrounding the waterfront, and 500 new police were sworn in. But as an atmosphere of panic swept the business community, Quin describes the "almost carnival spirit" that appeared in working-class neighborhoods. "Laboring men appeared on the streets in their Sunday clothes, shiny celluloid buttons glistening on every coat lapel. Common social barriers were swept away in the spirit of the occasion. Strangers addressed each other warmly as old friends. Labor wore its new-found power with calm dignity." Speaking in the language of the times, Quin expressed the social psychology of the industrial working class:

> After all, this great intricate mass of steel, stone and machinery was their baby. They built it and they ran it. They knew every bolt and cog and screw in the apparatus of civilization. They were as familiar and at ease with its mechanical complexities as they were with the insides of their pockets. They could turn the whole thing off at will, or start it up again in a minute if they pleased. They were organized.[23]

Meanwhile, red-baiting intensified as the *Chronicle* ran editorial after editorial warning that radicals controlled the strike and they wanted no settlement: "What they want is revolution. Organized labor and communism have nothing in common. There are no unions in Russia, where these radicals get their orders." This line had been perpetrated by U.S. ruling groups since 1877; in 1934 it had become obsolete.

On the second day of the general strike, the National Guard, in concert with the San Francisco police, initiated a series of raids on "reds and aliens." They smashed the Marine Workers' Industrial Union headquarters as the symbolic command post of the Communist Party of the United States operating within the industrial union movement. Over 450 people were arrested for vagrancy, only a few of whom were Communists. The American Legion organized shotgun squads which demanded the "death penalty for reds."

When the strike was in its third day, the press announced that both sides desired arbitration and that the "reds" who had been preventing a settlement were locked up in jail. On July 19, the strike committee, dominated by its old-line craft union officials, voted 191 to 174 to call off the strike and submit the issues to a federal arbitration board. According to the *Examiner*, "Mayor Rossi danced around his office with joy when notified by Edward Vandeleur, president of the AFL craft-dominated strike committee, that the strike was over." The mayor then issued the following proclamation:

> I congratulate the real leaders of organized labor on their decision. San Francisco has stamped out without bargain or compromise an attempt to import into its life the very real danger of revolt.
>
> San Francisco was founded by liberty-loving people. Its traditions are sacred to us. We will tolerate no tyranny, either of Communism or any other interference with constituted authorities.[24]

On October 12 the mediation board announced its award. The longshoremen won the six-hour day, thirty-hour week, and time and a half for overtime. They had asked for a base pay of $1.00 an hour and won $.95. The key issue had been control over hiring and the board set up a dispatching hall run jointly by the employers and the union, although "the dispatcher" was to be selected by the union. This breakthrough was later to be consolidated by a Left-led longshoremen's union that in the future, through more struggle, would win the best conditions for comparable work in the country.

Minneapolis: The General Truckers Strike

At the same time that the maritime workers on the West Coast were engaged in large-scale industrial warfare with waterfront employers, the Minneapolis truckers, also under radical leadership, were in the process of constructing the most powerful independent union in the country. Despite the fact that a progressive Farmer-Labor Party had elected a New Deal governor in the elections of 1932, Minneapolis retained its reputation of being an open-shop town. The city was firmly under the grip of the Citizens' Alliance, one of the most powerful and efficient business associations in the country. It possessed "a permanent and well-paid staff, a corps of undercover informers, . . . a membership of eight hundred businessmen," and a record of successfully breaking every major strike in Minneapolis for more than a generation.[25]

Minneapolis still had a tradition of industrial-union militancy, however. Thousands of itinerant lumberjacks, miners, harvest hands, and railroad construction workers in the period preceding World War I had built IWW Local 10 of Minneapolis into one of the largest Wobbly locals in the nation. Many of its members became "double-headers," joining AFL craft unions while retaining their Wobbly cards. Railroad workers who had been followers of Eugene Debs preserved their loyalty to socialism and industrial unionism. Immigrants from Sweden, Norway, Germany, Denmark, and Finland brought their socialist beliefs with them. Then in 1934 there occurred a fusion of native-born and immigrant labor militancy around the issue of industrial unionism and once again the workers chose socialist leaders to design strategies of class warfare over economic issues.

Vincent Raymond Dunne and Karl Skoglund, leaders of the great truckers' organizing drive, symbolized this unity. Dunne, the son of a Kansas streetcar mechanic, went to work at the age of fourteen as a lumberjack in the Minnesota woods, joined the IWW, worked as a harvest hand throughout the Northwest, and finally settled in Minneapolis as an express truck driver and active revolutionary socialist. Skoglund, a skilled worker in a Swedish pulp mill, was blacklisted in Sweden for being a trade unionist and socialist militant and immigrated to Minnesota where he worked as a lumberjack, building-trades mechanic, car repairman in the railroad shops, and coal hauler. Dunne and Skoglung became members of the newly formed Communist Party, in 1919 and 1920, and both were expelled in 1928 for supporting Trotsky over Stalin; they then moved to establish the pro-Trotsky Communist League in Minneapolis. In 1934 they organized rank-and-file coalyard workers and drivers to launch the first successful strike Minneapolis had experienced in decades. Sixty-five out of sixty-seven coal yards in the city were shut down with precision and military efficiency on February 7, 1934.

Farrell Dobbs, one of the ablest rank-and-file leaders produced by this strike, describes the first battle in the war that was to break the open shop in Minneapolis:

> The strike hit the industry with a bang. Characterized by militant mass picketing from the outset, the whole operation was both audacious and efficient. The pickets, mainly young workers in their first labor struggle, reinforced the careful planning by experienced leaders with courageous actions during which they came up with some innovations of their own. Development and use of cruising picket squads was an outstanding example of rank and file ingenuity.[26]

Dunne, Skoglund, and their radical group chose an existing AFL union, Local 574, chartered as a "general" local in 1915 and so weakened that it contained only seventy-five members, as the empty vessel into which they could pour the content of industrial unionism. As Dobbs explained, the drive was opened in the coal yards because Communist League members, including the Dunne brothers, were employed there. Moreover, "the coal yards were the strategic place to start the action because of the subzero Minnesota winters," meaning that "a well-timed and properly conducted strike could win a relatively quick sttlement in the union's favor, even though it might only be a partial victory."[27]

The strike was seen as the first step in the organization of the entire trucking industry in Minneapolis. The organizers planned to tap the spirit of revolt sweeping through the ranks of the nation's unorganized industrial working class and to mobilize the militants of past struggles: "In Minneapolis there were numerous trade-unionists who retained memory of radical unionism in the past. Some considered themselves socialists in a loose sense. Others had kept alive a spark of militancy from their IWW days. Once a real strike got under way in the city, many of them could be expected to rally like old warhorses responding to the sound of a bugle."[28]

Local 574: the building of a rank-and-file union

The key issue in the San Francisco longshoremen's strike proved to be the longshoremen's support of the demands of all the striking maritime unions and their refusal to accept a separate settlement. In Minneapolis, on the other hand, the principle of working-class solidarity was expressed by the scope of union recognition. Local 574 had organized not only truck drivers, but also helpers, yard workers, platform hands, shipping-room employees, packers, and other inside workers on jobs loosely associated with trucking operations. It was these "inside workers" who became the key issue in the strike. The question of solidarity among all categories of workers was an essential characteristic of industrial-union consciousness during the thirties.

Caught by surprise and under pressure from a public demanding immediate delivery of coal in freezing weather, the employers indirectly recognized the union by informing the NLB they would submit to collective bargaining. This was the first victory for the unorganized workers of Minneapolis in twenty years, and it marked the first time a teamster's local set about organizing on an industrial union basis, that is, taking all workers in a given enterprise into a single union, drivers and nondrivers alike.[29]

The rank and file of Local 574 proceeded to set up an organizing committee that by-passed the old-line AFL executive board of the local. Their aim was to organize all workers in the Minneapolis trucking industry. Organizing squads soon covered the whole city: "Meetings were held with each group of workers to formulate specific demands for their particular section on the trucking industry. They made the decisions on all items relating to wages, hours, and working conditions."[30] Organizers followed the tactic of the coal miners, who had employed the slogan: "President Roosevelt wants you to join the union." In Minneapolis, Local 574 distributed leaflets all over town announcing that Governor Floyd Olson would address a mass meeting called "The Right to Organize." Olson, his hand forced, sent to the meeting a representative who read a strong statement urging the truck drivers to "band together for your own protection and welfare."[31] By April 1934, Local 574 had grown from 75 members to 3,000.

The class-based organizations that confronted each other in Minneapolis replicated the polarization characteristic of the San Francisco General Strike. On one side, representing capital, was the Citizen's Alliance, which had united all employers to maintain the open shop at all costs; on the other side was a rank-and-file organizing committee, representing the industrial working class. This committee outmaneuvered local and national AFL leaders, successfully forcing the AFL Central Labor Council to go on record in support of its demands. The formerly effective alliance between businessmen and craft union officials was thus broken. Charles Rumford Walker, author of the definitive work on the 1934 trucker's strike, *American City,* interviewed A. W. Strong, head of the Citizen's Alliance. Strong told him: "I can conceive of dealing with a conservative and responsible labor leader, but certainly not with any of the A. F. of L. leaders in Minneapolis, or with the leadership of Local 574."[32]

Local 574 climaxed its whirlwind organizing drive with a huge rally at the Shubert Theater. On April 30, Local 574 put forth its demands to all the major trucking and allied businesses in Minneapolis: "the closed shop, shorter hours, an average wage of $27.50 a week, and premium pay for overtime."[33] The Citizen's Alliance held a strategy session at the West Hotel, where "a spokesman for the Alliance told representatives of the eleven major trucking firms that it had smashed the 1916 drivers' strike at a cost of $25,000 and that it could do the job again inexpensively."[34] The alliance then set up a special organization to represent the trucking industry, called the Minneapolis Employers of Drivers and Helpers. On May 7 this organization "categorially rejected" Local 574's demands, announcing that the central issue was the "closed shop" and that the trucking companies "would never agree to an abridgment of the liberties of the individual workman."[35] Local 574 then withdrew its demand for the closed shop and offered to arbitrate the wage demand. The trucking companies refused to bargain, mediation by the governor and the Regional Labor Board failed, and on May 15 the membership of Local 574 voted overwhelmingly to strike the entire trucking industry. The great trucking strike began on May 15, 1934.

Minneapolis business interests understood that a change in organizational form implied a change in the rules of the game; it was a matter of control. Craft unions under "responsible leaders" could be controlled; broad industrial unions representing the most exploited workers meant a loss of management control. Both the San Francisco and Minnesota labor upheavals undermined the divide-and-rule craft–business alliance that had blocked labor progress for more than fifty years.

The leaders and rank-and-file committees of Local 574 prepared the Minneapolis truckers' strike with meticulous care. Alliances were made with the unemployed and progressive farmers' organizations and a women's auxiliary was set up. The union rented a large garage building at 1900 Chicago Avenue as a strike headquarters, and the seventy-five-member strike committee established numerous subcommittees to handle all matters from legal aid to complaints. Farrell Dobbs and Ray Dunne were placed in charge of all picketing assignments. Like front-line commanders, they planned the tactical operations of the battle. Dobbs describes the first day of the strike:

> When the sun rose on May 16, 1934, the headquarters at 1900 Chicago Avenue was a beehive of activity. Union carpenters and plumbers were installing gas stoves, sinks, and serving counters in the commissary. The Cooks and Waiters Union sent experts on mass cooking. . . . Working in two twelve-hour shifts, over 100 volunteers served 4,000 to 5,000 people daily. . . .

Committees were set up to promote material aid. They solicited friendly grocers for staples to be used in the commissary and to help out needy families of strikers. Similar donations were also received from sympathetic farmers. The committee fought city hall to get public relief for union members and the facts of life were explained to landlords who pressed the workers for rent payments. Money donations from other unions helped to stock the commissary, as well as to buy gasoline for the cruising picket squads and medical supplies for the union's emergency hospital. Even Governor Olson contributed $500 to Local 574.[36]

A doctor and two interns from the University of Minnesota hospital volunteered to work in the union's makeshift hospital. Auto mechanics set up shop to keep the strikers' cars in operation, guards maintained order in the headquarters building, general meetings were held each evening to keep the workers informed of developments, and cots were set up so that key personnel could remain near the center of action. Teenaged volunteers on motorcycles operated a scout service for the headquarters. Local 574 became famous for its cruising squads, which covered every district in the city on the lookout for scab trucking operations. "Scooting around the city under strict orders to stay out of the fighting, they served as the eyes and the ears of the picket dispatchers and as a swift means of contact with picket captains," Dobbs wrote.

A majority of the city's population proved sympathetic to the strike and soon a spontaneous intelligence service was in operation. People telephoned reports of scab activities, and other information was mailed anonymously, often with the postage being paid by some unknowing employer. Typists, even personal secretaries, slipped an extra carbon to make a copy for the union when the boss dictated something they felt the strikers should know about. Material arrived that had obviously been salvaged from wastebaskets, some of it coming from the offices of the Citizens' Alliance.[37]

By the second day of the strike Minneapolis was effectively shut down: "Nothing moved on wheels without the union's permission."

The Citizens' Alliance established a law-and-order committee, organized special deputies to coordinate strikebreaking activities with the police, and imitated Local 574 by setting up their own headquarters equipped with a hospital and commissary for their army of deputies. On May 19, fights broke out between strikers and hired strikebreakers backed by police and Citizens' Alliance deputies; many of the unarmed union pickets were badly injured and hospitalized. That same evening, a police agent gained access to the union loudspeaker at strike headquarters and called for two or three truckloads of pickets, including women, to cover an emergency at the loading docks of Tribune Alley. When the pickets arrived they were ambushed by the police and beaten

mercilessly. The women pickets were brought back to strike headquarters unconscious. Skoglund tells the story:

> I remember the night. They brought the women in, and the other pickets
> from Tribune Alley, and laid them down in rows at strike headquarters. All
> the women were mutilated and covered with blood, two or three with
> broken legs; several stayed unconscious for hours. Saps and night clubs
> had been used on both men and women. When the strikers saw them lying
> round with the nurses working over them, they got hold of clubs and swore
> they'd go down and wipe up the police and deputies. We told them no, the
> Alley was a trap. "We'll prepare for a real battle, and we'll pick our own
> battleground next time." That night, all next day, and the next night,
> fellows began to collect clubs. They'd gone unarmed before that. Now they
> got sticks, hose and pipe. You'd see men all over headquarters making saps
> and padding their caps for battle. One picket would crack another over the
> head and say, "Does it hurt?" And he'd say, "Yuh, I can feel it. I'll put in
> some more." That's the way it went, the fellows were wild there for a
> couple of days.[38]

Local 574 selected the market area for their battleground and secretly
concentrated 600 strikers, armed with clubs, in an AFL hall near the
market to await the battle, planned for Monday morning. At 9:00 a.m.
when scab drivers attempted to drive loaded trucks out of the market
and were blocked by pickets, the police charged and the battle was on.
The 600 reserve union troops moved out in military formation and
routed both police and deputies. More than thirty police were hospitalized. According to Dobbs, some 20,000 people jammed the market area
the next day (Tuesday). Thousands of citizens lined up on the rooftops
to watch the battle, just as they had done in San Francisco. Strikers and
their supporters drove 1,500 policemen and hundreds of deputies out of
the market that day. Injuries were heavy on both sides and two special
deputies were killed. One of them was Arthur Lyman, an attorney and
member of the board of directors of the Citizens' Alliance. Workers all
over the country saw newsreel films of strikers clubbing police and
broke out in cheers when the police went down in defeat.

Governor Olson called for a truce and ordered out the National
Guard. Under pressure from the governor and the NLB, strikers and
employers agreed to a compromise settlement: the drivers' pay, which
had been raised by $1.50 an hour before the strike in an effort to defuse
the union's organizing drive, was to continue at the new rate for one
year; other issues were referred to arbitration. As in the coalyard strike,
the employers indirectly agreed to recognize the union when 166 of
them signed an NLB consent order.

In Minneapolis, Roosevelt allowed Governor Olson to shoulder the
responsibility for mediation of the Minnesota class war virtually alone.

Olson manipulated a settlement of the key issue covering the scope of recognition by proposing a new formulation of the recognition clause. Union recognition was to include drivers, helpers, and "such other persons as are ordinarily engaged in trucking operations."[39]

Local 574 consolidated its organization and expanded its membership to 7,000 in the weeks following the May settlement. The three Dunne brothers, Carl Skoglund, and Farrell Dobbs were employed by the union as full-time organizers, earning $25 a week, the average truck driver's wage. Then, in mid-June, the Citizens' Alliance began a new drive to break the union. The NLB made no effort to enforce the terms of the settlement, individual employers refused to bargain with the union over "inside workers," and Olson hedged on the issue by suggesting it be submitted to arbitration. The NLB ruled that the union had the right to represent only drivers, helpers, and platform workers "directly engaged in loading and unloading trucks." The union responded: "the Labor Board has 'generously' ruled that Local 574 shall have the right to represent almost half its membership."[40]

Local 574 then began preparing for another strike over the key issue of full recognition and over immediate wage increases. Capital, speaking through the Citizens' Alliance, launched a united propaganda campaign to educate the public on the distinction between "legitimate and American-minded trade unions from the terroristic Communist-led Truck Drivers' Local 574." The Employers' Advisory Committee placed a full-page advertisement in the Minneapolis press, headed: "Must Minneapolis Be Penalized by a Strike to Satisfy a Handful of Communist Agitators Who Plan to Make Minneapolis the Birthplace of a New Soviet Republic?"[41]

Following the San Francisco formula to the letter, Minneapolis business interests called forth the historic corporate–craft union alliance by enlisting Daniel Tobin, president of the International Brotherhood of Teamsters, in the campaign to destroy Local 574. Just as William Green had joined the San Francisco employers in attacking the longshore strike leadership, Tobin joined the employer coalition in Minneapolis to overthrow the rank-and-file teamster leaders. Tobin called on the membership of Local 574 to rid themselves of the "infamous Dunne brothers" and the other "semi-monsters who are creeping into our midst and getting into some of our newly organized local unions, creating distrust, discontent, bloodshed and rebellion." Tobin's direct attack on the leaders of industrial unionism was republished in a full-page ad paid for by Minneapolis business interests in the July 7, 1934, *Minneapolis Daily Star*.[42]

Both sides prepared for the new showdown. The employers, like their counterparts in San Francisco, engaged in daily planning sessions with the Minneapolis mayor and the chief of police. On July 16, the day on which Local 574 voted unanimously to strike, Chief of Police Johanes asked the city council for a 100 percent increase in the police budget. He wanted machine guns, 800 rifles with bayonets, 800 steel helmets, 800 riot guns, and 26 additional motorcycles.[43] Local 574, for its part, organized labor support throughout the city, began to publish the first daily labor newspaper in the country, and prepared even more carefully for the second campaign than it had for the first.

The Minneapolis newspapers announced that the San Francisco general strike had been broken by "armed bands of vigilantes" and the *Milwaukee Journal* called for using the same method to break the truckers' strike in Minneapolis.[44] The strike began peacefully, however, and on July 18 the union avoided a carefully planned police trap designed to lure the pickets into an attack on a truck purported to be carrying hospital supplies. On Friday, July 20, employers sent letters to all strikers containing an ultimatum that each striker had three days to report to work or be replaced. At 2:00 p.m. on the same day a scab truck pulled away from a loading dock in the market escorted by 50 police on foot carrying service revolvers, riot guns, and clubs, and another 100 police in squad cars. Once out in the street, the scab truck was followed by an open truck loaded with unarmed strikers. Dobbs describes what happened next:

> Suddenly, without any warning whatever, the cops opened fire on the picket truck, and they shot to kill. In a matter of seconds two of the pickets lay motionless on the floor of the bullet-ridden truck. Other wounded fell to the street, or tried to crawl out of the death trap as the shooting continued. From all quarters strikers rushed toward the truck to help them. . . . Many were felled by police as they stopped to pick up their injured comrades. By this time the cops had gone berserk. They were shooting in all directions, hitting most of their victims in the back as they tried to escape, and often clubbing the wounded after they fell. So wild had the firing become that a sergeant was shot by one of his own men.[45]

This police riot resulted in the serious wounding of sixty-seven people, including thirteen bystanders, two of whom died. The incident, called "Bloody Friday," took about ten minutes. As in San Francisco, the strikers organized some 20,000 workers in a mass funeral march to strike headquarters, where under a black flag the truckers paid tribute to their martyrs.

Farrell Dobbs wrote later that a special investigating commission appointed by the governor after the strike reported that police took direct aim at the pickets and fired to kill; the physical safety of the police was at no time endangered; there were no weapons in the pickets' possession in the truck; and at no time did pickets attack the police. It was clear that pickets came unprepared for such an attack.

On July 23, federal conciliators proposed that Local 574 have the right to represent the inside workers provided that the union was able to win a poststrike election, and that the union members be granted a 2.5¢ per hour wage increase and arbitration of all wage scales. The governor threatened martial law if the proposal was not accepted by both sides. The union accepted by a vote of 1,866 to 147, but the employers' association refused, stating: "We cannot deal with this Communist leadership. . . . This whole strike is the result of misrepresentation, coercion and intimidation." The governor, professing sympathy with the strikers, then declared martial law. However, the National Guard permitted more than half of the trucks in the city to operate without union permission, in effect breaking the strike. Local 574 leaders visited the governor to demand that he halt all truck movement or they would continue to picket all trucks regardless of the existence of martial law.

Olson then concocted a rather bizarre strategy. He ordered a military force to occupy strike headquarters, arrest the strike leaders, and incarcerate them in a military stockade. He planned to call for the rank-and-file election of a new strike committee that would be "truly representative" of the Minneapolis truckers, with which he personally, as governor, would negotiate a strike settlement. On August 1 at 4:00 a.m., a Colonel McDevitt, accompanied by several hundred guardsmen, a detachment of machine gunners, and a battery of light artillery, surrounded Local 574 strike headquarters. V. R. Dunne was placed under arrest, but in the confusion Farrell Dobbs and Grant Dunne escaped out the back door.

Charles Rumford Walker has described the reaction of the rank-and-file truckers to the arrest of their leaders. He was told by a member of Local 574, "In place of the South Eighth Street Headquarters we established 'curb' headquarters all over the city. We had twenty of them." Walker adds:

> And in place of the eight leaders walled up in the stockade, fifty-odd picket captains took charge of the strike on their own. They were fighting mad and utterly fearless. In the next twenty-four hours, the vigor, the scope, and the fury of the picket actions terrified the city and gave pause to the Governor himself. According to the press,
>
> "Marauding bands of pickets roamed the streets of Minneapolis today in automobiles and trucks, striking at commercial truck movements in widespread sections of the city. . . . National Guardsmen in squad cars made frantic efforts to clamp down. The continued picketing was regarded as a protest over the military arrest of Brown and the Dunnes, strike leaders, together with sixty-eight others during and after Guardsmen raided strike headquarters and the Central Labor Union."[46]

Governor Olson carried out the second step of his plan by engineering the election of a two-man rank-and-file strike committee to settle the strike. The strikers, believing that they had to negotiate with someone, went along with this plan, electing Ray Rainbolt, a Sioux Indian, and another militant, Kelly Postal. Rainbolt reported on their talk with the governor: "We met with the Governor, Kelly and I. He said to us, 'Well, boys, we've got to settle this thing.' We said to him, 'First you let out our leaders; after that we'll talk.' Kelly called him a copper-hearted son-of-a bitch and I said to him, 'Governor, you're right in the middle, on a picket fence. Watch your step or you'll slip and hurt yourself bad.'"[47]

Olson, seeing that his actions had only increased the militancy of the rank and file, reversed his strategy, met privately with Grant Dunne, and agreed to free the strike leaders and restore the strike headquarters to Local 574. Then on August 4 he ordered the National Guard to raid the headquarters of the Citizens' Alliance. The soldiers seized documents from the employers' headquarters, but tipped off in advance, the Citizens' Alliance had already shipped out its confidential files. Since 900 out of a total of 13,000 trucks in the city were operating under military permits issued by the National Guard, Local 574 appealed to the AFL Central Labor Council for a general strike. Olson then issued an ultimatum to the Citizens' Alliance: unless a settlement was reached by midnight August 5, he would halt all trucking in Minneapolis. The employers sought a court injunction against the governor, declaring that his declaration of martial law was "an unconstitutional deprivation of property under the due process clause of the Fourteenth Amendment." Olson announced that he would personally argue the state's case.

The Minneapolis employers sent a delegation to see Roosevelt, who was passing through Minnesota by train after his summer trip on the U.S.S. *Houston*. They branded the strike leaders "communistic" and held the union solely responsible for the violence and the rejection of key Regional Labor Board rulings.[48] The next day, August 8, a group of Minnesota labor leaders also visited the president's train, which was stopped in Rochester, and were received by presidential assistant Louis Howe. The labor leaders argued that the key issue of the strike was collective bargaining and that the way to a settlement was being blocked by the Citizens' Alliance. Governor Olson also traveled to Rochester to confer with Roosevelt.[49]

Olson returned to Minneapolis and argued his case before Federal Court, which sustained his power to invoke martial law. The employers were thus isolated from their traditional allies, the executive department of the government and the courts. On the other hand, the strikers were exhausted by five weeks of violence and the strike committee was running out of money. After a number of local mediation plans collapsed when the union refused to participate, the White House intervened directly in the dispute:

> Once again, Jesse Jones, presumably at White House initiative, came to the rescue. On the evening of August 18 he phoned Haas (the local mediator)

to learn, in effect, what it would take to settle the strike. The mediator reported that two assurances to the union were needed: allowing strikers to vote even if they were charged with committing acts of violence and requiring arbitration of wages above the minima. Jones phoned Barton [a local official of the Reconstruction Finance Corporation and leader of the Citizens' Alliance] that evening and must have taken a hard line indeed. On August 19 resistance among the trucking companies collapsed; they conceded on both points.[50]

Ratification of the agreement by both sides occurred on August 21. The trucking companies promised to give preference to strikers in reemployment. Irving Bernstein sums up the business surrender in what he labels "the Appomattox of the Minneapolis civil war":

> Within 10 days the labor board would hold elections both among the drivers, helpers, platform men, and inside workers of the 22 market firms and among the drivers, helpers, and platform workers of the 144 other companies. Only those on the payrolls on July 16 would be eligible to vote. Representatives chosen by the majority would bargain for all and "each employer shall deal with such person, persons, or organization . . . for purposes of collective bargaining." Minimum wages would be 50¢ for drivers and 40¢ for others; rates above these minima would be arbitrated by a tripartite board. Hours and overtime would conform to the NRA codes.[51]

Under its radical leaders Local 574 would push on in the next few years to organize the over-the-road drivers throughout the Northwest and contribute to making the teamsters one of the most formidable of the new industrial and semi-industrial unions.

General Strike in Textiles

During the course of 1934 the National Guard was called out in sixteen states as tens of thousands of workers from coast to coast rose in rebellion against industrial serfdom. In a virtual civil war fought out from Maine to Alabama, the textile workers, constituting the most exploited labor force in the country, suffered a tragic defeat at the hands of ruthless mill owners and reactionary state governments.

Workers in the textile industry earned from $5 to $6 a week in most mills during the early 1930s. They worked at a minimum a fifty- to fifty-five-hour week; night work by women was widespread; and textile employers were notorious for employing child labor. Worst of all was the constant speed-up, or "stretch-out" as it was called in the textile mills, which required workers to work ever more looms. Novelist Martha Gellhorn made a tour of the textile towns of New England and the South in 1934 and sent reports to Harry Hopkins, Roosevelt's key assistant, on conditions there. She found the textile worker living in "feverish terror." Children were deprived of all education past the fourth grade and malnutrition among textile workers was extensive. The overall picture Gellhorn found was "terribly frightening." Many textile workers who worked part time were "worse off than those on relief"; children did not have enough to eat or wear; and the young people in the textile towns were "apathetic and despairing." Unemployed textile workers (layoffs were frequent) were "consumed with fear," Gellhorn reported to Hopkins, "fear, driving them into a state of semi-collapse; cracking nerves, and an overpowering terror of the future." Such was the setting of the bloodiest battle between capital and labor waged during the thirties.[52]

Roosevelt signed the Code of Fair Competition No. 1 on July 9, 1933. The code, set up under the NIRA, established a minimum wage of $13 in the northern mills and $12 in the South, except for cleaners, outside workers, and "learners." The code included Section 7a covering the right of workers to choose their own union, the forty-hour week, and a prohibition on child labor under the age of 16. The code was placed under the administration of George A. Sloan, head of the Cotton Textile Industry Committee. The United Textile Workers of America (UTW) represented only 15,000 to 20,000 of the workers in an industry employing more than 300,000 workers, larger than the total labor force in the steel industry.

According to Bernstein, the UTW had "virtually no cotton membership in the South, where the industry was concentrated, having missed the bus in the great 1929 strikes in that region. Furthermore, the union was broke, and except for its vice-president, Francis J. Gorman, was without effective leadership."[53] Under the code production increased, and by April the labor force in the cotton mills increased to 440,000. Overproduction quickly ensued and by fall the companies laid off workers, cheated on the code, ruthlessly increased the work load of the cotton workers through the stretch-out, and fired workers for union activity. Despite a flood of complaints from employees to the NIRA Cotton Textile Board, which was under control of the mill owners, nothing was done.

In the summer of 1934 the code authority limited output in the industry to cut down excess stocks by cutting back work hours. This action meant that the workers would not earn enough money to feed their families. The UTW, which had built up its membership to 250,000, announced that if the NRA order to cut back hours went into effect on June 4, the UTW would call a general cotton-textile strike. NRA officials mediated a settlement by June 2 and appointed a UTW representative to the Cotton Textile Board. Production was then cut back 25 percent rather than 75 percent as planned. Some mills simply shut down every fourth week. Code minimum wages dropped from $12 to $9 a week in the South and from $13 to $9.75 in the North.

Workers in the industry denounced the settlement as a "sell-out," and on July 16, the Alabama State Council of Textile Workers voted 40 to 2 for a strike. "The response was impressive: 20,000 workers in 24 mills in northern Alabama went out. They demanded a minimum wage of $12 for a thirty-hour week, abolition of the stretch-out, a reinstatement of mill hands fired for union activity, and recognition of the UTW. The employers made no concessions and the strike was to drag on for two months."[54] On August 14, 500 UTW delegates met in New York City and the militant representatives from the South introduced over fifty resolutions demanding a strike of the whole industry and a condemnation of the NRA. On the fourth day of the convention, with no opposition, a resolution was passed that made it "mandatory upon the officers to call a general cotton-textile strike on or about September 1." The convention also authorized strikes in silk, wool, and rayon, but let the union officers set the dates. Gorman was elected chairman of the emergency strike committee.

The Cotton Textile Board, in Bernstein's words, "floundered in the storm," and it was clear that the industry looked forward to a test of strength with its workers, which it believed it could win. The greatest textile strike in U.S. history began on September 1, when the UTW struck the cotton, silk, woolen, and worsted mills. "Flying squadrons" of workers sped throughout the South from one mill to the next to extend the strike, which by September 4 had spread to every textile center in the country. Cotton workers struck in Georgia, South Carolina, Tennessee, Virginia, Pennsylvania, Rhode Island, Massachusetts, New Hampshire, and Maine. Silk workers shut their mills down in New Jersey and the workforce walked out at the New Bedford woolen mills. In all, 376,000 workers struck in what was to become one of the largest strikes in U.S. history.

One historian wrote, "the 1934 general strike in the textile industry was unquestionably the greatest single industrial conflict in the history of American organized labor."[55] Whether or not that was the case, it was unquestionably one of the bloodiest. The mill owners imported armed guards, evicted strikers from their homes, used pressure to cut off public relief for any worker on strike, utilized wholesale terror against striking workers and union members, and called on the governors in the textile states to order out the National Guard. On September 5 at Trion, Georgia, a union supporter and one deputy were killed and twenty others wounded. The next day six pickets were killed by deputy gunfire in a town in South Carolina, five more at Honea Path, and one at Greenville. On September 10 riots broke out in textile towns in Rhode

Island, Connecticut, Massachusetts, and Maine; two strikers were killed, twenty more wounded.

Roosevelt appointed Governor John G. Winant of New Hampshire to head the Board of Inquiry for the Cotton Textile Industry. Gorman, speaking for the UTW, wired Roosevelt on September 8 to stop "the further slaughter of [UTW] members," and called for arbitration of the dispute. The employers refused to deal with the union and ignored all efforts to arbitrate the strike. Instead, they succeeded in calling out the National Guard, supplemented the troops with thousands of special militia, and were able to keep their mills open in Alabama, Mississippi, Georgia, and North and South Carolina. Bernstein records the letters of Mollie Dowd of the National Women's Trade Union League on the desperate position of the UTW in the southern states:

> She reported mills with machine gun nests in fixed positions at the corners with guards armed wth shotguns patrolling on foot. Union organizers were run out of town; at Albertsville the police threatened to jail a sympathizer for talking to a striker; the employer at Pritchard fired anyone who talked with the girl who led the strike.[56]

Families were evicted from company-owned houses in the middle of the night and in Alabama the relief administration "automatically cut off relief to strikers." By October Miss Dowd wrote, "Some of these folks are literally starving."

Rioting continued throughout New England mill towns far into September. It then became clear that the combination of mill owners and armed troops had swung the balance of power in favor of the mill owners. Winant sent his report to the president on September 20. It argued that the union's demand for recognition was "not feasible," called for an end to "stretch-out prior to February 1, 1935," and asked the UTW to call off the strike. On September 22 the strike committee ordered the strikers back to work. Roosevelt pleaded with the textile employers to rehire strikers, but they ignored his request and by October 23 the UTW reported that 113 northern and 226 southern mills had refused to rehire strikers. "The great textile strike of 1934," in Bernstein's words, "left no heritage beyond bitter memories."[57]

Detroit: Auto Workers Open a New Front

While the cause of the textile workers was drowned in blood and choked off in hunger, the auto workers of Detroit prepared to open a new front in the fight for industrial unions. The capitulation of the Auto Board, set up under the NIRA after the 1933 strike at Briggs Auto

Manufacturers and the 1934 strike at Hudson Motors, contributed to the 1934 strike wave in the auto industry. Workers realized they could not depend on New Dealers to represent their interests. By May 1934 the auto workers' union possessed a membership of 275 workers in Detroit, including 55 members at Budd Manufacturing, 50 at Chevrolet, 30 at Hudson Motors, 25 at the Dodge plant, 45 at Murray Body, and 70 at Ford. From this handful of workers who stood up to company terror came the impetus to create an industrial union eventually embracing a membership of 1 million workers.

Five groups were active in organizing the Detroit auto workers during the NRA period. The Communists, who had assumed leadership of the auto workers' union, were for years the only aggressive force in the auto industry. With only a few members, they succeeded in organizing shop meetings and publishing shop papers. In addition, there were the AFL and its full-time representatives, who were inactive when it came to organizing; the International Workers of the World, particularly strong at the Murray Body plant; a small group of Socialist Party intellectuals who were not particularly active in Detroit; and most importantly, skilled tool and die makers of the Mechanics Educational Society of America (MESA), who made up the largest group of organized workers in the Michigan auto shops. MESA was an independent union dominated by Scotch, English, and Irish skilled workers who brought to America their experience in the British trade union movement. Many of the skilled tool makers had come to Detroit from abroad during the twenties and by the end of 1934 the organization they had built came to 17,000 members. Despite leaders who professed Marxism, MESA remained firmly independent, refused to join the CIO when the organizing drives erupted, and never realized its potential. In the end MESA was by-passed by history.[58]

Wyndham Mortimer, the veteran Communist auto worker, recognized as one of the key figures in the organization of the industry, describes the sabotage of the industrial union movement by the AFL old guard, a pattern followed throughout the country. In June 1934 Mortimer attended an AFL-sponsored conference of auto workers in Detroit. When Mortimer pressed the issue of building "an international industrial union of all automobile and parts workers," William Collins, the AFL official in charge of organization in the auto industry and chairman of the meeting, pounded his gavel and shouted: "Sit down! I know who you are speaking for. Every time I hear the words 'international industrial union' I know where it comes from. It comes straight from Moscow."[59] Whether in San Francisco, Toledo, Minneapolis, Detroit, or Akron, the issue was the same—industrial unionism struck at the very foundations of the corporate–craft union organizational structure of the American system.

Mortimer returned to Cleveland, where he was elected president of Local 18463 by unanimous vote of the workers in the White Motor Plant. He then went on to organize the Cleveland District Auto Council, where once again he was elected president. The Auto Council united all the federal auto industry locals in Cleveland—Fisher Body, Hupmobile, National Carbon, Baker Rau Lang, Bender Body, Willard Storage Battery, and White Motor, the latter being the largest local of auto workers in the city. The new Auto Council was "immediately denounced and ordered to disband by the Executive Council, the Central Labor Council, and the Metal Trades Council, on the grounds that it was against AFL policy and that a charter would not be issued for such a body."[60] As a result, the Auto Council operated without an official charter from the AFL and began to function as a dual center of power for the auto workers in Cleveland. It began to publish its own paper, *The United Auto Worker,* bringing the historic struggle between the AFL and the new industrial-union movement for the allegiance of the auto workers into the open. For a time, the AFL thwarted rank-and-file control over the newly formed federal union, expelling the elected leaders, sending letters to all federal union locals forbidding participation in the Auto Council, which it labeled "Moscow insired," and appointing the leaders of the AFL international auto union.

Organizing from the Bottom Up

While rank-and-file organizing movements appeared in all major industries in the United States in 1933 and 1934, the key to the future of the American labor movement was the mass organizing effort in the automobile, rubber, and electrical industries.

Workers in these industries all began to organize on their own. In July 1933, 350 workers struck the Philadelphia Storage Battery Company, owned by Philco Radio, over a temporary extension of the work day to ten hours. The strike paralyzed the work of an additional 2,000 workers. A few days later, on July 15, the company signed an agreement with the American Federation of Radio Workers, led by 21-year-old James Carey. Within a few years Carey would become secretary-treasurer of the CIO. In 1933, however, Carey, like the longshoremen, the truckers, and the auto workers, attempted to affiliate with the only national labor organization in existence, the American Federation of Labor. Since the masses of workers who wished to join the AFL were not craft workers but unskilled, the AFL either did not want them, or if it did, hardly knew what to do with workers who had organized themselves. In the case of Carey and the radio workers, as in the auto and rubber industries, the AFL set up federal unions—large locals that could absorb many different types of workers and were semi-industrial in form.

A long series of negotiations between the new radio locals and the AFL repeated the experience of the other recently organized industrial unions: the AFL refused to grant charters to independent unions. Nevertheless, a Radio Council was established, similar to the Cleveland District Auto Council set up by Mortimer, and it was soon joined by electrical workers who had independently organized union locals at the giant General Electric and Westinghouse plants. The council agreed not to affiliate with or become a subdivision of any craft union, an action that soon brought it into collision with the AFL hierarchy.[61]

Fearful that a nationwide movement of the unskilled might sweep them from their posts, the AFL craft union leaders followed Gompers' advice (given at the 1903 AFL convention) "to stem the tide of expansion madness" before they were engulfed by it. They did everything in their power to sidetrack, stop, or turn back the labor revolt from below. There were, however, two leaders of the largest industrial unions within the AFL who saw that the future lay with industrial unions: John L. Lewis of the United Mine Workers, and Sidney Hillman of the Amalgamated Clothing Workers. Lewis' own miners had begun the mass movement from below in the summer of 1933, and Hillman had utilized Section 7a of the NIRA to build his union from 50,000 to 125,000 members during the months following the passage of the act. Both Lewis and Hillman had a hand in writing Section 7a, and on June 9, 1933, three days before its promulgation, Hillman argued in a radio address that the new legal reaffirmation of the right of workers to organize and bargain collectively would exist only "on paper, void of results, unless labor takes full advantage of it."[62] The AFL officialdom needed the advice; the industrial workers did not.

3

The CIO:
Organization of a
Social Movement

The great strikes generated by the industrial workers in San Francisco, Toledo, Minneapolis, and throughout the textile industry frightened U.S. corporate elites, but the Committee for Industrial Organization (CIO) posed an even greater threat. It linked labor rebellion with a network of organization that reached into every corner of the U.S. industrial system.

Communists, Trotskyists, Socialists, and Left-syndicalists organized and created the social movement that came to be identified with the CIO. Traditional unionists either moved left or were by-passed by a historic campaign for social justice and collective industry, a mass movement directed against industrial peonage.

Early Challengers: John L. Lewis

On Labor Day, 1934, with the shock waves of the labor revolt still reverberating across the nation, John L. Lewis, former Gompers protégé, declared that the AFL must adopt a policy of industrial unionism in the mass production industries. On October 10, speaking to the industrial and financial elite at the Commonwealth Club in San Francisco, he warned his corporate audience that if the Morgan-Dupont-Rockefeller opposition to unionism and the New Deal continued, it would result in "an industrial revolt" leading to a fascist or communist dictatorship. This was one of the last times Lewis would publicly utilize the fear of communism to spur the business community into a recognition of "responsible" unionism. Within a short time, Lewis himself would become the target of a wave of red-baiting directed against the industrial-union movement and his position as its symbolic leader.[1]

Lewis launched his official one-man offensive to achieve industrial unionism within the American Federation of Labor at the 1934 AFL convention in San Francisco during the second week of October. Dubofsky and Van Tine note that while Lewis invited the business elites gathered at the Commonwealth Club to "support the New Deal in seeking a 'middle-way' for the United States," he followed a more militant approach when addressing AFL leaders in San Francisco:

> He told the A.F. of L's resolutions committee and its 1934 convention delegates that there was only one way to organize the nation's mass production workers, and it was not the "middle-way" preferred by craft unionists. Mass production workers could not be parcelled out by trade to competing craft unions, nor could the less skilled among them be offered an inferior status.[2]

Lewis found his efforts blocked by the most powerful of the old-guard AFL leadership—Wharton of the Machinists, Hutcheson of the Carpenters, Tobin of the Teamsters, John Frey, president of the AFL Metal Trades Department, and Matthew Woll, an official of the Photo-Engravers and a prominent ideologue of craft unionism. "The primary means by which the old guard preserved its power was through enforcement of the principle of exclusive jurisdiction. The Federation parcelled out territories, real as well as imaginary, to the internationals, which then became inviolate."[3] All the crafts fought each other over jurisdictional issues involving workers they claimed to be in their own trade, no matter where they might work. The Iron Workers fought the Carpenters, the Brewery Workers fought the Operating Engineers, and all argued about whether craft workers in the auto industry should be placed in temporary industrial units, made to join federation labor unions, or turned over to the Machinists. In the last half of 1933 the AFL granted 1,006 federal union charters, which were in effect temporary organizational expedients to take in new members and later divide them up among the crafts.

The newly organized industrial unionists in auto, rubber, and the electrical industries hoped to turn the AFL federal locals into permanent new national unions; the craft union officials wanted to absorb the rapidly expanding membership of the federal locals into the already established craft union structure. At the 1933 AFL convention, John Frey, head of the Metal Trades Department, introduced a resolution to require the AFL "to take such immediate action as is necessary to prevent the inclusion of any mechanic or laborer over whom the International Unions have jurisdiction through the charter rights given to them by the American Federation of Labor."[4] Woll supported the resolution that federal locals could be organized only with the consent of the international unions. Charles P. Howard, president of the Typographical Union, who would soon join John L. Lewis in setting up the Committee for Industrial Organization, sponsored a minority report that warned that the "future of this organization . . . depends upon molding our policies to fit new conditions"; the American labor movement "cannot stand still"; and the demands of mass production workers required "organization on a different basis."[5]

After the 1934 national wave of strikes and spontaneous organization in the mass production industries, it was clear that the unskilled laborers of the nation would organize themselves, either within the AFL or outside it. Pressured by John L. Lewis and the mass movement he was beginning to speak for, the 1934 AFL convention delegates passed a compromise resolution stating that industrial charters would be issued to unions in the automotive, cement, aluminum, and other mass production industries, while at the same time "the jurisdictional claims of existing unions" would be preserved. How this contradictory policy was to be carried out was not specified, but Lewis, according to Dubofsky and Van Tine, believed that he would be able to dominate the AFL Executive Council and "had no intentions of splitting the labor movement or forming his own industrial union federation."[6]

Lewis continued his campaign to create organizational structure for the newly organized industrial workers at the AFL Executive Council meeting in January 1935. He argued that the American Federation of Labor was weak in the auto industry because it had no organization among auto workers and was thus ignored by the Roosevelt administration. "It is axiomatic," he declared, "that you can get just about what you are ready to take."[7] He then presented a detailed proposal for organizing the industry. He put forward a motion to "postpone the settlement of jurisdictional claims in the auto industry until after the workers were organized." The executive board members, understanding very well that once the workers were organized on their own terms it would be too late to successfully reimpose the craft framework on a surging social movement, voted the Lewis proposal down by a vote of 12 to 2. David Dubinsky of the Ladies' Garment Workers was the only executive board member to support Lewis.

At the same executive board session, Lewis proposed that the AFL organize the steel industry and that this could be accomplished only by putting all the workers in one union. The board members refused to grant an industrial charter in the steel industry and instead set up a committee of Lewis, Tobin, and Wharton to negotiate with the Amalgamated Association of Iron, Steel, and Tin Workers over the question of industrial unionism. The Amalgamated refused to give up its jurisdiction in steel "or to allow a special AFL committee to organize steel for them," and the Executive Council dropped the matter.[8]

Rebuffed by the AFL leaders, Lewis decided to force the issue at the next executive board meeting, scheduled for May. Operating out of the headquarters of the United Mine Workers, he began to make contact with rank-and-file industrial unionists. In April, Lewis "welcomed union insurgents from the steel industry to meet with him in his office at UMW headquarters. The same local leaders expelled from the AA for their alleged Communist connections were embraced by the president of the mine workers."[9]

When the AFL Executive Council met from April 30 to May 7, Lewis put forth new ideas on a campaign for industrial unionism among the rubber workers. He warned the old guard that six months had passed since the San Francisco convention "and there has been no administration of that policy and no execution of the promissory note that the Federation held out to millions of workers in the mass production industry . . . and neither do I understand that there is any immediate desire to carry out that policy."[10] While the AFL board was meeting, Louis Stark, a journalist close to Lewis and the Mine Workers, reported in the *New York Times* that the United Mine Workers union was now ready to create a new labor federation dedicated to the organization of workers in the mass production industries, because the AFL had repudiated the San Francisco resolution on industrial unionism.

By the summer of 1935 Lewis had turned to those whom he had warned the craft union leaders against—the Left. In July, he put on the Mine Workers' payroll a group of socialists who had opposed him within his own union in the past and ordered them to contact rank-and-file unionists in the mass production industries—John Brophy, Powers Hapgood, and Adolph Germer. Hapgood wrote to his wife on July 24: "It's surprising how many radicals think I ought to see Lewis, saying it's much less of a compromise to make peace with him and stay in the labor movement than it is to get a government job and cease to be active in the class struggle."[11]

By the summer of 1935 social forces led by the industrial-workers movement generated powerful currents to produce new coalitions and break old ones. As Lewis moved within the economic sphere to connect with the labor revolt, Roosevelt, in search of new bases of power, followed him. At the crest of the nationwide strike movement in 1934, the president was confronted by a faltering National Industrial Recovery Act and the desertion of his business allies. In August, the American Liberty League, representing a coalition of corporate and conservative national elites, launched its public offensive against the New Deal. Roosevelt told Secretary of the Interior Harold Ickes that big business was bent on sabotaging his administration. However, the congressional elections of 1934 reflected the radical upheaval sweeping the country: Roosevelt won the greatest majority either party had ever held in the Senate, and the House of Representatives held 322 Democrats to 103 Republicans. The great social movement from below thus strengthened the independence of the executive branch of government. As Leuchtenberg asserts, "Roosevelt was riding a tiger."

The Wagner Act

The break between Roosevelt and those sectors of the business community that supported the NRA regime came in the spring of 1935, significantly over the National Labor Relations Act, known as the Wagner Act. The Wagner Act was the most radical legislation enacted during Roosevelt's tenure, yet he neither initiated nor supported the bill until the last minute. The Senate passed the legislation by a vote of 63 to 12 on May 16, 1935. Only after it had passed over to the House on May 24 did Roosevelt come out openly in support of the Wagner Act, since it was headed for passage with or without his support. Roosevelt's decision to take his stand on the side of the labor movement served as a clear-cut break with the United States Chamber of Commerce leaders who had conditioned their continued support of the Democratic administration on opposition to and defeat of the Wagner Act.

A series of Supreme Court decisions in May virtually struck down the New Deal. It was clear to Congress that the NIRA as a whole would soon be invalidated and that Section 7a as the only existing legal statement of labor's rights might soon be cast out. By passage of the Wagner Act, Congress was attempting to block the traditional anti-labor course of the highest court in the land. On May 27 the Supreme Court, by unanimous decision, declared the NIRA unconstitutional; John L. Lewis responded by declaring, "It is a sad commentary that every time the Supreme Court renders a decision it is along the lines to fatten capital and to destroy labor."[12] Congress passed the Wagner Act in June, and Roosevelt signed it in July.

For the first time in American history the traditional united front against labor by business, the government, and the judiciary was broken. In the summer of 1935 both Congress and the executive department of the federal government sided with labor against business and the Supreme Court. Roosevelt, in his effort to strengthen the executive power of the state, now needed labor support to fight the Supreme Court, which was bent on invalidating the major legislative actions of the New Deal. Roosevelt's subsequent assault on the Supreme Court by attempting to pack it with his own supporters created a political storm.

Often referred to as the Magna Carta of labor, the Wagner Act granted labor the greatest power it had ever possessed in U.S. history. It outlawed company unions, declared traditional anti-union practices by employers illegal, legalized union organizing efforts, and established the National Labor Relations Board (NLRB) to administer all provisions of the act. "Never before had the federal government . . . offered the union organizer and the worker eager to join a union such substantial protection against employers."[13] The way was now open for the fusion of organization represented by John L. Lewis and the substantial treasury of the United Mine Workers and the social revolt organized by rank-and-file industrial workers in the key industries of the nation. In the political sphere Lewis moved rapidly to forge a coalition with Roosevelt:

> Speaking to a Labor Day rally in Fairmont, West Virginia, on September 2, the largest outdoor meeting ever held in the area and attended by 40,000 coal miners and their families, Lewis demanded the reelection of Franklin D. Roosevelt. In the same city where ten years earlier on Labor Day he had been served with a fistful of anti-labor injunctions, Lewis now told an enthusiastic audience that "the era of privilege and predatory individuals is over." He called on American workers to join Roosevelt in a struggle against the Liberty League and the reactionary elite that for too long had dominated the United States.[14]

The Break with Business Unionism

Once the groundwork was laid for the alliance of industrial unionism with the executive department, Lewis was ready to break with the quarter-century-old corporate–craft union establishment. He went to the 1935 Atlantic City AFL convention prepared to support the young left-wing militants from rubber, auto, and steel centers and their crusade to organize the basic industries. He set up a separate United Mine Workers headquarters from which he received delegations of supporters for the cause of industrial unionism. Lewis opened his attack on the old guard at the October AFL convention by introducing two resolutions directed at Matthew Woll and John Frey, the symbolic representatives of the business–craft union alliance. The first declared that any official who held office in the National Civic Federation (NCF), the business-sponsored organization that from 1900 had linked the AFL to the largest corporations, could not simultaneously serve as an officer of the AFL. The resolution was adopted and Woll, who was acting president of the NCF, was forced to resign. The second resolution declared that the official press organ of the AFL could not publish advertisements by anti-union corporations. This too was rapidly adopted.[15]

On October 16 the convention debated a minority report advocating a massive organizing campaign among industrial workers. Charles P. Howard of the Typographers called for the adoption of an all-out drive to recruit millions of workers in the mass production industries into newly chartered industrial unions. Woll, as usual, opposed the idea, as did the rest of the AFL hierarchy. Then Lewis, in one of the most dramatic speeches of his career, rose to condemn the AFL for its failure over a quarter of a century to organize workers in the steel, rubber, glass, lumber, copper, and other mass production industries. Lewis no longer warned that communism might result from the federation's failure to organize the unorganized; now he warned of the danger posed to the U.S. labor movement by fascism, which had wiped out the labor movement in Germany and Italy. The burning question, he proclaimed, was whether the AFL would establish industrial unions, and he made it clear that if they did nothing, he and his supporters would take on the task themselves.

The coalition being forged between the president of the UMW, the largest industrial union within the AFL, and the left-wing rank-and-file delegates speaking for the unorganized mass production workers was symbolized by the alliance between John L. Lewis and Wyndham Mortimer, a rank-and-file auto delegate at the convention. As Mortimer describes it:

> During the debate on the minority report I tried repeatedly to get the floor, but the chair would not recognize me. John Brophy came to me and said, "John wants to see you." I went to the Miners' delegation where President Lewis was, of course, seated. He said, "Wyndham, I notice you have been unable to get the floor. Now, let me tell you how to do it. Just go up to the platform and stand behind Bill Green, and when the present speaker is through talking, step quickly to the microphone and begin talking. Green does not have enough courage to stop you. I know Bill Green."[16]

Mortimer followed Lewis' advice and spoke effectively for the cause of industrial unionism. He was immediately followed by a rank-and-file delegate from the rubber industry who was then called to order by Big Bill Hutcheson, the elephantine, three-hundred-pound president of the Carpenters Union. Lewis then took the microphone to protest the tactics of the AFL hierarchy, who consistently attempted to rule out of order rank-and-file delegates speaking in support of industrial unionism. Lewis remarked contemptuously: "This thing of raising points of order all the time on minor delegates is rather small potatoes." Hutcheson replied from the floor: "I was raised on small potatoes, that is why I am so small." When Lewis passed by the carpenters' delegation on the way back to his seat, Hutcheson called Lewis "a bastard." Most historians quote Edward Levinson's description of what happened next:

> The mine leader's right fist shot straight out. There was no swing to the blow, just a swift jab with 225 pounds behind it. It caught the carpenters'

president on the jaw. Instantly other carpenters' officials rushed at Lewis, and as suddenly, the latter's colleagues sprang from their near-by seats. Hutcheson went crashing against his long table, which went over under the impact of more delegates pushing, elbowing, punching. Others rushed to separate the fighters and in a few minutes the battle was over. Hutcheson was lifted to his feet. Blood streaked one side of his face from his forehead to his chin. Friends guided him to the washroom. . . . Lewis casually adjusted his collar and tie, relit his cigar, and sauntered slowly through the crowded isles to the rostrum.[17]

To the tens of thousands of workers engaged in the greatest labor revolt in U.S. history, Lewis' action represented an example of class struggle American-style. Thousands took vicarious pleasure in the blow struck against the feudal structure of craft unionism. Lewis, a coal miner, had replaced Gompers the cigar maker as the symbol of the labor movement in the largest industrial country in the world.

The Birth of a New Organization: The CIO

On November 10, at a meeting in the Washington headquarters of the United Mine Workers, John L. Lewis and ten other union leaders set up the Committee for Industrial Organization. Lewis was made chairman, Charles Howard of the Typographical Union was made secretary, and John Brophy was made director. This self-appointed subcommittee of the AFL was little more than a symbol for the rank-and-file organizing drive that was sweeping the country. Len DeCaux, an ex-Wobbly who became loosely associated with the Communist Party, was brought in to edit the *CIO News*. Dubofsky and Van Tine state: "In late 1935, the CIO amounted to scarcely more than Brophy and his two secretaries, Len DeCaux, a cubbyhole for an office, and Lewis' dream."[18]

It is clear that Lewis originally planned to organize the steel industry and its captive mines in order to safeguard the gains won by the UMW. However, this strategy was preempted by the mass movement created by the workers in the auto, rubber, and electrical industries. In the final analysis, then, these workers confronted a major section of the U.S. corporate elite, defeated them in battle, and delivered steel to Murray and Lewis. Auto, rubber, and electrical were organized from the bottom up; steel was organized from the top down. Recognizing the sequence of the struggle is essential to understanding the outcome for industrial organization in the basic industries.

The CIO was at this point little more than an extension of the United Mine Workers. In the first two years of its existence, according to John Brophy, the United Mine Workers provided between two-thirds and three-quarters of the money for the CIO. Many of the full-time organizers assigned by Lewis to the CIO remained on the UMW payroll. In the main, however, the CIO did not organize from the top down: its staff aided workers in the process of organizing themselves. Heber Blankenhorn, who reported to the top National Labor Relations Board officials on the progress of union organization in the basic industries, kept his superiors advised on Lewis' role in the new movement. At the end of March 1936, he wrote: "A significant factor is Lewis' heavy emphasis to local leaders, 'You have got to do the leading.' He is not at all dictating to them, he is discouraging the myth 'Lewis will lead us' and says privately that a principle job is to develop young leaders. That does not sound like precipitate action."[19]

By the end of 1935 the CIO included Lewis and eight other AFL union presidents: Sidney Hillman of the Amalgamated Clothing Workers; Charles Howard of the Typographers; David Dubinsky of the Ladies' Garment Workers; Thomas McMahon of the Textile Workers; Max Zaritsky of the Hat, Cap, and Millinery Workers; Thomas Brown of the Mine, Mill, and Smelter Workers; and Harvey Fremming of the Oil Workers. Lewis was ready to break with the AFL; some of the others were not. Howard, Dubinsky, and Zaritsky wished to move cautiously and were behind the moderate statement of purpose issued by the new committee:

> The Committee will work in accordance with the principles enunciated by these organizations (the eight founding unions) at the Atlantic City Convention of the American Federation of Labor. It is the purpose of the Committee to encourage and promote organization of workers in the mass production and unorganized industries of the nation and affiliation with the American Federation of Labor. Its function will be educational and advisory and the Committee and its representatives will cooperate for the recognition and acceptance of modern collective bargaining in such industries. Other organizations interested in advancing organization work along the lines of industrial unionism will be invited to participate in the activities of the Committee and name representatives to join in its work.[20]

The UMW, Amalgamated Clothing Workers, and the Ladies' Garment Workers each put in $5,000 to begin the organizing work.

Lewis responded to the grass-roots demand for organization with an enthusiasm unmatched by other AFL leaders who associated themselves with the founding of the CIO. Dubinsky, for example, eager to avoid a split within the AFL, devoted most of his energy to unity negotiations with the craft union hierarchy. Neither Hillman nor Murray was overly enthusiastic about rank-and-file control of the new organizations that were being created. Moreover, Hillman, Dubinsky, and Murray were all united in their opposition to the Lewis policy of opening CIO doors to Communist Party members.

Lee Pressman, the Communist lawyer who was soon to become

chief legal counsel of the CIO and Lewis' right-hand man, describes the differences between Lewis and Hillman in their overall approach to organization:

> There were many things about the development of the CIO in which it just grew like Topsy. There was no organization to it. Hillman always commented: "You just don't get more people demanding membership than you can handle." You had to do it in an orderly way. As far as Lewis was concerned, he didn't mind if ten thousand people tried to get in at one time, and if your organizers couldn't get around fast enough to organize them, don't try to stop them from standing up. He just had the ability to visualize the thing on a grand scale.[21]

Lewis consistently fought for the creation of an independent power base composed of the newly organized industrial working class; Hillman accepted his role as Roosevelt's representative to the CIO. The standard interpretation of American labor history fails to come to grips with the Lewis–Left alliance. Cochran makes a solid contribution to the subject by filling in the lacunae:

> When the CIO undertook to organize steel and led the assault on other open-shop strongholds, Lewis and his associates embarked on the fight of their lives—as they well understood. Not only could civil war be anticipated in major industrial centers, but the CIO was moving toward the kind of massed confrontation in which labor had always come out the loser. Labor history was dotted with the tombstones of lost strikes and crushed organizations. . . . Consequently, Lewis was not merely disposed to accept whatever allies were available in the desperate war that was in the offing. He could not do without the support of the radicals—and the 1930s, radicals meant primarily Communists. It was not that man-for-man Communists were necessarily superior organizers or agitators than non-Communist radicals. The contrary was demonstrated in the Minneapolis and Toledo strikes. But whatever their qualities, non-Communist radicals were few in number. The American Socialist Party was only a shell, and the radical splinter groups, so-called, were less than that.[22]

Following the adjournment of the 1935 AFL convention, Mortimer, at Lewis' request, visited the mine union chief at his Washington headquarters. Lewis questioned Mortimer on the progress of organization in the auto industry and then promised to aid the rank-and-file auto worker organization in every way he could. In January 1936 Mortimer, acting through his District Auto Council in Cleveland, sponsored the first historic mass meeting of unorganized industrial workers in the Cleveland public auditorium. It was here that Lewis launched the public CIO organizing drive in the basic industries of the country. Mortimer got the rubber workers to organize a similar meeting on the following day, and a caravan of twenty cars accompanied Lewis to Akron, where he addressed an overflow meeting.

The first efforts: the rubber industry

The rubber workers, like the mass production workers in other basic industries, had begun to organize in response to massive wage cuts and intensified speed-ups initiated by the tire corporations in the early 1930s. Between 1922 and 1933, the average weekly wage of rubber workers was slashed from $29.58 to $13.67. Despite the reduction in the number of employees, man-hour output of tires doubled between 1922 and 1931, while some 42,000 workers were displaced by advanced technology. Thousands of rubber workers then flocked into AFL federal unions set up during the NRA.

The corporations refused to recognize the new industrial unions, however, and Akron employees, following the coordinated policies of the National Association of Manufacturers, set up company unions, which they then argued were in compliance with the spirit of Section 7a of the NIRA. These company unions were supplemented by the corporate practice of labor espionage, the use of undercover agents, and the massive purchase of guns and tear-gas equipment. At the same time, the craft unions undercut the efforts of the rubber workers to set up their own unions by cannibalizing the membership and subjecting the new unions to debilitating jurisdictional disputes. The rubber workers, pursuing the same tactics as their fellow workers in the auto industry, forced the AFL to set up a national council to link all the federal unions in the rubber industry. Strikes for recognition began to spread throughout the industry, and, again following the national pattern, the disputes between the rubber companies and the workers ended up in the lap of the federal government and the National Labor Relations Board. But despite repeated NLRB rulings that the employers had to bargain with a union representing a majority of employees, the companies refused to bargain with any union. Businessmen throughout the country had little doubt that the Supreme Court would once more come to their aid and invalidate the Wagner Act just as it had overthrown Section 7a. In the meantime, they had no intention of legitimating the rights of labor by bargaining with the new unions.

Breakthrough in rubber

But workers had learned not to depend solely on the government to win bargaining rights for them. In February 1935 Akron rubber workers supported a strike at the Ohio Rubber Company, and when the company used strikebreakers, tear gas, and assaults by company guards, the workers threatened a general strike in Akron. Workers at the big three rubber companies—Goodyear, Firestone, and Goodrich—called for a strike vote; the companies, in turn, prepared for a showdown by constructing barbed-wire fences around their plants, organizing citizen vigilante committees, and bolstering the city police by purchasing new weapons and swearing in new deputies. With another general strike imminent, Secretary of Labor Frances Perkins brought the disputing parties to Washington. The result was the Teacup Agreement, a sexist reference to the female mediator of the undeclared rubber war in Ohio.[23]

The agreement proved to be a Pyrrhic victory for the union. Although the companies agreed "to meet with employees," it was soon evident that they had no intention of recognizing the United Rubber Workers as their employees' collective-bargaining agent. The personnel director of the Goodyear Tire and Rubber Company, F. W. Climer, in a classic letter addressed to the special conference committee representing the rubber companies of Akron, illuminates the strategy of the corporate–craft union response to industrial unionism:

> Knowing the interest that all members of the Special Conference Committee must have in the Akron labor situation and in the negotiations which led to the settlement of the threatened strike in Akron, I will make an effort to cover in this letter only those points which may not have been thoroly [sic] explained in the newspapers.
>
> I would like to point out that at no time during the negotiations in Washington did the representatives of the three rubber companies meet with the representatives of the Union. All negotiations were conducted with Miss Perkins who personally, or thru her assistants, acted as intermediary between the two groups, and as far as we are concerned the agreement published in the newspapers was signed between the three rubber companies and Miss Perkins.
>
> When news of the agreement first reached Akron, it was the opinion of all of us that the Union leaders would have difficulty in selling the agreement to the local unions. It was also our thought that in order for them to sell it, they would have to go as far as possible in bragging about having obtained a signed agreement with the rubber companies. The Union leaders must have cooled down considerably after their visit to Washington because at their meeting with the locals here, they stated that because of their small membership they felt that they had gotten as much out of negotiations as could be expected. While there was quite a bit of dissatisfaction among the radical element of the three locals, the agreement was ratified by a vote of something like 9 to 1.[24]

The last paragraph of this revealing document shows corporate confidence that the labor movement could be contained within the bounds of the thoroughly tamed AFL:

> We are today cautioning the members of our industrial Assembly, as well as the members of our supervisional forces, to be very careful about any talk of this proposed agreement. Our thought is that if our organization goes out and attempts to belittle the A.F. of L. and the outcomes of the threatened strike, this attitude would have the effect of solidifying the

Union organization, whereas if we keep quiet about the whole situation and proceed as we always have, we have every reason to hope that the union movement in Akron may completely disintegrate.[25]

A twenty-five-day strike over the issue of wages, conditions, and union recognition occurred soon after the signing of the April agreement; it ended in defeat for the union. As a result, the company publicly repudiated the Teacup Agreement, apparently believing that the radicals had been successfully isolated and unionism was dead in Akron.

In fact, however, this defeat only made it clear to the rubber workers that they could not rely on either the government or the AFL. They began to desert the AFL in droves, and by mid-September the AFL rubber union was down to 4,000 members. These were the events that prompted rank-and-file rubber workers to make contact with John L. Lewis at the 1935 AFL convention and bring Lewis to Akron to address the mass meeting of rubber workers in January 1936.

Lewis, in a hard-hitting speech, attacked the rubber companies' assertion that labor and capital were partners in the process of production. Labor and capital may be partners in theory, Lewis declared, but "they are enemies in fact." Citing Goodyear's vast profits, he compared "these untold millions" with the "constant struggle for its workers to live at all." After delivering a detailed description of the corporate policy of systematic exploitation, Lewis pounded the podium and shouted: "Organize! Organize! Go to Goodyear and tell them you want some of those stock dividends. Say: 'So we're supposed to be partners, are we?' Well, we're not. We're enemies." Ruth McKenney describes the closing moments of the speech:

> He said these words to an increasingly excited audience. He evoked a dream in the minds of men, a dream of security, and a dream of freedom.
> Suddenly, he stopped speaking. There was a long pause. Then he said quietly, and very earnestly, "I hope you will do something for yourselves."[26]

Ten days later, workers at the Firestone plant unleashed a new weapon of industrial warfare—the sit-down strike. This involved 500 tire builders and resulted in the reinstatement of a worker suspended for union activity. A few days later Goodyear was hit with another sit-down, protesting layoffs and a 10 percent wage cut; the company shut down all production, idling 14,000 workers. Then, on February 8, 1,500 workers at Goodrich staged a sit-down over the reduction of wage rates for workers transferred from one machine to another. A total of forty-three strikes, involving 76,699 workers with a loss of 477,286 man-days of production, were recorded in the rubber industry in 1936—an all-time high for the industry.

Despite the organization of an Akron vigilante Law and Order League, court injunctions, and a request by the Goodyear Industrial

Assembly to Governor Davey to call out the militia, all attempts to open the factories failed. The five-week Goodyear strike, aided by full-time organizers sent in by the CIO, resulted in a company agreement to negotiate grievances with "duly chosen representatives for purposes of negotiations on all questions in which there is mutual interest" to rehire all strikers without discrimination, to establish a thirty-six-hour week and six-hour day shifts in the tire and tube division, to set up grievance machinery, and to provide representatives of the workers with lists of those to be laid off for union inspection. This was a considerable victory, even though union recognition as such was not won. On the other hand, the initial strike was only the beginning of a longer process of struggle. Once workers had won de facto bargaining rights, they still had to fight for each new shop rule they wished to establish, and these would subsequently have to be translated into written contracts. Then, once union recognition was won, worker participation in decisions governing the work process and a weakening of iron-clad management prerogatives had to be wrested from bitterly anti-union corporate representatives.

Harold Roberts, the senior economist of the National War Labor Board, in his comprehensive history of the rubber workers, wrote that in addition to the demands won by the union, "the strike also gave the workers an opportunity to gauge their collective strength. They had effectively met the largest tire and rubber company in the industry, maintained strict discipline in the face of trying and difficult circumstances, and won the support of the people of Akron. It established the rubber workers as a force to be reckoned with."[27]

In fact, it did more than that. While corporate management across the country had pooled its experience and adopted coordinated policies, now the workers began to do the same. Auto workers aided the rubber workers and thus gained experience that they would put to use in the organization of their own industry. Each strike became a laboratory in which the tactics for the next strike were tested.

Building Alliances

Lewis recognized the need for an alliance with the radical rank-and-file leaders of the organizing drives in the rubber, auto, and electrical industries and carefully went about building one. He utilized the socialist opposition leaders in the UMW—Brophy, Hapgood, and Germer—to make contacts with class-conscious organizers of the revolt from below. With only rare exceptions, such as the top-down appointment of the steel union officials, the new leaders of the key industrial unions in the CIO had three qualities: they were on the Left, they were young, and they were workers in the industry they organized. Mortimer spells out the significance of the new alliance:

> These two huge mass meetings, the first in the country held in behalf of the CIO, demonstrated beyond question the eagerness of workers in the mass industries for organization. While I am confident that we could by our own efforts, eventually have organized the auto industry, the arrival of President Lewis and the CIO on the scene helped enormously. Without him, the road would have been longer and much more difficult. We were no longer fighting alone against the auto manufacturers and the AFL Executive Council.[28]

Len DeCaux, editor of the *CIO News*, hired by Lewis to set the left-wing ideological orientation of the early CIO, recently told me that he was astonished in the 1970s when a prominent labor historian asked him why the Communists allowed Lewis to use them. He said he answered: "Why, what the hell, we were using him." Such is the nature of political coalitions. When I asked Blackie Myers, the openly Communist leader of the National Maritime Union, what he received out of his close relationship with Lewis in 1935 and 1936, he replied: "Guns, funds, and automobiles."

Lewis widened the split between the newly established CIO and AFL leaders by resigning as a vice-president of the AFL on November 23, 1935. From that point on, William Green openly accused the CIO of splitting the labor movement. In a letter to Green, Lewis offered to make Green chairman of the CIO "in my stead." Green replied that in his more than thirty years in the labor movement "I have never aligned myself with any . . . dual movement."

By the beginning of 1936, industrial locals across the country that had been denied charters by the AFL were openly requesting affiliation with the CIO. By early 1936 the AFL Executive Council issued a declaration stating that the CIO constituted "a challenge to the supremacy of the American Federation of Labor and will ultimately become dual in purpose and character to the American Federation of Labor." It then demanded that the CIO be immediately dissolved. The United Mine Workers responded to the demand at their Washington convention at the end of January 1936. Philip Murray told the delegates that if the AFL continued its "carping criticism . . . the sooner we get the hell away from them the better." Lewis told the delegates that he took orders only from the UMW and that if the miners told him to dissolve the CIO he would; otherwise, "all the members of the Executive Council of the American Federation of Labor will be wearing asbestos suits in hell before that committee is dissolved." The miners gave a unanimous standing vote of approval for the CIO, authorized Lewis to deliver a series of addresses on network radio in favor of the CIO, and empowered the Executive Council to hold payment of per capita taxes to the AFL.[29]

Although a committee was set up to mediate the differences between the two labor organizations, it was clear that the split was irrevocable. The two organizations fought their first battle in the auto industry.

John Brophy, the CIO's director of organization, sent Adolph Germer to Detroit to aid the organization of auto workers. Germer worked to unite the many factions of unionists in the auto industry but soon found himself obstructed by Francis Dillon, head of the AFL Auto Council, who had direct connections to AFL president William Green. Dillon antagonized rank-and-file organizers by calling them "NRA crybabies" and denounced Mortimer as a Communist. In the spring of 1936 all factions had agreed to call a convention under the auspices of the AFL Auto Workers' Union. When the convention met on April 27 Dillon was isolated and the Progressive caucus, a group of left-wing auto unionists, had little difficulty electing their slate of officers.

The Communist-led Progressive caucus that dominated the convention backed Mortimer for president of the union. Mortimer withdrew, perhaps because as an avowed Communist his election would only succeed in drawing additional fire against the first industrial union in the auto industry. In any case, the convention made a historic mistake by electing Homer Martin, a former Baptist minister from Missouri, as the auto union's first president. Mortimer was elected first vice-president; Ed Hall, a non-Communist who had joined the Progressive caucus, was elected second vice-president; Walter Wells, a master mechanic, was elected third vice-president; and George Addes, a leader of the left-wing Progressive movement in Toledo, was made secretary-treasurer. Leftists dominated the eleven-man executive board of the union.[30] The great majority of the rank-and-file auto leaders were under 35. By July the new union had united all the organized locals except for 1,000 skilled workers in the Mechanics Educational Society Association led by a British sectarian Marxist who refused to go along with the CIO. On July 2 the UAW affiliated with the CIO, with about 40,000 members out of an industry containing a labor force of 1 million. Mortimer, Henry Kraus, and Robert Travis, all Communist Party members, together with the Reuther brothers who were Socialists dedicated to industrial unionism, laid the foundations for the organization of the auto industry.

Early efforts in the auto industry

Following a successful sit-down at the Bendix Products Corporation in South Bend, Indiana, which succeeded in winning partial bargaining rights for the UAW, Communist Party members led the first successful sit-down strike at the center of the auto industry in Detroit. Twelve hundred workers sat down at the Midland Steel Products Company, which produced steel frames for Chrysler and Ford, causing the lay-off of more than 53,000 workers at Plymouth, Dodge, Chrysler, Lincoln-Zepher, and the Briggs auto body shop. The resulting victory was heralded by the UAW as "the most significant union victory in the history of the automobile industry."[31] Greater concessions might have been won except for the fact that Ford threatened to remove all its business if the company made any more concessions to the union. According to Sidney Fine, "the Midland sit-down demonstrated graphically how a strike in one key automobile plant could paralyze the operation of other motor-vehicle factories that depended on its product." Moreover, "the strike also gave evidence of the sense of solidarity, that bond among the automobile workers and the rubber workers that was to characterize the sit-down era in automobile history."[32] Mortimer and his colleagues would take the Akron sit-down technique and use it effectively against the largest corporation in the world—General Motors.

UE: Independent Unionism

At the same time that the rubber and auto workers were carving out the framework of industrial unionism in their industries, the electrical workers were carrying on similar struggles. In the spring of 1936, UE Local 103, operating as an independent union alongside a company union at the Radio Corporation of America (RCA) went on strike because of the refusal of the company to grant the union a signed agreement. A violent strike ensued, featuring mass back-to-work movements sponsored by RCA, mass picket lines, aided by Camden shipyard workers, the assignment of Powers Hapgood from the CIO to aid the strike, and the arrest by police of Carey and other UE leaders.

The strike was expensive for the company, which spent at least $244,000 to fight it, plus another $586,000 getting its orders filled elsewhere. John L. Lewis personally entered into the negotiations with the company and an agreement was signed on July 21 in which the company agreed to an NLRB election. UE won, despite a boycott organized by the company union, but it failed to gain a majority of the total number of workers employed in the plant. Although UE was certified by the NLRB, RCA hired Hugh Johnson, the former head of the NRA, and he refused to recognize UE. After a long struggle, the company finally recognized UE as the exclusive bargaining agent for all employees at RCA.[33]

While the radio industry was important, the electrical industry, dominated by one of the giants of U.S. capitalism, presented the greatest challenge to industrial unionism. General Electric (GE) is a particularly interesting case because the company's president, Gerard Swope, was the consummate corporate liberal. He deserves the assessment of Irving Bernstein as "bold and imaginative, without parallel among contemporary industrialists."[34] During World War I, Swope joined the War Industries Board at the request of Bernard Baruch. By 1922 he had become president of General Electric. Swope was, indeed, an anomaly in the corporate world of the 1930s. Bernstein records that in 1926 Swope and Owen Young of General Electric met secretly with William Green of the AFL to attempt to persuade Green to launch an AFL organizing drive in General Electric plants. Swope told Green that if the AFL should undertake this task the only condition he demanded was that "the union with which GE would bargain must be industrial."

Swope was one of the few far-sighted industrialists prescient enough to recognize the decline of traditional craft unionism and ready to act to transform the corporate–craft union alliance into its next stage. Swope was very frank about his motives: "It was simply good sense for a man in my position to take the first steps." He did not wish to confront a union that might become "a source of endless difficulties." What he wanted was "an organization with which we could work on a businesslike basis."[35] Green, of course, had no intention of organizing any industrial unions and Swope never heard from him again. What is signficant for the theory of corporate liberalism is the fact that when GE finally got its industrial union it proved to be the strongest left-wing union in the country. Workers in the 1930s fought corporate paternalism as hard as they fought corporate intransigence. The Communist-dominated United Electrical Workers, which was the first great independent union to affiliate with the CIO, was not quite what Swope had in mind.

The drive for industrial unionism in the General Electric empire in 1936 was led by Julius Emspak, who at the age of 14 had gone to work at the Schenectady plant as an apprentice. Along with other left-wing rank-and-file leaders he experienced the great 1919 strike when more than 28,000 workers struck GE and then went down in defeat. Emspak and his fellow workers had to wait seventeen years before they had a chance to take over the company union and run it for themselves.

In September 1936, UE Local 301 at Schenectady asked for a representative election. When the company consented, UE, led by Communists, won by a vote of 5,111 to 400. However, when it came to bargaining with Local 301, the company stalled on every issue. Emspak recalls that Swope was none too eager to codify any of the agreements reached between the company and the new CIO union: "It's significant— he did not run to us, or GE did not run to us with a collective bargaining agreement. We didn't achieve a national collective bargaining agreement with GE until 1938, which was a year after the steel agreement."[36]

Gerard Swope, the symbol of corporate liberalism, differed very little from his big-business colleagues when it came to recognizing the legitimate rights of industrial unions. On February 24, 1937, while riding home on the New York subway, the president of General Electric read the headlines announcing that Walter Chrysler had agreed to meet with Lewis and the UAW leaders to negotiate a contract. "Swope" he said to himself, "it isn't time for you, a little king, to say you won't meet with anybody."[37] The next day Swope overruled the other executives at General Electric and agreed to meet with James Carey of the United Electrical, Radio, and Machine Workers, CIO, to sign a national agreement for all the major GE plants. This would not become effective until April 1, 1938.

Given its long-standing policy of paternalism, it was ironic that of the three great American corporations—General Motors, General Electric, and United States Steel—GE was the last to sign an agreement with a CIO union.

The United Electrical, Radio, and Machine Workers, which was to become the third largest union in the CIO after auto and steel, was an amalgam, as its name makes clear, of three separate strands of industrial unionism. It was led by James Carey, the youthful organizer of the radio industry, Julius Emspak, the skilled tool maker at General Electric, and James Matles, a machinist who became active in the Communist-led Trade Union Unity League, which organized medium and small machine shops. It was these diffused and local origins that gave UE its rank-and-file character.

UE provides the best example of the type of bottom-up organizing true of rubber, auto, and the electrical industries. Matles, in noting the differences with mass production industries, compares in particular the structural differences of the organizing campaigns in the steel and electrical industries:

> The 1937 drive on the open shop steel industry was mainly conducted from outside the plants by the Steel Workers Organizing Committee, with publicity men, statisticians, batteries of lawyers, thirty-five subregional offices, one hundred fifty-eight field directors and full time organizers, eighty-five part-time organizers, supplied largely by the manpower and financial resources of the United Mine Workers.
>
> This organizing strategy was employed in steel. Not so in electrical manufacturing. The UE grew indigenously in most shops, giving it a character in its origins which remained throughout the years and had an all-important bearing on its development and survival. In Schenectady, not even a single full-time organizer from the UE international union was assigned to the campaign. On the contrary, Local 301 helped the international union.[38]

The policy of electing rank-and-file negotiating committees, a practice followed to one degree or another by most left-wing unions, was deeply rooted in UE tradition from the very beginning. This practice resulted in the establishment of permanent conference boards composed of representatives from local unions embracing all the plants of a particular corporation. Thus, there was a GE Conference Board, a Westinghouse Conference Board, a Radio Conference Board, and so forth, made up of rank-and-file delegates who negotiated on an industry-wide basis. These boards were responsible, "with the assistance of the international union and its top leadership, for preparing demands and negotiating national contracts with the corporations."[39]

> The rank and file committee members carried the ball in negotiations with GE. Some, like Turnbull and Coulthard, had put in years in the shop, accumulating plenty of trade union experience. All committee members were acquainted at first hand with present conditions and problems on the job. None of the international leaders, at this early point in their careers, were in a position to make the contributions to negotiations which lay within the competence of the rank-and-file committee people. Such a setting as negotiations with General Electric, in fact, furnished an excellent chance for the young international union officers to gain necessary leadership education.[40]

Both Matles and Emspak recall an incident in early negotiations when James Carey, the president of the international union, was excluded from the negotiations by the rank and file because he made a serious mistake in confronting GE corporate executives. This occurred long before the split in the leadership, and at a time when both leadership and rank and file were united in their views and purpose.

The UE soon gained a reputation in the press as a Communist-dominated union that never deviated from the party line. While there was some substance to the first charge, the union throughout its history turned out to be fiercely independent. At the birth of industrial unionism in 1935, the Communist line was to join the AFL, but Emspak and other union activists organizing in the electrical industry would under no circumstances join the AFL, which they believed to be organizationally bankrupt. A decade later when the Communist line was to remain within the CIO, the UE walked out. All of the truly radical unions in the CIO retained over the years much of what the rank and file had put into them.

Industrial Unionism as a National Institution

By the fall of 1936, the upsurge and coordinated actions of the industrial working class had transformed the skeleton Committee for Industrial Organization into a powerful national institution that was able to influence the politics and economics of the United States. Both the United Electrical Workers and the United Rubber Workers voted to affiliate with the CIO at their fall national conventions. On the West Coast, Harry Bridges and a progressive slate of candidates were elected by a referendum vote of all Pacific ports to lead the West Coast district of the International Longshoremen's Association. Shortly thereafter, all seven West Coast maritime unions decided to present common demands on September 30 and thus present a solid front to the ship owners. On October 30, these unions struck the West Coast together. The ship owners closed down operations and prepared for a long strike in the hope that the unions could be broken. The strike lasted ninety-nine days and was joined by the East Coast seamen, who established the National Maritime Union under Communist leaders and soon affiliated with the CIO. In Detroit, the auto workers opened their offensive against General Motors, and by the end of the year had occupied the property of the largest corporation in the country, an action that precipitated a national crisis.

An exception to the CIO victories was in trucking. The Minneapolis teamsters, led by the Dunne brothers, William Brown, and Farrell Dobbs, had organized most of the trucking industry in Minneapolis into industrial unions, and wished to join the CIO. Local 574 leaders in Minneapolis consulted with John Brophy, the organizing director of the CIO, and were told that the CIO had no plans to organize the trucking industry. The result was that the teamsters would re-affiliate with the AFL, whose leaders, confronting a crisis, belatedly decided that they would compete with the CIO in recruiting industrial unions. Charging that the CIO was Communist dominated, the AFL updated its ideology to pit American industrial unionism against unionism originating in Moscow.

The Communists and left-wing militants did not do the job alone, but without them it might not have made much headway. At its height, the CIO drive had profound political implications, which were not lost on the corporations, the government, or the press. Whether the movement could be contained within narrowly defined economic boundaries must have appeared problematic to observers of the dynamic social assault that swept over the nation's productive centers in the mid-thirties. In historical terms, industrial unionism cannot be equated with revolution, but it required a degree of class interest, consciousness, and organizational solidarity strong enough to withstand the bullets, spies, intimidation, and coercive power wielded by the largest corporations in the country. American workers in the 1930s were motivated by other than entrepreneurial instincts. For a number of years, business unionism went into retreat.

4

The Roosevelt-CIO Coalition

In mid-1935 Roosevelt set himself a new course. Having abandoned
the NRA experiment of enticing capital and labor to enjoin a social
bargain at the top, he embarked on a new strategy designed to isolate his
business opponents, contain the social movement of which the CIO was
the most powerful organized force, and capture the judiciary for his
policies. The Supreme Court, in particular, continued to cling to
nineteenth-century precedents and stubbornly opposed all social legislation sponsored by the federal government. The court overturned the
NIRA in 1935 and then moved rapidly within the next year to wipe out
the Agricultural Adjustment Act and the Guffey Coal Act, and surprised
even conservatives by declaring invalid a New York State minimum
wage law. "In the field of labor relations, the Court seemed to have
created, as President Roosevelt protested, a 'no-man's land,' where no
government—state or federal—could function."[1] It was clear that both
the Wagner Act and wages and hours legislation would be next on the
list of victims for the Supreme Court axe. In these circumstances,
Roosevelt embarked on his campaign to reorganize the court by
enlarging its membership and packing it with his own supporters. This
maneuver proved to be one of the most controversial political acts of his
presidency and Roosevelt needed all the allies he could get, and the most
powerful ally available was the CIO.

Arthur Schlesinger, Jr., defines the New Deal at this point: "Its
intellectual content and its political method had undergone striking
changes. It had renounced the dream of national planning through
national unity and had become a coalition of the nonbusiness groups,
mobilized to prevent the domination of the country by the business

community."[2] In more specific terms, Thomas Corcoran, a close adviser to Roosevelt during the thirties, has recently described the circumstances under which Roosevelt made his historic shift to the newly organized industrial union constituency. Corcoran comments that "labor's political significance dawned on Mr. Roosevelt's brain trust slowly." Section 7a of the NIRA and the Wagner Act were viewed as economic moves to "pump up worker's purchasing power. But not long afterward the political advantages also became apparent."

Corcoran remembers the day in 1936 when, acting as Roosevelt's agent, he stopped by the office of John L. Lewis to pick up a $500,000 check as an industrial union contribution to the Roosevelt reelection campaign. "That labor money carried a lot of political whack," Corcoran told a *Wall Street Journal* reporter in 1979. The reason Roosevelt was unable to embrace the labor movement too soon, he argues, was because "Mr. Roosevelt's 1932 victory was based on Southern support and he couldn't risk alienating the Solid South—at least not until after the 1936 election." According to Corcoran, once the election was won, "Roosevelt substituted the labor movement for the aristocratic South. But the transition from South to labor movement was a delicate political operation. The key was timing, and the Old Man had an absolutely magnificent sense of timing."[3]

Consequently, Roosevelt forged a coalition with the CIO to win reelection in 1936. He built his campaign around an attack on the large corporations and a call for a "people's government" in Washington. The angry working-class crowds that had elicited a class line from John L. Lewis demanded the same from Roosevelt, and the president and his followers gave their audiences the message they wanted to hear. An example of the general tone of the campaign was a speech delivered by Pennsylvania Governor Earle to a predominantly working-class crowd in Pittsburgh waiting to hear the president himself. Earle defined the enemy:

> There are the Mellons, who have grown fabulously wealthy from the toil of the men of iron and steel, the men whose brain and brawn have made this a great city; Grundy, whose sweatshop operators have been the shame and disgrace of Pennsylvania for a generation; Pew, who strives to build a political and economic empire with himself as dictator; the duPonts, whose dollars were earned with the blood of American soldiers; Morgan, financier of war.[4]

The people Earle was talking about were perfectly aware of the issues at stake. The Republican National Committee labeled Roosevelt "the Kerensky of the American revolutionary movement." Al Smith declared that Roosevelt could go to Russia and take his Brain Trust with him, while other Republican speakers asserted that the president had "gone over hook, line and sinker to the Communists and Socialists by whom he is surrounded." Ernest T. Weir, the anti-union spokesman of the steel industry, warned in an article in *Fortune* Magazine that Roosevelt was opposed not by a small minority, as he claimed, but "almost unanimously by the business and professional men of the country."[5]

Roosevelt and Lewis, of course, had very different motivations for forming a coalition. Dubofsky and Van Tine describe the political partnership as based on common necessity, rather than shared values, and note that during the summer of 1936, Lewis subordinated his campaign to organize the steelworkers to the reelection of Roosevelt because he felt that the future of the CIO "depended upon a sympathetic government." In April the mine union leader joined with Sidney Hillman to set up Labor's Non-Partisan League, dedicated to the reelection of Roosevelt. Lewis, however, was determined that the CIO and the labor movement must be independent of the Democratic Party. Once the CIO had organized the mass of industrial workers, it would, in Lewis' estimation, be able to exert political power on its own.

In June, Lewis met with Roosevelt, who promised to support the CIO's drive to organize the steel industry. Lewis then told the press that he fully supported Roosevelt's reelection platform. Notwithstanding this show of support, Lewis a week later attended a conference sponsored by Robert LaFollette, Jr., to lay plans for the creation of an independent farmer-labor party. The nation's press was quick to charge that a deal had been made by two of the country's most powerful figures. According to press speculation, Lewis had promised support for Roosevelt in 1936 in return for the president's promise to back Lewis as the Democratic nominee for president in 1940. Although Lewis never lent any substance to this charge, he did not deny that he was seeking to establish an independent labor party by the next election. He told the *New York Times*: "We cannot forecast the future. There may be new alignments in the next few years. It may be well to be prepared with a strong labor movement so that we can shift our weight around."[6] Speaking to the first convention of Labor's Non-Partisan League in August, Lewis stressed "the absolute necessity for labor to preserve its own autonomous political organization."[7] In September, Lewis attended a conference of "progressives" in Chicago chaired by Senator LaFollette that included eighteen congressmen and governors and twenty-seven labor leaders "who endorsed Roosevelt, but not the Democratic Party, and promised an inevitable future realignment of party politics."[8]

All through October, Lewis campaigned for Roosevelt in the industrial states of the East and Midwest. At the end of the month, he addressed 20,000 union supporters at Madison Square Garden and another 8,000 massed in the streets outside. Lewis called on labor to "organize politically as well as economically to free workers from the clutches of an unscrupulous economic dictatorship."⁹ Two days later the CIO leader gave the last speech of his tour, appearing jointly with Roosevelt at Wilkes-Barre, Pennsylvania.

After his landslide victory, Roosevelt had to face the fact that it would not be easy to defuse that victory of its class content. The CIO organizing drive was rapidly enlarging the influence of the Left in most of the strategically located industrial centers of the country and Lewis wasted no time reminding the president publicly that it was the workers who had elected him. The *New York Times* and other commentators expressed the opinion that Lewis had won a greater victory than had Roosevelt and predicted that Lewis would organize an independent labor party in 1940. The combined categories of semi-skilled and unskilled workers, representing close to 30 percent of the labor force, made this sector of the industrial working class the largest single occupational grouping in the nation in 1935. These were the troops commanded by the CIO in 1936, and, with the addition of the poorest of the farmers and farm workers plus extensive sections of the middle class, they gave Roosevelt a national majority. This was the base of power for the strongest federal executive apparatus in American history. Roosevelt commanded a broader base of support than did the CIO, but in 1936 and 1937 the CIO had become the most highly organized and articulate component of the national Roosevelt coalition. During that crucial period, the contention for power between the Roosevelt-CIO coalition and the traditional Big Business–American Federation of Labor alliance had a decisive influence on the politics of the nation as a whole.

CIO influence and power as an independent force in relation to the Democratic administration depended on the success of the rank-and-file organizing campaign in heavy industry; CIO power was directly related to rank-and-file victories in the great strikes of the period.

The General Motors Sit-Down Strike

Following the 1936 election, the industrial workers associated with the CIO continued to hold the initiative. On December 18, Lewis and Brophy held a conference in Washington with United Automobile Workers' leaders Mortimer, Hall, Martin, and McCabe. The meeting was called to map out a strategy to cope with strikes that had broken out in General Motors plants in Atlanta and Kansas City, and the GM policy of provoking local strikes at times and places of its own choosing. The result was a formal announcement that the CIO would seek national collective-bargaining rights with General Motors. Brophy was dispatched to Detroit, where he presented a letter from the UAW to

General Motors proposing a discussion of general grievances, including speed-up, discrimination against union members, job security, and the "abuses of the present piece-work system of pay." General Motors replied that all questions put forth by the union must be settled locally on a plant-by-plant basis. On December 28 the rank and file took matters into their own hands and staged a sit-down strike at the Cleveland Fisher Body plant. Mortimer hurried to Cleveland from Detroit and announced that there would be no settlement of the Cleveland strike without a national agreement.

Two days later, workers at the Fisher Body Plant No. 1 in Flint, Michigan, spurred on by Mortimer and Travis, but lacking any previous authorization from Lewis and other CIO leaders, occupied the plant. The auto workers thus preempted the Lewis strategy of organizing steel before attacking the auto industry. Nevertheless, that evening Lewis spoke on the radio to the nation, giving all-out support to the automobile workers and demanding that Roosevelt and the Democratic Party pay their debts to the workers who had voted them into power. He also directed pressure on the Senate, which had just established the LaFollette Civil Liberties Committee to investigate business violations of the right of workers to organize unions and bargain collectively: "May I humbly warn the Senate that labor wants the LaFollette investigation pressed home and wants industry disarmed lest labor men on their march to industrial democracy should have to take by storm the barbed-wire barricades and machinegun emplacements maintained by the rapacious moguls of corporate industry."[10]

On New Year's Day, 1937, workers in Ohio struck Fisher Body and Chevrolet in Norwood, followed by the Guide Lamp plant in Anderson, Indiana. Between January 1 and February 1, sit-downs and walkouts occurred at the Toledo Chevrolet plant, the Chevrolet and Fisher Body plants at Janesville, the Cadillac and Fleetwood plants in Detroit, the Fisher and Chevrolet plants in Oakland, and the Chevrolet Plant No. 4 in Flint. On January 4 the UAW leadership under Homer Martin announced eight demands it was seeking in a national collective bargaining agreement with General Motors. These were:

> a national collective-bargaining conference; the abolition of all piece-work systems of pay; the thirty-six hour week, the six-hour day, and time-and-a-half compensation for overtime; establishment of a minimum rate of pay; reinstatement of employees who had been "unjustly" dismissed; seniority based on length of service; recognition of the UAW as the "sole bargaining agency" for GM workers; and the mutual determination by management and union committees of the speed of production in all GM plants.[11]

The key demand from the union's point of view was the call for recognition of the union as the sole bargaining agency for GM. The workers, on the other hand, were more concerned with speed-ups and steady work. Alfred Sloan, the president of General Motors, responded with a classic management statement. The real question, he declared, was: "Will a labor organization run the plants of General Motors . . . or will management continue to do so?"[12] The company refused to recognize any union as the sole collective bargaining agent and was immediately backed by its old ally, the AFL craft union hierarchy. On January 7 the Metal Trades, Building Trades, and six affiliated international unions, led by John Frey, president of the Metal Trades Department of the AFL, sent a telegram to General Motors protesting any exclusive bargaining rights to the UAW.

In 1934, class-conscious rank-and-file leaders had initiated and led the great national labor revolt. In 1937, the Left-Lewis alliance produced the greatest industrial union victory in the history of the United States. Left-wing union organizers led the historic General Motors strike: Wyndham Mortimer and Robert Travis, both Communists, the Reuther brothers, both Socialists, and Ed Hall, George Addes, and other class-conscious trade unionists. Within the national office of the CIO the key figure besides Lewis was Lee Pressman, the CIO general counsel, who had been a member of the Communist Party as late as 1936. While Mortimer and Travis mapped out the strike strategy at the Detroit and Flint GM plants, Lewis and Pressman coordinated a bargaining strategy that took into account the pressures brought to bear on the strikers by the corporations, the government, and the courts. Maurice Sugar, a local Communist attorney, worked with Pressman on legal tactics to block corporate-judicial attacks on the union. Another Communist, Charles Kramer, who served as the chief investigator for the newly established LaFollette Civil Liberties Committee, exposed the strikebreaking activities of the auto companies. These investigations in turn fed the press releases of left-wing journalist Carl Haessler, who handled publicity for the strike. During the final negotiations Lewis, Pressman, and Mortimer represented the UAW at the bargaining table.

The key to the General Motors strike was Fisher Body Plant No. 1. On December 30, the workers informed Robert Travis that the company was attempting to remove critical dies from the plant, presumably to resume production in Grand Rapids or Pontiac, Michigan. As workers poured into the union hall across from the plant to discuss this crisis, the men inside took possession of the plant. The dies were thus captured. In Bernstein's words, "By the end of the first week of the New Year, the great General Motors automotive system had been brought to its knees."[13] Walter Galenson, another well-known labor historian, called the GM strike the most critical labor conflict of the 1930s.

Three days after Fisher Body Plant No. 1 was occupied, GM attorneys obtained a circuit court injunction ordering the Flint strikers to leave the plant immediately and prohibiting them from further picketing. Pressman and Sugar discovered that the judge who had issued the injunction, Edward Black, owned more than 3,000 shares of General Motors stock. They therefore argued that the injunction was without legal force and would be ignored by the union. An embarrassed General Motors then announced that its suit would be transferred to another court.

GM next resorted to a classic strikebreaking strategy: it formed a front committee called the "Flint Alliance—for the Security of Our Jobs, Our Homes and Our Community," and used it to initiate a back-to-work movement. The alliance pressured employees of the struck plants to sign back-to-work petitions. Roman Catholic Bishop Gallagher of Detroit declared: "We're fearful that it's Soviet planning behind them [the sit-downs]," and the press began to call for presidential intervention in the strike.[14] General Motors apparently believed that in its own city of Flint it would be able to smash both the strike and incipient unionism in the auto industry. GM officials announced that they would not bargain until the plants were evacuated; the union declared that it would not leave the plants (unless GM closed them) until a settlement was reached. In addition, they insisted the company promise not to remove machinery and end its back-to-work campaign.

It was the extraordinary organization and solidarity of the workers that made the GM strikes successful. At Fisher Body Plant No. 1, a strike committee of seventeen constituted the "chief administrative body . . . whose decisions were subject to daily checkup of membership meetings. These meetings were like the townhall gatherings of a basic democratic society. The entire life of the sit-down came into review here and most of its ideas and decisions originated on the spot." All the strikers were organized into groups of fifteen, "each headed by a steward." The groups generated the warmth of families and Henry Kraus quotes one worker, after the strike was settled, as saying, "The first three days after the strike before the plant reopened were the lonesomest of my life." There were special committees on sanitation and security, food deliveries were organized, regular hours were set aside for bathing, and rules were enforced by impromptu courts. "It was like we were soldiers holding the fort. It was like war. The guys with me became my buddies," recalled one of the sit-downers in Chevrolet Plant No. 4. Wives of strikers organized an emergency brigade to aid the strike and soon became the most enthusiastic troops in the battle. One striker's wife was quoted as saying, "I'm living for the first time with a definite goal. . . . Just being a woman isn't enough any more. I want to be a human being with the right to think for myself." Another woman activist wrote: "Women who only yesterday were horrified at unionism, who felt inferior to the task of organizing, speaking, leading, have, as if overnight, become the spearhead in the battle for humanism."[15]

As Dubofsky and Van Tine put it, "The solidarity established by the strikers on the inside and their families and supporters on the outside provided Lewis with the power that enabled him to play the role of negotiator-extraordinary." Lewis utilized that power to the fullest:

> Uninvolved in the more conventional activities of the strike, Lewis concentrated on eliciting federal and state support for the sit-downers and forcing General Motors to the bargaining table. Put another way, during the General Motors strike, the sit-downers personified labor power, power that Lewis could exert to win for unionism an unprecedented triumph in mass-production industry.[16]

GM's strategy was to break the strike at its weakest point, and on January 11 the Flint police moved in on Fisher Body Plant No. 2, held by only 100 strikers. The company turned off the heat and company guards prevented union men and women from bringing food into the strikers. Victor Reuther and the strikers in the plant fought back. The incident, called "The Battle of the Running Bulls" by the union, left the auto workers in command. Fourteen strikers and two spectators were wounded by police gunfire and a number of policemen wound up in the hospital.

As a result of this battle, Governor Murphy—newly elected, largely with auto worker support—called out the National Guard, which occupied Flint on January 12, and then the governor used his considerable prestige to compel GM to enter into negotiations with the union. But GM refused to bargain exclusively with the UAW, and invited the Flint Alliance to represent loyal GM employees and take part in the negotiations. In response, the strikers refused to leave the plant.

Secretary of Labor Frances Perkins, who kept in touch with the crisis in Flint, reported to Roosevelt that Lewis remained adamant in his refusal to recommend evacuation of the plants before concessions had been made by General Motors. Lewis then began to exert direct pressure on Roosevelt. On January 21, he announced at a press conference in Washington:

> We have advised the administration that for six months the economic royalists represented by General Motors contributed their money and used their energy to drive the administration out of power. The administration asked labor for help to repel this attack, and labor gave its help. The same economic royalists now have their fangs in labor. The workers of this country expect this administration to help the workers in every legal way, and to support the auto workers in the General Motors plants.[17]

The press responded with an attack on Lewis for daring to attempt to pressure the president and predicted the break-up of the Roosevelt-CIO coalition. But Roosevelt, who had run into a storm of opposition to his campaign to expand and pack the Supreme Court with his own supporters, still needed CIO support and attempted to walk a tightrope between capital and labor.

On January 23 Secretary Perkins issued a formal invitation to the chief officers of GM, the UAW, and Lewis as the representative of the CIO national office to attend a conference in Washington on January 27 "without conditions or prejudice." Lewis accepted, but Sloan refused, writing that GM would not negotiate until its plants had been evacuated, that the patience of GM management was running out in the face of the illegal occupation of its property, and that if the public authorities did not do something about it, GM might act on its own.

On January 26 Roosevelt told a press conference that Sloan's refusal was "a very unfortunate decision." Perkins went even further, telling reporters that Sloan was shirking his moral authority, ignoring the public interest, and that she could understand why the UAW leaders did not trust the word of GM. The sit-down strikers in the Fisher Body plant reported at a strike meeting on January 28: "Sloan has been criticized by Roosevelt and Perkins. We are in a better position now."[18]

As tensions rose, a LaFollette Committee investigator concluded that "civil war is not beyond the possibilities." While the company prepared for violence, stepped up its back-to-work movement, and escalated its anticommunist propaganda campaign in Detroit, Travis and Roy Reuther devised an ingenious strategy to once again take the initiative in the strike. They planned to seize Chevrolet Plant No. 4, which produced a million engines a year and was the most important plant in the GM system. Since a frontal assault on the plant, which was guarded by hundreds of company police, would be suicidal, Travis and Reuther called a special meeting where they knew company spies would be present and laid out plans to capture Chevrolet 9. On February 1 a large crowd of union men gathered before Chevrolet 9 shouting "Strike!" a battle with police ensued, and during this battle other strikers seized Chevrolet 4 and 6. The strikers thereby showed their power to escalate the strike at a time when General Motors was suffering severe economic damage.[19]

Seeking another injunction, the corporation told the court that GM production had fallen from 31,830 to 6,100 cars a week, while Ford and Chrysler were increasing production every day.

The company attempted to halt food deliveries to the strikers inside the plant on the basis that the workers occupying the plant were not employees but outsiders. Brophy called the governor and got permission to enter the plant, where he proved to the National Guard that all the sit-downers were regular employees. The food deliveries resumed. On February 2, GM obtained another court injunction ordering the evacuation of the plant and the union immediately announced that it would defy the injunction. At last the company agreed to bargain. The seizure of Chevrolet 4, the defiance of the court by the union, the refusal of the governor to resort to force, and the refusal of Roosevelt to intervene, added to continued financial loss, convinced GM officials that they must negotiate.

When Lewis arrived in Detroit from Washington on February 2 he found the occupied GM plants ringed with bayonet-wielding troops, who in addition to their rifles had set up machine-gun posts throughout the strike area. General Motors' negotiating team included William Knudsen, vice-president of the company, John Thomas Smith, chief attorney, and Donaldson Brown, representing the duPont Corporation, which owned a controlling interest in GM. The union committee consisted of Lewis, Pressman, and Homer Martin, president of the UAW. After the first day of negotiations with Governor Murphy and the GM team, Lewis met with Mortimer, George Addes, the secretary-treasurer of the UAW, and Ed Hall, the second vice-president, and said that he could not continue with "this man Martin," who he said was "totally unpredictable and I never know what foolish remark he will make next."[20] Martin was sent on a speaking tour around the country and Mortimer joined Lewis and Pressman on the union's negotiating team.

The GM negotiators refused to enter the same room with the UAW representatives, so Murphy shuttled between the two rooms. The key issues were evacuation of the plants, exclusive recognition for the UAW-CIO, and the duration of the contract. The strikers insisted on a one-year contract; GM wanted only a thirty-day contract, long enough to hold elections. Mortimer and Travis visited the strikers in Fisher Body Plant No. 1 to discuss the issue of contract length. The men in the plant were told that Roosevelt wanted a thirty-day contract and the union was demanding one year. "The sit-downers agreed that the union must insist on one year, but that we must not under any circumstances agree to less than six months," enough time for the union to solidify its base in all plants. When Mortimer and Travis reported back to Lewis, he said: "That is what I like about you fellows, you certainly know what you want."[21]

At this point, powerful forces throughout the nation began to mobilize against the auto strikers and their negotiating committee. The National Association of Manufacturers and the National Chamber of Commerce flooded Murphy with telegrams assailing him for failing to enforce the injunction against the auto workers who were occupying GM's factories. President Roosevelt added to this pressure. Mortimer records the following phone call:

A day later, the Governor came into the room and said, "John, Washington wishes to speak to you." Lewis picked up the phone, motioning me to listen in on the extension. President Roosevelt said, "John, I just had a talk with Sloan and I think I can get him to sign a thirty-day contract." Lewis replied, "Mr. President, it must be a six-month contract." Roosevelt said, "Maybe I can get him to agree to a two-month contract, I don't know, I will try." Lewis again answered, "Mr. President, it must be a six-month contract." Roosevelt was obviously irked. "Come, come now, John, this is no time to quibble." But again Lewis said, "Mr. President, it must be a six-month contract." The next voice we heard was that of Secretary of Labor Frances Perkins, who related the facts of the meeting with Sloan. She too, then hung up.[22]

And, finally, the AFL Executive Council sent a telegram signed by all members to Knudsen demanding that General Motors refuse to negotiate a contract with the UAW "since it would destroy the rights of AFL members in the General Motors plants" and threatened to strike GM if the company entered into an agreement with the UAW-CIO.[23]

Both Lewis and the chief officers of GM realized that only Murphy had the power to break the strike. Lewis got Murphy aside and told him: "President Roosevelt swept this state by nearly 200,000, you carried it by 40,000 because labor supported you. Labor put you there. . . . If you break this strike that washes us up and washes you up. General Motors fought you in the election and when we are gone you are gone. If you stand firm you will aggrandize your political position enormously and there will be talk of Governor Murphy in 1940." When Murphy begged Lewis to persuade the strikers to leave the plants, Lewis told him:

> I am not going to withdraw those sit-downers under any circumstances except a settlement. What are you going to do? You can get them out in just one way, by bayonets. You have the bayonets. Which kind do you prefer to use—the broad double blade or the four-sided French style? I believe the square style makes a bigger hole and you can turn it around inside a man. Which kind of bayonets, Governor Murphy, are you going to turn around inside our boys?[24]

During the final hours of negotiations, Lewis used a press report that revealed the assignment of a Pinkerton detective to watch his house in Alexandria, Virginia, to put the company executives on the defensive. He demanded to know: "Who sent that Pinkerton? Was it you Brown? Was it you Smith?" Knudsen replied, "Well, I guess it must be my department."[25] Then Arnold Lenz, the plant manager of Chevrolet Plant No. 4, endangered the negotiations by turning off the heat. The strikers, who had previously responded to this attempt to freeze them out by threatening to light bonfires in the plants, this time retaliated by opening all the skylights, an action that threatened to freeze pipelines and valuable equipment. Lenz mobilized 330 plant police to evict the strikers by force, a move quickly blocked by Knudsen. Travis and Roy Reuther entered the plant and convinced the workers to close the windows and skylights once the heat had been turned back on.

Finally, GM capitulated. According to Mortimer, Lewis was confined to his room with the flu. Smith, GM's counsel, entered the room, came over to Lewis' bed, and once more raised the question of a thirty-day contract:

> Lewis arose on his elbow and in his most sonorous voice asked: "You want your plants to reopen, do you not?" Smith replied, "Yes, yes, of course." "Well then, it is six months!" Lewis said, turning his back to Smith. The latter stood looking at Lewis for a few moments. "Very well, then, Mr. Lewis," he said and left the room.[26]

Mortimer went into an adjoining suite and met Knudsen, who had argued during the negotiations that it was impermissible for GM employees to wear union buttons inside the plants. Knudsen signaled an end to one of the great strikes in U.S. history by telling Mortimer: "Mr. Mortimer, let your people wear a union button, ten buttons, a hundred buttons, a thousand buttons, I don't care a damn. Let's get back to making automobiles." The final agreement was reached at Lewis' bedside, with the governor sitting on the bed. Smith, the GM lawyer, ended an epoch with the same corporate attitude with which it had begun. He told Lewis: "You beat us, but I'm not going to forget it. I just want to tell you that one of these days we'll come back and give you the kind of whipping that you and your people will never forget."[27]

The final agreement, signed on February 11 by Wyndham Mortimer for the UAW, John L. Lewis for the CIO, and Lee Pressman as the union's attorney, provided little more than a skeletal framework within which the struggle between company and union would continue. GM recognized the United Automobile Workers of America as "the collective bargaining agency for those employees of the Corporation who are members of the union," agreed not to "interfere with the rights of its employees to be members of the union," and not to discriminate against any employee because of union membership, and to take back all strikers without discrimination. Company and union agreed to open negotiations for a full collective-bargaining contract on February 16. The union agreed to terminate the strike and pending negotiations with the company no strikes or interruption of work would be undertaken by union members. Finally, the company agreed to resume operations as soon as possible and to dismiss injunction proceedings against the union.

Henry Kraus accompanied Mortimer to Fisher Body Plant No. 1, where Mortimer read the contract to the membership. They fired questions at him, mainly about "the speed of the line" and whether "the bosses" would be just "as tough as ever." One striker was cheered when he stated: "I'll be goddamned if I ain't gonna smack the first one that looks the least bit cockeyed at me." These were not the workers who had shut the plant down; desperate then, they were aware of their power now, but without illusions. One worker defined what had and what had not been won: "What's the use of kidding ourselves? All that piece of paper means is that we got a union. The rest depends on us. For God's sake let's go back to work and keep up what we started here."[28]

Mortimer described the difficulties facing the union when negotiations with GM opened on February 16: "Every meaningful demand put forward by the union was regarded as a challenge to the corporation's authority, to their property rights, which they regarded as sacred." When Mortimer commented at the bargaining table that GM profits were high enough to accommodate substantial wage increases, Harry Anderson, representing the company's personnel department, replied angrily: "Mr. Mortimer, our profits are none of your goddamned business."[29]

Irving Bernstein notes that General Motors' policy "was to contain the union, to yield no more than economic power compelled and, above all, to preserve managerial discretion in the productive process, particularly over the speed of the line."[30] GM officials were adamant in their refusal to agree to a shop-steward system that would allow workers to present their grievances to a steward rather than a foreman, and only agreed to a watered-down version after prolonged bargaining. They refused outright the union proposal for one steward for every twenty-five employees, agreeing only to the establishment of a shop committee with a maximum of nine committeemen per plant. The union was unable to win a shorter workweek or the abolition of piecework. Except for seniority rights and union recognition, every other gain of substance had to be won through further struggle, more strikes, more sit-downs, and direct action by the workers on the assembly line. As Bernstein put it, GM was inviting a sharp union reaction, one which would not be long in coming.

U.S. Steel Surrenders to the CIO

On March 8 the new auto union carried the battle to Chrysler and occupied nine of the main Chrysler plants. Murphy, who was prepared to use force to evacuate the factories, quickly arranged a meeting between Lewis and Walter Chrysler. After some negotiations, Lewis agreed to evacuate the plants in return for recognition of the union, a promise to bargain faithfully, and a guarantee not to resume production until an agreement was reached. On April 6 Chrysler signed an agreement almost identical to the GM settlement. With the negotiations at an end, Chrysler said to Lewis: "Mr. Lewis, I do not worry about dealing with you, but it is the Communists in these unions that worry me a great deal."[31]

With the historic capitulation to its workers by General Motors, the attention of the nation and the press turned to the steel industry, where the CIO was in the process of launching its next massive organizing campaign. The managers of United States Steel, however, who had observed the outcome of the great Detroit sit-down strikes in the auto industry, read the writing on the wall and voluntarily signed a contract with the CIO for all its production workers. In effect, the auto workers had delivered steel to the CIO without a strike. Lee Pressman later described the circumstances under which U.S. Steel renounced its fifty-year open-shop policy and surrendered to the CIO:

> The success or failure of the auto workers' strike meant the success or failure of the budding CIO. The loss of that strike might have been the end of the CIO. . . . At that time we did not have anywhere near approaching a majority of membership in their US Steel plants. It wasn't the pressure of union organization that compelled them or required them to recognize us.[32]

Myron Taylor, chairman of the board of U.S. Steel, conducted private talks with John L. Lewis during the peak crisis period of the General Motors sit-down. The General Motors settlement occurred on February 11, 1937, while the steel agreement was reached on March 2. In short, steel did not settle until the outcome of the General Motors strike had been determined. If cooptation had been wanted, U.S. Steel could have sent a message to its colleagues in arms at GM by settling first. However, it was the auto workers who sent the message to both General Motors and U.S. Steel.

As Dubofsky and Van Tine make clear, the steel contract signed on March 2, 1937, actually offered less to the Steel Workers Organizing Committee (SWOC) than the sit-downs were able to wring out of General Motors on February 11. U.S. Steel executives hedged their recognition of SWOC by establishing their legal right to deal with any other union that might appear in their shops. Myron Taylor never gave up his belief that the majority of workers in U.S. Steel plants would not choose to join the union.[33]

A further corroboration of the thesis that Taylor settled with Lewis as a direct result of the UAW victory against General Motors comes from Matthew Josephson. During the period of the auto breakthrough and the steel settlement, Josephson, who had extensive contacts on Wall Street, talked off the record with a prominent financial figure about the wave of industrial unionism sweeping the country. Josephson reveals that he talked with Leland Fraser, who was then president of the First National Bank, a member of the finance committee of U.S. Steel, and a member of the board of directors of U.S. Steel, General Motors, and A.T.&T.

He told me that when the General Motors sit-down strike was over, the problem of the U.S. Steel settlement came up and that he and Lamont favored making a reasonable settlement with the union. . . . This was the decision of the Finance Committee and the Board of Directors of Steel, . . . and that's what (Myron) Taylor, who was President, followed, you see; he followed those directives.

He was just a servant, you know, of the big banks.[34]

U.S. Steel was negotiating at that time with a representative of the British government to tie down a large armaments contract and thus feared a strike. A repeat of the Flint plant seizure in steel was too risky for a company that had carefully observed that the state had failed to play its traditional role of strikebreaker. Even *Fortune* Magazine admitted that if the workers could tie up the auto industry they could do the same in steel. On the other hand, Dubofsky and Van Tine explain why John L. Lewis agreed to settle for less in steel than he had in auto: "The steel union lacked the Mortimers, Travises, Simons, Johnsons, and Reuthers—militant cadres who could force the hands of both corporation executives and labor leaders."[35] By winning the confrontation with the two largest industrial monopolies in the nation, the CIO became the most important labor organization in American history. In three weeks, as Dubofsky and Van Tine assert, the CIO accomplished what the AFL had failed to achieve in half a century.

The historic agreement between U.S. Steel and the CIO unveiled the strategy the giant corporations would utilize in adapting themselves to the power of industrial unionism: wage increases would be matched with price increases, thus passing on the economic costs of labor settlements to the rest of society. In 1937 U.S. Steel set the precedent for socializing the costs of production. It was a formula that would eventually build inflation into the American system and in the long run produce a systemic crisis of an entirely different order. Bernstein describes the historic bargain that would shape the future of the American system: "With the current high volume of operations, the corporations could stand this amount (raising the basic labor rate in the North to 62.5¢ an hour), and, in fact, used this first labor agreement to institute the policy of raising prices immediately following the granting of a wage increase."[36] The head of the Federal Reserve Board, Marriner Eccles, wrote to Roosevelt informing him that the price increase instituted by U.S. Steel "has been greatly in excess of the rise that would be sufficient to compensate for the wage advance." The Bureau of Labor Statistics estimated that the U.S. Steel price increase was actually double the cost of the wage increase granted the Steel Workers Organizing Committee of the CIO.[37]

Two of the largest basic industries in the country had now surrendered to the CIO. The third largest was the electrical industry. The giants of that industry, General Electric and Westinghouse, faced by a militant Left-led union, were the last of the great corporations to sign with the CIO. General Electric finally signed in 1938 and Westinghouse stalled full recognition of the United Electrical Workers union until forced to do so by the Supreme Court in 1941.

Two of the other major institutional opponents of industrial unionism—the judiciary and the American Federation of Labor—were put on the defensive by the CIO sweep in the basic mass production industries. Already under attack by the executive department and Congress for invalidating New Deal legislation, the Supreme Court was profoundly affected by the LaFollette Committee exposures of American business–sponsored illegal anti-labor practices and by the CIO victories over General Motors and U.S. Steel. One month after the capitulation of U.S. Steel, the Supreme Court decisively sustained the constitutionality of the Wagner Act. Industrial unionism was given legal legitimation only after decades of bloody struggle. However, the court had only ratified what the workers had already won in their massive strike battles. By the end of August 1937 the CIO's aggressive organizing drive had produced a larger membership than that claimed by the AFL. The CIO, at its national conference in Atlantic City in October, claimed 4 million members, 32 national and international chartered unions, and 600 local federated or industrial unions, and had established 80 state and city central labor councils. William Green complained to the AFL Executive Board: "The country seems to be filled with CIO organizers. Every town and every city, small and great, seems to be filled with organizers employed, appointed, and assigned to work for and by the CIO."[38] Industrial unionism, previously exorcised as un-American by business, government, and the courts, was now firmly implanted as a new institution of power in American society.

5

The Limits of Industrial Unionism Under the New Deal

Labor revolt and the emergence of the CIO as the organized expression of a coast-to-coast workers' movement for industrial unionism stand as the most significant events of American history in the mid-thirties. However, by the summer of 1937 the forward thrust of the CIO was blunted by a powerful counteroffensive launched by corporate capital and its political allies. Moreover, splits within the CIO over strategies, goals, and policies undermined the solidarity of the industrial-union movement and prevented it from breaking out of the straitjacket of economism.

While corporate capital attempted to crush the CIO through industrial warfare in the centers of production, conservatives in Congress joined the business lobby to repeal, rescind, or emasculate prolabor legislation produced by the New Deal. At the same time, the liberal core of the Roosevelt coalition and its major Catholic, Jewish, and social-democratic constituency within the CIO conducted a successful struggle to subordinate industrial unionism to the Democratic Party. Left-syndicalist forces were thus contained in their attempt to carve out an independent base for industrial unionism and the social movement it led.

Three major bulwarks against the continued advance of radical labor in the United States were the two-party system, the universally held belief in the major tenet of private property, and the continued division of the American working class into separate ideological, ethnic, and religious groupings.[1] While not strong enough to prevent the drive of industrial workers for self-organization, these forces prevented the leap from economic organization to a self-reliant political movement. What solidarity there was in the CIO was achieved through common struggle, not through the social cohesion of its membership. Thus, ethnic, cultural, religious, and political differences contributed to separate ideologies and political strategies, and once the common struggle subsided, the component parts of the CIO fell apart. The three main ethnic and political blocs of the industrial-union movement of the thirties were the Catholic workers from Eastern and southeastern Europe, Jewish and European workers with social-democratic traditions, and national Protestant, Jewish, and European-born workers imbued with a Left-syndicalist world outlook. In essence, the politics of the CIO involved the struggle between the Left-syndicalist group represented by Mortimer, Myers, Bridges, Emspak, Matles, and John L. Lewis, and the Catholic-Jewish bloc of liberal Roosevelt supporters represented by Murray, Hillman, Carey, and Brophy plus Communist Party functionaries who shared a similar strategic if not ideological outlook with the liberal bloc. That strategy sought acceptance of the CIO within the state by making alliances at the top. The Lewis-Mortimer-Bridges rank-and-file syndicalists fought for a line of independent economic and social power for the CIO; they had no real political strategy. Their lives and their world outlook encompassed struggle and continued organization of the unorganized and because of this they more truly represented the spirit of the age for which the CIO had become the symbol.

The Corporate Strikebreaking Counteroffensive

In the spring of 1937, Eugene Grace of Bethlehem, Tom Girdler of Republic, Ernest Weir of National, Frank Purnell of Sheet and Tube, and Charles Hook of ARMCO coordinated a violent offensive that succeeded in taking the lives of scores of steelworkers and stopped the CIO organizing drive in its tracks. During May, Girdler spent $50,000 on munitions, increased his private security force to 370 men, and equipped them with 552 pistols, 64 rifles, 245 shotguns, 143 gas guns, 58 gas billies, 2,707 gas grenades, 178 billies, and 232 night sticks. He also hired a New York public relations firm to distribute 43,800 copies of a pamphlet entitled "Join the CIO and Help Build a Soviet America." Then on May 20, he locked out 9,000 steelworkers from his main plants in Massilon and Canton, Ohio. One foreman told the president of the local CIO union at Massilon: "When we get through starving you out, you won't want to strike."[2]

Philip Murray, in command of the CIO steelworkers' organizing drive, committed a strategic blunder by then striking the plants of Republic, Inland, and Sheet and Tube on May 26. At Republic and Sheet and Tube plants in Youngstown, Ohio, 23,600 workers went out, and 2,500 workers struck the South Chicago Republic plant although the company continued production with scabs and supervisory personnel. Having forced the strike, the steel companies methodically put into effect a refined and updated strikebreaking strategy based on the "Mohawk Valley Formula" developed by James Rand, Jr., to smash a union of office and equipment workers at the Remington Rand Company plant in New York State in 1936. The Mohawk Valley anti-union prescription was simply a distillation of standard strikebreaking procedures developed throughout the country during the industrial wars of the early thirties. Union leaders were branded "agitators," the union was red-baited, local bankers, businessmen, and real estate operators were mobilized into a traditional "citizens committee" to oppose the strike, a vigilante force was created, and extensive violence was used to keep the struck plants open. Most of the "improvements" to the Mohawk Valley Formula came in the area of violent tactics.

When the strike was called at the South Chicago Republic plant on May 26, approximately 150 Chicago policemen were already stationed inside the plant gates, where a police headquarters was established; city policemen were fed at company expense. During the first hours of the strike, in an illegal effort to prevent picketing, police arrested twenty-three strikers for unlawful assembly and disorderly conduct. A riot occurred on the third day, when union men marching to the plant to set up mass picketing were dispersed with gunfire and clubs.

On May 30 the Steel Workers Organizing Committee (SWOC) called a mass meeting to protest police restrictions on picketing. Some 2,500 strikers and their supporters, including women and children, assembled to listen to speeches by strike leaders in front of the strike headquarters, a few blocks from the Republic mill. The chairman was Joe Weber, a steelworker and Communist Party member who was an organizer on the SWOC staff. At the end of the meeting, the crowd marched behind U.S. flags up to the gates of the plant in an attempt to form a mass picket line. The rest of the story has been recorded in history texts, on newsreel film, at Senate hearings, and in fiction. The Chicago police fired point-blank into the crowd, continued firing at the backs of those who fled, beat the wounded who had fallen, dragged those who were shot to waiting police vans, and refused first aid to the victims. As the LaFollette Committee, after the investigation of the Memorial Day Massacre, commented, "Wounded prisoners of war might have expected and received greater solicitude."[3] Despite national outrage, the police were never prosecuted and Republic Steel continued strikebreaking. John L. Lewis called Tom Girdler "a heavily armed monomaniac, with murderous tendencies who has gone berserk."[4]

The next application of the updated version of the Mohawk Valley Formula was carried out in Johnstown, Pennsylvania, by the Bethlehem

Steel Company. Of the 15,000 workers at Bethlehem's Cambria Works, 12,000 walked out on June 11, 1937. The mayor, Daniel Shields, working closely with Bethlehem Steel executives, deputized dozens of American Legionnaires as vigilantes and then informed a meeting of business and professional leaders that the plant would remain open. He subsequently told a radio audience that "Johnstown is our city," asked whether the community was going to allow "outsiders" to come in and destroy it, and called on all "red-blooded Americans" to rise up and prevent "communism and anarchy" from taking over. Bethlehem provided the mayor with thousands of dollars to carry out his strike-breaking plan. On June 18, Shields sent a telegram to Roosevelt informing him that the CIO "can only mean blood in our streets" and that it "is a Russian organization." On June 19, Governor Earle declared martial law in Johnstown and closed down the Cambria Works. Bethlehem Steel responded by hiring a Pittsburgh advertising agency to conduct a national campaign to force the reopening of the plant in the name of "law and order." Full-page ads, partially financed by Ernest Weir of National Steel and Richard Mellon of the Mellon National Bank, were placed in major metropolitan newspapers. Earle buckled under the pressure and lifted martial law; Bethlehem immediately organized a back-to-work movement to break the strike.[5]

In the meantime, Girdler had refused to sign a contract with SWOC, had refused to meet with Lewis, and had turned down all mediation efforts by Roosevelt. Governor Davey of Ohio wired Roosevelt, pleading that he "intervene on behalf of the Federal government." Roosevelt finally gave in and by executive order created the Federal Steel Mediation Board, with Charles Taft, who had mediated the Auto-Lite strike, as chairman and Lloyd Garrison and Edward McGrady, who had been active for the federal government in the San Francisco General Strike, as co-members. Girdler still refused to meet with either Lewis or Murray. On June 19 a riot broke out at the Republic plant at Youngstown; two strikers were shot to death, and forty-two pickets, including several women, were seriously injured. Davey called out the National Guard, ordering those plants that were working to remain open, those that were closed to remain closed.

On June 21, Lewis told a press conference that as a result of the deaths of twelve steelworkers over the past three weeks and ten more "gasping for their lives in hospital beds," all victims of company terrorism, "labor will await the position of the authorities on whether our people will be protected or butchered."[6] But the president, astutely observing that the pendulum was once again swinging against labor, refused to take a stand. Roosevelt informed reporters that he had just spoken to Charlie Taft, the federal mediator of what became known as the Little Steel Strike, who had told him: "The majority of people are saying one thing: 'A plague on both your houses.'" Newspapers around the country announced that the president was fed up with both the CIO and the steel companies, and the CIO could no longer count on his support. It was now clear that the president would grant to the CIO no more than its own power could achieve.[7] The CIO thus lost a major campaign; the bloodied strikers trooped back to the mills after the union and companies fixed their signatures to "a statement of policy," but all the Little Steel companies refused to sign a collective-bargaining agreement. The SWOC won recognition for its members only and a rehiring of strikers without discrimination. "The union had saved a little face . . . from what otherwise would have been the total disaster of the Little Steel Strike."[8] Years later Pressman remarked: "We took a terrific drubbing on that Little Steel Strike—a terrific drubbing."[9]

One of the last great organizing drives of the CIO was led by Sidney Hillman, who set up the Textile Workers Organizing Committee (TWOC) and opened a great textile drive in the spring of 1937. Like the Steel Workers Organizing Committee run by Murray, the TWOC was run from the top down, but unlike Murray, who allowed the Communists to take the risks at the bottom, Hillman saw to it that there were no Communists or radicals at any level in the unionization of the textile industry. The Mortimers and Travises were kept out of the textile drive, which proved to be one of the greatest disasters in CIO history.

> In the fall of 1937, TWOC suffered two devastating blows. In late September textiles were struck by a severe recession that immediately threw the union on the defensive. Significant new organization was now out of the question and the union strove desperately to hold on. In October American Woolen laid off three fourths of its labor force. In December the New Bedford Textile Council, a UTW affiliate, accepted a 12.5 percent wage cut in the local cotton mills without the knowledge or consent of TWOC. Despite the expulsion of seven locals, the reduction spread through the cotton industry, North and South. Woolens instituted a similar cut in the face of defensive strikes. The same story unfolded in carpets in the spring of 1938.[10]

Throughout the country the corporations organized carefully planned lockouts to destroy the newly won bridgeheads of organized labor. The UE was particularly hard hit, facing more than fifty strikes and lockouts in 1938. The most publicized was at the Maytag plant in Newton, Iowa. Maytag was a family-owned business and Newton was a one-shop company town. After its contract expired on May 9, 1938, the company introduced a "take-it-or-leave it" wage cut and virtually threw the contract out the window. When the workers refused to accept the company ultimatum, the company locked out its 1,600 employees; the union responded by voting to strike. The Mohawk Valley Formula was brought into play, and the National Guard was called out after the strikers mixed with a crowd of scabs entering the plant and, once inside the plant, staged a sit-down and occupied the factory. Police then escorted the scabs out and the strikers remained in control of the plant. After a long and bitter struggle involving the arrest of the UE leader, Bill Sentner, a Communist Party member and organizer of the electrical industry in St. Louis who was indicted on criminal syndicalist charges, the strike was broken.

The UE strike leaders, sensing that the strike would be broken under the guns of the National Guard, argued that the workers should return to work, preparing to fight on from the inside. The strikers reluctantly agreed, but issued the following statement to the press: "We are returning to work under the forces of military intimidation and coercion. But at the proper time, and in the proper manner, Local 1116 will again present its demands to the Maytag Company."[11]

After weeks of negotiations, the union won a contract without a wage cut and with a restoration of all the clauses the company had demanded be removed from the original agreement.

Disunity Within the CIO

As the CIO began to lose momentum in the downturn of the economy in the second half of 1937 and faced the mobilization of national forces to oppose its further advance, the internal conflict within the CIO that had always existed began to surface. The conflict was clearly symbolized by the differences in personality and outlook of the CIO's two most powerful leaders, John L. Lewis and Sidney Hillman.

The difference between the social-democratic world outlook of Hillman and the class-conscious syndicalist stance of Lewis is clearly revealed by Lee Pressman in his oral memoirs. Hillman had played a "lone wolf game" by building the Amalgamated Clothing Workers outside the framework of the AFL. "He made friends in high places" and followed a strategy "to organize from the top, to establish good relations with employers, so that they wanted you in the industry." From the very beginning of the New Deal under the Roosevelt adminis-tration, Hillman "was right on the doorstep of the White House, trying to get all he could out of the fact that he had good relations with Roosevelt and the White House." Roosevelt decided very early in the game to use Hillman as his spokesman. According to Pressman, Hill-man "was terribly frightened about sit-down strikers." Lewis, on the other hand, would reply to Hillman's stated fears by saying, "Well, I didn't start it." Since the sit-downs were spontaneous creations of the workers, Lewis warned Hillman: "Don't try to put out the fire. If you do you'll loose your forces."[12]

Whenever Hillman disagreed with what Lewis was either doing or saying he would seek the aid of Philip Murray and the two would attempt together to counter the Lewis line in the CIO. Pressman captures the essence of the difference in personality and world outlook of a Lewis, who reflected the militancy of millions of industrial workers who were attempting to put their stamp on an entire society, and a Hillman, who believed that social gains might be won through negotiations with the holders of power:

> The word "compromise" was extremely important in Hillman's vocabulary. He was also accustomed to dealing with low-paid industries, clothing workers. For Lewis, the word "compromise" was very, very foreign to him. Not that he negated it, it was simply foreign to him. He didn't consider it a favor to be permitted to come to the White House. His position was that considering what organized labor did in '32 and '36 on behalf of the administration, as a matter of right, they were entitled to go to the White House, as representatives of organized labor, just the way representatives of organized industry had a right to walk into the White House under Hoover.[13]

Lewis, as Pressman confirms, would not tolerate a paternalistic attitude from the president toward organized labor. Pressman states that Lewis criticized both Murray and Hillman for their gratitude to Roosevelt for any prolabor position the president took. "Why be appreciative of a thing like that?" Lewis would say. "The thing to do is to say, 'Roosevelt, why aren't you doing more?' More of that to which we are entitled." The key to the Lewis stance was the question of CIO independence. This was a notion, according to Pressman, that Philip Murray never grasped. "Lewis had a vision for himself and the CIO, that the labor movement should become so powerful that it would not be beholden to political persons or parties."

Murray, on the other hand, did not "want to bite the hand that fed him." Pressman quotes him as saying: "The thing to do with Roosevelt is to . . . cultivate him. We shouldn't antagonize him. John L. Lewis is just John L. Lewis, and by god, he'll antagonize anybody else and give him his complete works, and it's wrong, it's wrong, it's wrong." During the General Motors strike, "both Murray and Hillman thought that Lewis was absolutely crazy to antagonize the President of the United States who makes a point of getting them (the auto workers) that kind of an agreement for three months."[14] Apparently, the fact that Lewis and the sit-downers were able to wring a six-months agreement out of General Motors had no educational effect on either Murray or Hillman.

Pressman reveals that Lewis once told him, "For God sakes, why doesn't Murray understand that if we all stuck together and showed Roosevelt that he couldn't play one against the other, maybe we'd get much more that way, than we'll get just as a matter of favor." Lewis made a bid to organize the 3.5 million workers enrolled in the federal Works Progress Administration (WPA) program and told Harry Hopkins, "It's the least the administration can do for the CIO." But Roosevelt said no.[15] By the end of July, Roosevelt had resolved to break the political strength of the CIO; he unveiled a double-edged strategy of playing the AFL against the CIO, and breaking the CIO coalition from within.

The New Deal and the Ideology of Nationalism

In the political sphere, the New Deal, following in the footsteps of all the crisis regimes in American history, had become a nationalizing force. The collapse of the business society of the twenties had shifted the responsibilities for industrialization from the business community to the state. The purpose of the welfare state, in every nation as well as in the America of the thirties, has been to ameliorate class struggle and "to make the nation more solidary, more cohesive, more interdependent of its growing diversity; in short to make the nation more of a nation."[16] The "liberal coalition" led by Roosevelt monopolized the ideology of nationalism, and nationalism historically has had a long record of success in subduing ideologies based on class struggle. The CIO was only one main component of the New Deal coalition and within the political arena Roosevelt commanded a majority of the constituent parts of the New Deal electorate. In times of crisis the ideology of power generated by the state becomes a substitute for the goals of achievement usually associated with the economic sector of the social order.

In response to the crisis in the economy, Washington had become a boom town as immense new centers of bureaucratic power were hastily erected. Professionals of all kinds, particularly liberals and radicals, flocked to the capital to take part in the exciting task of policy formation concerned with national reconstruction. Most avenues of upward mobility were captured by the state as the economy foundered. This great new instrument of national patronage gave Roosevelt the kind of power previous presidents had only dreamed about. Robert Wohlforth and Matthew Josephson, reminiscing about the halcyon days of the New Deal, describe the heady atmosphere created by state power in the mid-thirties:

> *Wohlforth:* Now don't forget, we all went to Washington as crusaders. This was the way you saved the country. Everything was going to hell in a bucket; there were no jobs; and here was this great effort to get rid of the "merchants of death" and to make labor organization possible and everybody get a fair wage and buy a new automobile, you know. We all went for that. We were all red hot stuff.

Josephson: But wasn't there something exciting though, about a lot of young lawyers and young writers coming down and becoming big bureaucrats who gave hell to those bosses and laid down the law and began to tell them what. This was an exciting life. Bob was one of the many New Dealers working day and night for what? $60 a week? And they were attacking gigantic multi-millionaire corporations with $60 a week job holders, like Bob. That was the picture. And they had great enthusiasm and great joy in working on this, doing something constructive.[17]

The CIO and the Democratic Administration

In the absence of an independent labor party, the politics of the mid-thirties was shaped by the struggle for control of a transformed Democratic Party. Neither Roosevelt, the master of the political sphere, nor Lewis, the personification of the social movement arising in the economic sphere, had any intention of becoming a tail on the other's kite. However, only left-wing leaders in the CIO shared with Lewis the vision of industrial unionism as an independent and self-reliant social interest. In 1936 and 1937 that vision lay in the future. In the early days of CIO strength, concessions and power were extracted from Roosevelt even within the realm of the state itself. Carl Haessler, the capable left-wing journalist whose career was interlocked with the rise of the UAW in Detroit, describes one aspect of the political division of labor during the height of the Roosevelt-CIO coalition:

> Before the (GM) negotiations ended I was called to Washington because President Roosevelt's crusade against the reactionary Supreme Court had begun, and Labor's Non Partisan League, of which Lewis was president, needed a public relations man on the labor side to handle the press there.
>   Roosevelt, whether formally or informally or just through subordinates, had apparently delegated to Labor's Non Partisan League what you might call the rough and tumble end of the Supreme Court fight. Roosevelt, himself, and the New Deal generally maintained a more or less dignified front. But the labor and liberal side needed a more lusty attack. Labor's Non Partisan League took that on.[18]

In the second Roosevelt administration left-liberals and Communist professionals were in on the ground floor of the construction of social administrative agencies, particularly those related to labor. Nathan Witt, a Communist, became chief counsel for the National Labor Relations Board (NLRB) while John Abt, who would later become the chief counsel for the Communist Party, played a key role in the LaFollette Civil Liberties Committee in 1936. Charles Kramer, another Communist, was a key investigator for the LaFollette Committee, and Lee Pressman, before he became the key legal aid to John L. Lewis in the

CIO, first worked for Jerome Frank as assistant general counsel to the solicitor in the U.S. Department of Agriculture. The government was flooded with Harvard and Yale law graduates in the early thirties. Witt, Abt, and Pressman all moved from the Agriculture Department into labor affairs. In the early days of the second New Deal, Roosevelt delegated some power to the Left in return for support of his policies. The Left utilized that power to set up one of the most effective legislative committees of the decade—the LaFollette Civil Liberties Committee.

Despite the passage of the Wagner Act in May 1935, its administration was constantly undermined by the employers, the AFL, and the press. Radicals, leftists, and prolabor staff members of the National Labor Relations Board searched for some way to counter the sabotage of the Wagner Act and finally found a way in which public opinion might be rallied to the cause of industrial unionism by creating a Senate Committee that could conduct an offensive against the corporations and their strikebreaking, anti-union record. The LaFollette Committee was set up to conduct political warfare against the corporations, the National Association of Manufacturers (NAM), and the National Lawyers Committee of the American Liberty League, which had united to launch a multipronged attack on the constitutionality of the Wagner Act. The chairman of the National Labor Relations Board, J. Warren Madden, responded to the declaration of war on his administrative agency by stating that "this kind of incitation to disobedience" made the administration of the Wagner Act "impossible."[19]

Heber Blankenhorn must be given the most credit for the creation of the LaFollette Committee. Blankenhorn, an experienced newspaperman who served as a special investigator for the NLRB, had supervised the famous Interchurch Investigation of the 1919 Steel Strike and ever since had dedicated himself to exposing the violent methods corporations utilized to prevent the unionization of their industries. As an aide to Senator Wagner, Blankenhorn was transferred to the NLRB, where he carried on his lifelong goal of helping to create a strong labor movement by winning over public opinion to the cause of labor.[20]

In the winter of 1935–1936 Blankenhorn proposed to Senator LaFollette that an investigation of industrial espionage, strikebreaking, deputy sheriff systems, factory arsenals, and labor detective agencies be conducted by a special Senate committee. Blankenhorn soon had the support of NLRB members Madden and Carmody and Senator Robert Wagner. On March 23, Senator Robert LaFollette submitted Senate Resolution 266 to Congress. The resolution authorized and directed the Committee on Education and Labor "to make an investigation of violations of the rights of free speech and assembly and undue interference with the right of labor to organize and bargain collectively." The principle behind the proposed investigation was that the right of workers to organize unions was "an important civil liberty."[21] After long hearings, Senate Resolution 266 was passed on June 6, 1936, and the LaFollette Civil Liberties Committee went into operation as a de facto political arm of the National Labor Relations Board.

Although Congress gave the committee only $15,000 to carry out its operations, it was able to rely on the staff of the NLRB for research and investigation. The committee and the CIO soon were coordinating their activities with the CIO organizing drive. As soon as the committee was set up, John L. Lewis came to its chairman, Senator LaFollette, and said: "Why don't you investigate U.S. Steel? Get busy on this. What are they doing with their arms and cars?"[22]

The LaFollette Committee played a historic role in exposing the American corporations' practices of hiring professional thugs, storing huge arsenals in their plants, spying on unions, and breaking strikes through the use of terror. The committee made headlines every week during the years its investigations educated a whole nation in the anatomy of class oppression. Lee Pressman notes that the LaFollette investigations "unquestionably had an impact on the justices of the Supreme Court" when they finally upheld the Wagner Act.[23] While tireless investigators like Charles Kramer exposed the illegal activities of General Motors during the sit-down strike, other investigations won over the public to the necessity of the Wagner Act if the corporations were to be prevented from violating the U.S. Constitution. John L. Lewis was soon prompted to comment: "My god, what a blessing LaFollette's Civil Liberties Committee has been in our efforts to organize CIO."[24]

It was inevitable that the corporations would not suffer these attacks on both the economic and political fronts without protest; they mobilized all their resources to smash the combined attacks on the corporate power structure, targeting especially the CIO, the National Labor Relations Board, and the LaFollette Committee, all of which were declared to be hotbeds of communism. By the end of the decade, Big Business and its political allies had regained much of the influence that had been stripped from them by the industrial uprising that gave birth to the CIO.

During the first six months of 1937, Roosevelt needed the support of the CIO. But once he had consolidated power, concessions to his CIO allies became fewer and he began to dictate the terms of the alliance. Lewis clearly understood the choice confronting the CIO; it could become subordinate to the president and the Democratic Party, seeking favors for good behavior, or it could continue on the road of building an enlarged base among the industrial workers and follow self-reliant economic and political strategies.

Throughout the summer of 1937, Lewis criticized the Democratic

Party for allowing a clique of conservatives in Congress to block reform legislation and once more raised the question of a third party made up of farmers and workers.[25] Then on September 3, in a national radio address, Lewis directly attacked Roosevelt. Referring specifically to the Little Steel Strike, he intoned: "Labor, like Israel, has many sorrows. Its women weep for their fallen, and they lament for the future of the children of the race. It ill behooves one who has supped at labor's table to curse with equal fervor and fine impartiality both labor and its adversaries when they become locked in deadly embrace."[26]

Roosevelt, however, was not yet ready to break openly with the most radical sectors of industrial unionism. When asked by reporters for his reaction to the speech by Lewis, the president replied, "There wasn't any."[27] Roosevelt apparently agreed with Tugwell, who had recommended that the president "hold Lewis's hand once every three weeks. Life for all of us will be so much easier if you will."[28]

Economic Downturn and the Conservative Backlash

At the end of August 1937 a sharp economic decline set in. Within nine months production fell 30 percent and employment declined by 23 percent. From 1937 to 1939 per capita disposable income fell from $552 to $537. The steep economic downturn undercut Roosevelt's congressional coalition and allowed conservative forces in both the political and economic spheres to stage a comeback.

> Whereas the 1933 emergency had been the "Hoover Depression," the new crisis became the "Roosevelt Recession," and New Deal claims returned to haunt the President. The recession was a decisive event in the growth of congressional conservatism. It confused Roosevelt, making him indecisive and dilatory; it eroded more of the fabulous Roosevelt magic; it destroyed the unity and resolve of the New Deal coalition; and it caused some congressmen to grope toward a bipartisan coalition.[29]

The Fair Labor Standards bill was sent back to committee by a vote of 216 to 198 in the House, indicating that the New Deal congressional coalition was coming apart. Congressman Baily of North Carolina defined what was at stake in a letter to a friend: "It seems to me that we are now at the crossroads where it will be absolutely necessary either to turn further to the left and control practically all business and agriculture or some concession will have to be made so that industries in the United States can look forward with some degree of certainty to an uninterrupted program."[30] Secretary of the Interior Harold Ickes noted in a letter that "it looks as if all the courage had oozed out of the president . . . he has let things drift."[31]

In January 1938 Roosevelt held a series of conferences with corporate leaders and appeared to be flirting with the idea of a return to NRA-style corporatist solutions. Harold Ickes wrote in his diary: "The President, after letting Jackson and me stick our necks out with our anti-monopoly speeches, is pulling petals off the daisy with representatives of big business."[32] Despite the fact that many Americans in the early months of 1938 were nearing starvation, that WPA rolls in the major industrial towns had "increased at a staggering pace," that relief funds were exhausted, and that deaths from malnutrition, starvation, and suicide were commonly reported in the press, despite all this, "by 1939, Congress was moving aggressively to dismantle the New Deal. It slashed relief appropriations, killed Roosevelt appointments, and, in a deliberate slap at the Keynesians, eliminated what was left of the undistributed profits tax. Faced by the need to make concessions, Roosevelt threw his opponents some of his less popular experiments."[33]

The Business-AFL Coalition

With the economic downturn in 1938 and the corporate-congressional attack on the CIO, the AFL gained new strength in its own struggle to fight off the radical challenge posed to traditional business unionism by the millions of newly organized workers in the basic industries. It not only committed financial resources—Bernstein's research reveals that the "AFL payroll for organizing shot up five times" after the spring of 1937—but it reinforced the traditional weapon of ideology. Class-conscious unionism was equated with communism. The AFL Executive Council demanded tests of loyalty from all local bodies; the charters of CIO locals were revoked and CIO officers were expelled from AFL state federations and city labor councils. The issue was no longer one of industrial unionism per se, but of AFL respectable industrial unionism versus CIO un-American industrial unionism. The Carpenters, Machinists, and International Brotherhood of Teamsters all threw their forces and considerable union treasuries into the organization of industrial unions. The AFL's success after 1938 can be accounted for in part by "the decision of many employers to do business with the more conservative AFL unions in order to forestall the drives of the more radical CIO group."[34] For more than half a century corporations had utilized craft unions as the first line of defense against the organization of industrial workers; after 1938, the employers, with the help of the president, used the AFL to block any further advance of the CIO.

AFL leaders turned against the Wagner Act soon after its passage, calling it a CIO law. In Pressman's words, it "was so good, so specific, so all embracing, so clear in its purpose and intent and provisions" that "all labor needed was someone willing to carry out the statute."[35] The AFL immediately demanded that the new industrial bargaining units be carved up into twenty or thirty units along craft lines, while the CIO fought to keep the industrial structure intact. When the NLRB supported the CIO claims, the AFL demanded the heads of the board members.

> Concern over the designation of appropriate bargaining units was not confined to employers. The craft leaders of the AFL, harassed by the militancy of industrial unionists led by Lewis, were similarly fearful lest an unsympathetic board join these forces against them. The NLRB, for example, might decide that drivers working for a brewery were part of a unit comprising all its employees, hence presenting the Brewery Workers rather than the Teamsters with a majority.[36]

During 1938 and 1939 the resurgent AFL, in coalition with congressional conservatives and representatives of corporate management, launched a two-pronged attack against the LaFollette Committee and the personnel of the NLRB. Jerold Auerbach, in his well-researched book on the committee, argued that by 1938 the committee had amassed evidence that "seemed to confirm the most pessimistic Marxist forebodings about the nature of capitalist society. The LaFollette Committee did not warn of the imminence of class warfare; it documented its existence. . . . Committee disclosures pointed to class warfare as the dominant fact in American life."[37]

Opponents of the committee declared that it was simply a front for the Communist Party and the CIO. Unfriendly witnesses called before the committee publicly stated that it was "the culmination of a conspiracy entered into between John L. Lewis, representatives of Communist and other red organizations, and . . . Senator LaFollette." Other prominent critics claimed that the "Committee and the NLRB have made a hell on earth for one industry after another. . . . They have been the most effective recruiting agency of the CIO."[38]

The red-baiting attack accelerated into a national campaign that culminated in the establishment of a right-wing counter-committee, the House Committee on Un-American Activities, headed by Martin Dies of Texas. Auerbach places the relationship between the two committees in historical perspective. One committee represented "the aspirations of those who looked to the New Deal for social and economic justice" and the other stood for "the antithesis of all that the New Deal represented." The Dies Committee thus quickly established itself as "the investigative counterweight to the LaFollette Committee."[39]

It was no surprise when the Dies Committee directed its first investigation against the CIO and the LaFollette Committee, nor that the main witness should be John Frey, president of the Metal Trades Department of the AFL. Frey attempted to tie together in one great conspiracy the CIO, the Communist Party, and the LaFollette Committee. Corporate undercover agents working within the unions complained before the Dies Committee that they had been fingered by Communists and their dossiers turned over to the LaFollette Committee. Dies later boasted that his investigations were responsible for Senate action in cutting LaFollette Committee appropriations.[40]

After the 1938 elections, conservative members of Congress voted for an investigation of the NLRB, and together with the AFL Executive Council put pressure on Roosevelt and Secretary of Labor Perkins to change the composition of the board, which they claimed was pro-CIO. They also charged that some of the board members were procommunist, particularly Edwin Smith. Roosevelt succumbed to the pressure and Chairman Warren Madden was forced to resign and Donald Wakefield Smith, Edwin Smith, and the board's left-wing attorney Nathan Witt were purged. Strict administration of the Wagner Act was abandoned and the way was prepared for its replacement by the Taft-Hartley Act following World War II.[41] The essentially conservative character of the most powerful bourgeois society in the world was reasserting itself, and the CIO, the most powerful labor movement in American history, lacked both the unity and the ideology necessary to transform industrial unionism into a viable form of working-class political action.

6

Roosevelt Captures the CIO

From 1934 to 1940 corporate interests that had dominated the business society of the 1920s lost control of the social order they believed to have been completed. In the most turbulent years of the 1930s, capital, labor, and the state fought for control over national policy. By 1938 the CIO had swept into its organizational net the bulk of the workers in the basic mass production industries. The key CIO unions included the United Mine Workers, the United Automobile Workers, the United Electrical Workers, the United Rubber Workers, the Aluminum Workers, the Oil Workers, the Marine and Shipbuilding Workers, and the Packinghouse Workers. The CIO was also entrenched in the maritime industries, in transport, the garment and textile industries, communications, and retail stores and had a hold on the state, county, and municipal workers and a number of other key industries from farm equipment to newspaper reporters.

During the heyday of CIO power, the Left controlled larger sections of the American labor movement than it had at any time since the American Federation of Labor was founded in 1886. The Communist-controlled unions contained about 25 percent of the CIO's total membership and Communists wielded considerable influence in unions with another 25 percent. The Left had a firm ally in the most powerful union leader of the thirties, John L. Lewis, had another ally, Len DeCaux, as editor of the national CIO news, and could claim the support of the chief legal counsel of the CIO, Lee Pressman. The prestige of Harry Bridges, Julius Emspak, and James Matles equaled that of any other national trade union leaders in the country. In the final analysis, the future of class-conscious unionism in the United States was determined in the struggle for control over CIO policy between those forces willing to trade off labor independence to the state in return for legal collective-bargaining rights and those forces fighting for an independent labor base that might then be converted into working-class political action. In retrospect, it is clear that to have maintained an independent base for class-conscious unionism, the Left would have required control of the auto, steel, coal, electrical, and trucking industries. Together with the maritime, packinghouse, transport, farm equipment, and western metal mining industries, these bastions of industrial unionism might have had a major influence on the shape of an advanced industrial society.

While there was nothing inevitable about the outcome, the correlation of corporate power, liberal politics, and anticommunist ideology, a configuration legitimated by a war economy, blocked the further advance of class-conscious industrial unionism in the United States. Nevertheless, that outcome emerged only after a long and protracted struggle to eliminate the Left from a movement that could not have been created without it. By 1940 the state proved to be the instrument capable of coercing a new national consensus in a climate of war-inspired crisis. In the classic manner, class conflict was dissolved in the heady brew of nationalism.

Roosevelt, who skillfully built the most powerful executive apparatus of state power in American history, utilized that power to break the leading coalition within the CIO and thus undermined the influence of the Left in the industrial-union movement. The history of the struggle to eliminate the Left in the CIO is not as simple as either anticommunist or procommunist historians sometimes attempt to make it. The Communist Party of the United States, in the final analysis, shared with its social-democratic rivals, Hillman and Murray, the same desire to secure positions of power by creating alliances at the top, an orientation that guaranteed the eventual purge of the Left from the CIO.

Roosevelt's drive to isolate the Left within the CIO was paralleled by a campaign to isolate and remove its influence within the executive agencies of the government administering labor affairs, notably the NLRB. Roosevelt worked together with Daniel Tobin of the Teamsters to contain the influence of the CIO and its supporters within the National Labor Relations Board. At the same time, he cultivated relations with CIO Democrats to isolate the Left in the CIO and subordinate industrial unions to the Democratic Party. In this effort, he was greatly assisted by the Catholic church. The full history of the Catholic church and its role in the CIO is yet to be written.

Roosevelt and the Catholic Church

During the early years of the depression, the American Catholic church began to move in a liberal direction. Much of the New Deal reform legislation paralleled Catholic teachings on social justice. Roosevelt, astute politician that he was, quoted from a papal encyclical (*Quadragesimo Anno* of Pius XI) during a major campaign speech given in Detroit on October 2, 1932:

> It is patent in our days that not alone is wealth accumulated, but immense power and despotic economic domination are concentrated in the hands of a few, and that those few are frequently not the owners but only the trustees and directors of invested funds which they administer at their good pleasure. . . . This accumulation of power, the characteristic note of the modern economic order, is a natural result of limitless free competition, which permits the survival of those only who are the strongest, which often means those who fight most relentlessly, who pay least heed to the dictates of conscience.[1]

Roosevelt called the encyclical "just as radical as I am" and "one of the greatest documents of modern times." Liberal Catholics were naturally delighted at this bow in their direction and were quick to note that Roosevelt had chosen two Catholics, Farley and Flynn, as his close advisers. Subsequent elections would show that Catholics were more susceptible to political influence because of their religion than were Protestants and that Mahatma Gandhi had been right when he had asserted that those who said religion had nothing to do with politics did not know the meaning of religion.

Pius XI had reaffirmed the ideas of Leo II, which encouraged the organization of unions to protect the rights of the laborer, but he developed new principles that distinguished the right of private ownership (which he defended) from the use of ownership, declaring that "ownership should be manifested with due regard for the common good as defined by the state." Moreover, the pope argued that increased social wealth ought to be distributed among individuals and classes for the common good, supported a living wage for labor "sufficient to support both the worker and his family," and stated that opportunity for work should be provided to all those willing and able to work. These segments of encyclicals and other church pronouncements were taken up by the liberal wing of the American Catholic church and made the basis of a program for social justice, including the rights of labor. In 1937, at the height of the CIO organizing drive, the Reverand John P. Monaghan established the Association of Catholic Trade Unionists (ACTU). The ACTU joined the Catholic Worker Movement in New York City, established by Dorothy Day in 1932, in the effort to keep the loyalty of Catholic workers, who might otherwise be attracted to

Marxism. Opposition to communism thus made the Catholic bloc in the CIO the natural ally of Hillman and Reuther, who would soon utilize the organizational skill and finances of the church to gain power in the CIO. In the next four years chapters of the ACTU were operating actively in Akron, Chicago, Cleveland, New York, Pittsburgh, Pontiac and Saginaw (Michigan), San Francisco, and South Bend (Indiana).[2]

By 1939 the Catholic church in Detroit and other industrial cities decided that rather than fight the CIO, a better tactic was to attempt to infiltrate the unions and capture the CIO. ACTU seminars, Catholic conferences on industrial problems, and training schools created a coordinated network of cadres and policies throughout the country to carry out the church line in the CIO. Within the Catholic parishes in industrial communities, ACTU members were carefully trained in seminars on labor issues, current events, and papal encyclicals, as well as how to effectively utilize parliamentary law. The coordinated strategy of Catholic factions within the various unions proved to be the most important organizational weapon against the Left.

This organizational weapon was first honed to perfection in the United Auto Workers' Union and then introduced into other CIO unions in the struggle against the Left. Catholicism was a strong force in Detroit all through the great labor wars of the thirties. Father Coughlin, the radio priest, had a national following and soon established bridge-heads in the newly formed auto workers' union. The union local at Dodge Motors, for example, was a Coughlin stronghold. The president of the Dodge local was Richard Frankensteen, who later played a key role in the factional politics of the UAW.

Carl Haessler, the left-wing journalist who worked closely with Walter Reuther in the Detroit West Side auto locals, provides an outline of the role of the church in the history of the UAW. Haessler was told by an AFL official in 1939, who was not himself a Catholic, "that it was touch and go whether the church or the Communists would control the CIO."[3] Philip Murray, Lewis' key lieutenant in the United Mine Workers union, put by Lewis in charge of the Steel Workers Organizing Committee (SWOC), was himself a devout Catholic. Together with Hillman, Murray played a decisive role in the internal politics of the United Automobile Workers. Wyndham Mortimer, the key figure in the organization of the auto industry, accurately assessed Murray. "Philip Murray, a devout Roman Catholic, was strongly influenced by the teachings of the church. He was guided more by the encyclicals of Pope Leo XII than by the principles of American trade-unionism."[4]

The UAW: Microcosm of CIO Politics

Much of the written history of the United Automobile Workers suffers from a bias introduced by the internal factional struggles for control of the union. Fortunately, a new generation of scholars has begun the task of setting the record straight. Roger Keeran's recent history of the role of the Communist Party within the UAW accurately assesses the key contribution of Communists in organizing the auto industry. Referring to the founding convention of the auto workers' union, Keeran states, "The UAW convention that opened in South Bend, Indiana, on April 27, 1936, represented the triumph of the Communist initiated Progressive movement for an industrial union that was controlled by the rank and file and geared to militant organizing and strike action."[5]

Rank-and-file delegates to the 1936 convention broke with the AFL, elected a majority of leftists to the eleven-member executive board of the new CIO union, and voted in favor of the full Progressive caucus program for organizing the auto industry. The one great historic mistake was the election of Homer Martin, a former Baptist preacher from Missouri, as president of the union. "Though the Progressives originally backed Mortimer for President, he withdrew."[6] Apparently Mortimer withdrew because as an avowed Communist he did not wish to draw additional fire against the UAW and wanted to prove that the Communists had no intention of controlling the union. Keeran's research substantiates the fact that the Communist Party did not, in fact, seek control of the UAW. At any rate, Mortimer, the number-one organizer in the auto industry, accepted the second-ranking position in the union, first vice-president. Homer Martin, who would later take a management job with the Ford Motor Company, then initiated a long and protracted factional struggle to break the auto workers' union from within.

Keeran argues that the factional strife in the UAW can be divided into two periods. During the first, from April 1937 until January 1938, "Homer Martin attempted to consolidate his control over the union by strengthening his administrative position and reducing the authority of the locals in general and Communists and Socialists in particular." In the second period, from January 1938 to March 1939, "the Communists and other dissidents waged a struggle against Martin and his policies."[7]

The seesaw struggle for power in the UAW continued when Martin took over the Progressive caucus and the Communists, Socialists, and rank-and-file militants set up a new left-wing caucus named the Unity caucus. Martin subsequently began a systematic purge of Communists, Socialists, and militant rank-and-file unionists from all positions of power in the UAW. In his drive to establish a personal dictatorship, Martin established a secret alliance with Jay Lovestone, who had once been general secretary of the American Communist Party and in 1929 had been expelled after a struggle with William Z. Foster over party policy. In the ensuing years Lovestone became a rabid anticommunist and finally an ideological hatchet man for the AFL. In the fall of 1937 "the conflict between Martin and the Left sharpened when the rank and file indicated that it favored the aggressive path (of organizing) advocated by the Unity caucus over the cautious one followed by the Progressive caucus."[8] A downturn in the economy resulted in the loss of 320,000 jobs for auto workers, "and reduced the membership of the UAW by three fourths." At this critical juncture, Martin, following Lovestone's advice, "responded to the crisis by pursuing a conciliatory attitude in the negotiations then in progress with GM and Chrysler." Then on September 16, "Martin sent GM a 'letter of responsibility' granting the company the right to fire any employee whom the company claimed was guilty of provoking an unauthorized strike."[9]

Most significant for the history of the United Automobile Workers was the breakup of the united front between the Communists and Socialists in the struggle against Martin. Keeran describes the historic break between the two radical factions in the UAW and the issues that brought it about:

> At a meeting of the Executive Board on January 13, Martin's supporters and the Socialists joined to endorse Congressman Louis Ludlow's proposal for a constitutional amendment requiring a national referendum before Congress could declare war (except in cases of invasion). Since the Communists believed that only a collective security alliance among non-fascist nations could guarantee peace, they naturally found much "discomfort" in the Executive Board's action and expressed regret that "the confusion sowed in progressive ranks throughout the country by the Ludlow war referendum amendment has also penetrated the auto union." In a press conference on February 3, Martin claimed the Communists wanted to drag America into war to defend Stalin, and declared that "Communists are Fascists in every sense of the word."[10]

From 1938 on, issues of foreign policy emerged as a major factor in destroying the unity of the industrial-union movement in the United States. The Socialists identified the foreign policy issue as "the main bone of contention in the union," and then, as Keeran states, "quickly moved from a rejection of the CP's stand on collective security to a rejection of all Communist trade union policies."[11] In short, the Socialists at a critical juncture in the union's history broke the Left alliance in the UAW and threw their support to Homer Martin in his fight to purge the Communists and other rank-and-file leftists from the UAW.

In the fall of 1938, when opposition to Martin was growing, the UAW's most prominent Socialist, Walter Reuther, expressed a willingness to support Martin's reelection. As late as February 1939, after Martin had lost nearly all support in the union and in the CIO, Norman Thomas declared that "Martin is, to a very considerable extent, the victim of the Communists and that it is a great weakness for us to desert the only labor leader who ever came near to endorsing our anti-war stand."[12]

Since both the Communists and the Socialists would switch their "principled" lines on foreign policy in the future, neither came out with clean hands in the factional fight that destroyed the unity of one of the key CIO unions.

George Addes, the secretary-treasurer of the UAW who emerged as a rank-and-file leader in the 1934 Toledo Auto-Lite strike, and Richard Frankensteen, who was an assistant to Martin, joined the Communist-led Unity caucus in the spring of 1938. A few months later, Martin put Mortimer, Hall, Frankensteen, and Addes on trial and expelled them from the UAW. The Communists responded by making public the private correspondence between Jay Lovestone and Martin proving that Martin was simply taking orders from Lovestone and by implication the auto companies and the AFL. "In June, the Detroit District Council, representing 200,000 UAW members, demanded the reinstatement of the suspended officers, and by July 15, 43 local unions made similar demands."[13]

At this point, John L. Lewis and the national office of the CIO intervened directly in the affairs of the UAW. Lewis forced Martin to reinstate the expelled auto union leaders to their officially elected positions and appointed Philip Murray and Sidney Hillman to supervise the UAW and mediate the factional struggle within the union. A committee to settle disputes in the UAW, consisting of Murray, Hillman, Martin, and R. J. Thomas, was set up in Detroit. However, as Irving Bernstein puts it, "The committee became a receiver in bankruptcy for the UAW and Murray and Hillman took over the union."[14] The Murray-Hillman takeover of the UAW soon had a profound effect on the history of the CIO and the future of industrial unionism in the United States.

The struggle for power over the future policy and orientation of the CIO emerged at the special convention of the UAW-CIO that opened in Cleveland on March 27, 1939. Once more the Left-center coalition led by Mortimer, Addes, and Frankensteen and their rank-and-file militant union supporters dominated the convention. As the first order of business, the delegates expelled Homer Martin from all offices and membership in the UAW. Martin, who had secret connections with Ford Motor Company executives, subsequently received a charter from the AFL to set up a new auto union to raid the UAW-CIO. This rump union soon failed and Martin was given a job by his Ford management backers. The next order of business involved the historic task of returning the union to the workers who had built it.

Since the Left-oriented Unity caucus represented 85 percent of the delegates, its members were ready to nominate either Mortimer or Addes for president of the union. However, Hillman and Murray utilized all their influence to prevent the Left from controlling the key union in the CIO. They countered the effort of the rank and file to make Mortimer or Addes president of the UAW by proposing the election of R. J. Thomas as top official of the new auto workers' union. Thomas, who had been vice-president under the Martin-Lovestone regime, was practically unknown to the auto workers. Moreover, he was, as Bernstein admits, a man "who had no intellectual or leadership qualifications for the presidency of the UAW."[15] The election of a nonentity as head of the most important industrial union in the CIO was the first step by the Roosevelt-Hillman-Murray coalition to capture leadership of the industrial union movement created by Left-syndicalists.

Both Hillman and Murray attempted to line up Mortimer behind the Thomas candidacy by telling him that Earl Browder, chairman of the Communist Party of the United States, supported Thomas. Mortimer refused, stating that he did not care whom Earl Browder supported and that "R. J. Thomas was the last man to desert Martin and Lovestone. He has done nothing and has said nothing to deserve such an office and would still be a Lovestonite except that he is being groomed for Martin's replacement. I cannot support him."[16] Mortimer commented years later that he "would have been just as glad to have had George [Addes] selected, since he was a very trustworthy man. He was also much younger than I, and I was never ambitious anyway."[17]

In any case, on the next day the hierarchy of the Communist Party mobilized to put pressure on Mortimer, the recalcitrant party member:

> The following day the Communist Party appeared in the persons of Louis Budenz, Bill Gerbert, Roy Hudson, and Earl Browder. I was approached by Budenz and urged to support the CIO and R. J. Thomas. I refused. I was then contacted by Roy Hudson who tried to tell me that Thomas was the choice of Lewis and the CIO. I told him I did not believe this and I would not support Thomas. I knew Lewis did not want R. J. Thomas as president of the UAW and I felt that Hillman and Murray had their own fish to fry.[18]

Bernstein confirms the reputation of Mortimer for impeccable honesty and for a lack of interest in personal power by stating that "Wyndham Mortimer, the Communists' most impressive figure, was too retiring" to fill the role of Communist candidate for the presidency of the UAW.

However, Mortimer was not so much "retiring" as he was independent in his loyalty to class rather than party interests.[19]

The Hillman–Murray–Communist Party alliance at the 1939 UAW convention was forged by common interests. This was a social-democratic elitist strategy of forming a united front from above with Roosevelt. Lewis and the Left-syndicalists were dedicated to expanding the independent power of the industrial workers movement in the strongest capitalist nation in the world. Thus Wyndham Mortimer had more in common with John L. Lewis than he did with his own party functionaries. That is why Mortimer stated: "I had, and still have the highest respect for John L. Lewis. In my opinion, he has done more for American labor than any other individual to date."[20] Murray and Hillman did not represent Lewis as they claimed at the UAW convention; instead, as Mortimer asserts, Thomas was used to attack Lewis and his followers.

Hillman and Murray moved decisively to cut down the strength of the Left in the leadership of the UAW. Not only was Mortimer denied the presidency of the union, but he was removed entirely from the executive board. The vice-presidential posts were eliminated and the Communist Party gave its consent to the virtual purge of the Left from the UAW leadership. "Thus, for the first time since the founding of the UAW, no officer or Executive Board member was a Communist."[21] Hillman and Murray then utilized the same tactics to cut down the Left in the CIO national office.

The anticommunist offensive within the CIO coincided with a nationwide red-baiting attack on the CIO by the AFL and prominent newspaper journalists. John Frey, the AFL leader, appeared before the House Committee on Un-American Activities (the Dies Committee) and named a number of CIO unions as Stalinist front organizations and claimed that between forty and fifty CIO leaders belonged to the Communist Party. Journalists like Louis Stark of the *New York Times* and Benjamin Stolberg echoed the AFL red-baiting attack on the CIO. The signing of the Nazi-Soviet nonaggression pact in August 1939 only added more fuel to the anticommunist hysteria that was beginning to sweep the nation. "The warm relationship between Lewis and the left wing troubled Hillmanites, one of whom warned Adolph Germer on September 12, 1939, that unless Lewis changed his tactics and restricted Communist influence in the CIO, the ACWA [Amalgamated Clothing Workers], like the ILGWU a year earlier, might be forced to secede from the organization."[22] When the 1939 national convention of the CIO opened in October, the split between the Lewis-Left forces and the Hillman-Murray-Roosevelt coalition was clearly revealed.

The 1939 CIO Convention: The Split Widens

In 1971 Mortimer finally disclosed facts about the 1939 CIO convention in San Francisco that he had kept secret until after the death of John L. Lewis. Lewis stopped him in the lobby of the Whitcomb Hotel and invited him to attend an enlarged meeting of the CIO Executive Board. Lewis announced that he would not be a candidate for reelection as president of the CIO. According to Mortimer's account, Hillman said: "Without John L. Lewis, the CIO is impossible." Lewis answered that since Hillman had entry to the White House and he did not, and since Hillman had the ear of the president and Lewis did not, and since the president no longer believed that Lewis spoke for the CIO, Hillman could do more for the membership than Lewis could. After a three-hour stormy session, Lewis was persuaded to remain for one year, but said it would be his last term.[23]

Lewis and the Hillman-Murray forces worked out a tenuous compromise at the 1939 CIO convention. Lewis shelved his original report to the convention, which criticized Roosevelt's domestic and foreign policies and openly criticized the Communists at a CIO Executive Board meeting on October 14. He warned that no known Communist was to be employed in any capacity by the CIO, and restricted the authority of Harry Bridges as West Coast Regional Director of the CIO to California. On the other hand, a resolution condemning the Communists was blocked by Lewis, who stated firmly that he was opposed to "witch-hunts" in the CIO. Lewis tried to handle the opening of what was to become a protracted campaign against the Left in the CIO with levity: "If we start removing people merely charged with membership [in the Communist Party] we will have to remove Lewis, Hillman and Murray," and then added: "If the Communists are good enough to work for General Motors, we have little choice but to accept their dues in the United Auto Workers."[24] However, Hillman and Murray consolidated their hold on the CIO national office by backing a slate for top leadership positions headed by R. J. Thomas of the UAW and Emil Rieve, the staunchly anticommunist president of the textile workers. The Hillman-Murray slate defeated the Communist-supported Left list of candidates. Despite this victory, Lewis still remained the most popular leader of the American industrial working class. Hillman and Murray were not yet ready to take over the CIO.

Matthew Josephson makes clear what most CIO activists understood during the waning years of the thirties. "Roosevelt feared greatly that the CIO, which had given him such mighty aid in the campaign of 1936, might be turned against him through the enormous influence of Lewis." Roosevelt thus initiated a policy of coopting key CIO leaders into an alliance with the state. He turned first to Hillman: "In Hillman the

President sensed a rival force within the CIO, one that might be used to divide the growing opposition in the labor movement or wean it away."[25] Hillman, on the other hand, "believed that his working alliance with the President was a good 'investment,' so to speak." Years later, Julius Emspak recalled that by 1939 Carey, Hillman, and Brophy had all become key Roosevelt supporters.

Throughout the year, Roosevelt utilized Hillman to promote unity negotiations between the CIO and the AFL. Roosevelt had already abandoned his role as a mediator of national class struggle through reform and was moving rapidly to dissolve class struggle by the creation of a national unity state in the fires of a war crisis. The major problem facing Roosevelt remained the Lewis-Left industrial-union movement and its opposition to his policies. Thus the president eagerly awaited the results of the CIO convention in San Francisco: "After the CIO Convention at San Francisco was over, Roosevelt sent Hillman an urgent message asking him to join him on his private train in order that he might be informed as to what had really happened at the convention, especially with regard to the question of reunion with the AFL. Roosevelt was quite worried about Mr. Lewis."[26]

Throughout 1939 Lewis and the left-wing CIO forces fought for what remained of the New Deal reforms. "The nation had no greater advocate of public employment programs, public housing projects, and Social Security improvements than John L. Lewis."[27] He continued to threaten that in order to achieve these goals the CIO would "build a left-wing, farmer-labor alliance that would incorporate student radicals and racial minorities either in an independent third party or as the dominant element in the Democratic Party."[28] Roosevelt, on the other hand, had turned to political conservatives and corporate elites for support of his defense program; the president "perceived fewer political benefits in Lewis's recommendation that a farmer-labor coalition become the core of the Democratic Party."[29]

The End of the Road for the CIO

As the possibility of building an independent radical labor party receded, Lewis turned on the Roosevelt administration that had betrayed the labor movement. Limited by his own nationalism, Lewis turned to Wendell Wilkie and the Republican Party in an effort to use the two-party system to oppose Roosevelt's oppressive policies. Given the historical cul-de-sac in which Lewis found himself, his action in supporting Wilkie, who was no less liberal than Roosevelt, is not as bizarre as many historians believe. Harry Bridges, another powerful radical labor leader, similarly announced a number of years later that he would register as a Republican in protest over the cold war policies of the postwar Democratic administrations. Under American historical circumstances there was no place else to go.

Other leaders turned in different directions during the key struggle for power in the UAW, abandoned the Left, and made an alliance with the ACTU, or Catholic caucus as it was known in the UAW. The Catholic caucus, which followed the advice of Archbishop and later Cardinal Edward Mooney, soon linked up with the Hillman-Murray-Roosevelt forces in the CIO.

Haessler sums up the political configuration of politics in the UAW: "The Addes faction leaned on Lewis and the Reuther faction on Hillman and Murray." When John L. Lewis arrived at the 1940 UAW convention he was met at the railroad station by a delegation of union leaders that included Walter Reuther. According to Haessler, "When the group lined up for photographers Reuther wormed very close to Lewis, but Lewis spread his arm and deliberately brushed him away so that Reuther was on the outskirts of the picture."[30]

However, Reuther could not be so easily pushed out of the picture. "The Church, with Reuther's help, won in the end. That is one reason why there are so many Catholics in the high command of the UAW under the presidency of Reuther, who never was a Catholic and through most of his life was not even a Church member."[31] Reuther understood the power of the organizational weapon offered to him by the Catholic church, whose finances and connections far outstripped those of the Communist Party. The lesson was soon learned by Murray, Curran (president of the National Martime Union), and James Carey, who followed Reuther's road to power.

At the 1940 UAW convention the two main issues were the election of officers and the inclusion of an anticommunist clause in the union constitution. The other major business was the position of the union in supporting the national defense program. On this latter issue Sidney Hillman attempted "to pressure the UAW into a defense straitjacket" by putting "a moratorium on union demands."[32] The Lewis faction, led by Addes, stood on labor's rights as the best posture for national defense in wartime. Class-conscious industrial unionists fought for a full partnership of labor with government and employers as the basis for a national unity regime and refused to accept a subordinate position for labor. The balance of union power remained basically the same as it had been in 1939 and the move by the Catholic caucus to ban Communists from the union was blocked.

However, the Catholics succeeded in driving a wedge into the constitution that enabled the anticommunists to win this victory a year later. The constitution was amended so that Article 9, Section S, now read: "No member of any local union located in the United States of

America shall be eligible to hold any elective or appointed position in this International Union or any local of this International Union if he is a member of any organization which is declared illegal by the Government of the United States through constitutional procedure."[33] The UAW convention was a dress rehearsal for the 1940 CIO convention, which would determine the historic fate of industrial unionism in the United States.

The year 1940 marked the victory for the state in capturing the leadership of the CIO. In January Lewis stood up before the Miners Union convention and made a clean break with Roosevelt and the Democratic Party. Lewis understood clearly that Roosevelt, by utilizing the power of the state and legitimating that power by a war emergency, was threatening the independent power of the CIO and attempting to subordinate the labor movement to the state. Lewis laid his case before the miners. Reminding his audience that the Democratic Party had won in 1936 only because of its coalition with organized labor, Lewis declared:

> In the last three years labor has not been given representation in the Cabinet, nor in the administrative or policy-making agencies or the government. . . . The Democratic Party is in default to the American people. After seven years of power it finds itself without solution for the major questions of unemployment, low income, mounting internal debts.
>
> Labor and the people are losing confidence. They fear for the future and rightly so.[34]

Lewis came out openly against a third term for Roosevelt. As Lewis traveled throughout the country in the first six months of 1940 attacking Roosevelt, Hillman followed on his heels speaking in favor of Roosevelt and the Democratic administration. Hillman led the movement to draft Roosevelt for a third term. In the spring of 1940 Roosevelt, responding to the German attack on France, established a national defense program, and on May 28, 1940, he announced the formation of the National Defense Advisory Council. Significantly, Roosevelt, without informing Lewis and the CIO, appointed Sidney Hillman and William Knudsen of General Motors as the key members of the seven-man council. Lewis was hardly paranoid when he charged Roosevelt with an attempt to control the CIO; in an interview with Saul Alinsky, he showed clearly that he recognized the symbolic importance of the Hillman appointment to a major position in the Roosevelt war administration.

Lewis told Alinsky that Roosevelt "has been raiding the CIO for the past three years. He has been carefully selecting my key lieutenants and appointing them to honorary posts. . . . He has been engaged in a deliberate conspiracy to wean away the primary loyalty of many of my lieutenants from the CIO to himself." Accusing the president "of boring from within." Lewis told Alinsky that the first he knew of the appointment of Hillman to the National Defense Advisory Council was when he read about it in the morning papers. He said that Hillman's "prime loyalty" would now be to the president and that he would maintain only "a secondary, residual one to the working-class movement from which he came, here, in this case, to the CIO." Lewis then accurately predicted the outcome of the Hillman appointment: "You mark my words, if Franklin D. Roosevelt ever tells Sidney Hillman to break a strike, Hillman will issue the order to break a strike."[35] Within a year Hillman would be active in breaking the North American Aviation strike led by one of the key representatives of the radical upsurge of American labor—Wyndham Mortimer.

All the historic forces destined to contain radical labor in America came together rapidly in the latter half of 1940. "In the first week of July, Philip Murray, head of the Steelworkers, and Thomas J. Kennedy, Secretary of the United Mine Workers, with R. J. Thomas and Richard Frankensteen of the Auto Workers, Dalrymple of the Rubber Workers, and Rieve, head of the Textile union, arrived at the Chicago offices of the CIO to help the draft-Roosevelt movement of the Democratic Party convention."[36] Lewis was silent until July 1, when he spoke to the United Automobile Workers convention and told them that "profitable defense contracts were being awarded to companies that violated the Wagner Labor Relations Act."[37] In October, Lewis was called to the White House, where he angrily told the president that he was being shadowed by the FBI and that his telephone was tapped. The president denied it. A week later Lewis made a nationwide radio address to 25 million listeners in which he accused Roosevelt of concentrating more power in the White House than had been done at any other time in American history. Determined to go down fighting, Lewis then dramatically announced that he recommended the election of Wendell Wilkie.

Lewis proclaimed that if Roosevelt was reelected he would resign as president of the CIO, while Hillman met with his own executive board of the Amalgamated Clothing Workers in preparation for the CIO convention. It was there proposed that the constitution of the CIO be amended to bar Communists, Nazis, and fascists. Hillman approved of putting into effect the formula worked out by the Catholic church in the UAW. The main business of the 1940 CIO convention duplicated the content of the UAW agenda—the election of officers, the exclusion of Communists from holding office in the CIO, and a policy establishing labor's role in defense production.

The CIO convention opened on November 18 and the majority of delegates appeared wearing huge buttons stating: "We Want Lewis." Lewis finally delivered the speech everyone had waited for and with his usual hyperbole indicated his decision to resign, adding that "we cannot stop to weep and wear sackcloth and ashes because something that happened yesterday did not meet with our approval, or that we did not have a dream come true." On the second day of the convention a dispute broke out over the resolution, probably written by Lewis, that censured the Roosevelt administration and the labor division of the National Defense Advisory Council, headed by Hillman. The Hillman faction countered with a resolution calling for unity negotiations with the AFL. Lewis made an impassioned attack on the AFL and its supporters, Dubinsky, Zaristky, and—by implication—Hillman. Lewis challenged the Amalgamated Clothing Workers to "clear out of the CIO" if they did not like its policies. Fearing that Lewis was stampeding the convention, Potofsky called Hillman in Washington, pleading with him to come and stop the Lewis steamroller.

The November 20 session of the CIO convention was described by the press as a "dramatic duel between labor's greatest showman and labor's greatest strategist." Hillman gave a long and well-prepared speech defending the record of the Amalgamated Clothing Workers and pledging that it would remain in the CIO. He defended the actions of the National Defense Advisory Council, stating that "I find no difficulty in reconciling the objectives of labor and the objectives of national defense; they are intertwined, they are inseparable." He then attempted to reach a reconciliation with Lewis by praising his role in building the CIO, stopping in the middle of his speech to shake hands with Lewis. He regretted that "John L. Lewis will not be leader of this organization," and then ended by saying that "it is my considered judgment that when John L. Lewis steps down there must be a demand for Phil Murray." Historians assert that Hillman killed the draft-Lewis movement, but it was clear to Lewis that if he remained, the CIO would be split. Indeed, there is little evidence that Lewis did not intend to resign.

The climax of what had been a historic struggle between the forces of class-conscious industrial unionism and the coalition that would subordinate labor to the state came with a whimper rather than a bang. The Roosevelt-Catholic coalition literally backed into power. On November 23, Philip Murray, a weak and fearful man, escorted to the CIO convention by a phalanx of Catholic priests who sat with him on the speaker's platform, was nominated for the presidency of the CIO by John L. Lewis, seconded by Hillman, and then elected by a unanimous vote of delegates who understood that the emergence of a national war economy was changing the historical rules of the game. It was clear that Roosevelt had mastered the crisis with labor and now commanded the national preparation for war.

Hillman's amendment to bar Communists from holding office was abandoned for the present, and a watered-down anticommunist resolution was substituted, since Lewis considered an all-out attack on communism a repudiation of his own administration of the CIO. Lee Pressman, general counsel of the CIO and the highest official spokesman for the Left in the national office, presented the watered-down resolution to the convention. The symbolic surrender of the Left to the new coalition of power allied to the state marked a bitter turning point for industrial workers who had fought their way into the system and now realized they had come to the end of the road.[38]

Pressman was the symbol of the Communist strategy, which aimed at its own acceptance as part of the historic bargain Hillman had negotiated with Roosevelt—the great trade-off in which power was granted to the state in return for the right of organized labor to bargain with capital. The alliance with Roosevelt exchanged power for money and guaranteed a separation of state and economy in a welfare-capitalist advanced society. Given the balance of forces, Hillman had the only viable political strategy and pursued it to the end.[39] By 1941 any problem concerning labor drew the same response from Roosevelt: "Clear it with Sidney."

However, Hillman was to be disappointed by Roosevelt. In April 1942 the president passed over Hillman and assigned the mobilization of America's civilian manpower to Paul V. McNutt, an Indiana politician. "The news hit Hillman very hard. He had tended almost to 'identify' himself with Franklin Roosevelt. Now, as one newspaper commentator observed, he was being shelved after two years of furious effort in the public service which had wrecked his health and exposed him to being 'ground to pieces between powerful, rival labor advocates.'"[40] Roosevelt would never grant labor the power or prestige that he showered on business.

The future of the Communist Party of the United States, on the other hand, which had become simply a tail on the social-democratic kite, was foredoomed by 1940. The party had begun to lose its identity as early as 1938 when it abandoned Mortimer and the class-conscious workers who had organized the auto industry for a spurious Left-center united front with Hillman and Murray. This was not a tactical error but a consistent policy followed in the National Maritime Union (NMU), the United Electrical Workers union, and many other CIO unions. Communist Party officials had become divorced from the workers they claimed to represent; party officials were rapidly becoming classless and their allegiance was to the party and not to the industrial-workers' movement.

At an early stage in the building of an industrial union in the East Coast maritime industry, the Communist Party chose Joseph Curran for president of the NMU despite the angry opposition of left-wing seamen who knew better. Blackie Myers, the most popular avowed Communist on the waterfront, warned the party leadership that Curran was not to be trusted and that it would be a serious error to place the fate of the East Coast seamen in Curran's hands. Myers, who had sailed with Curran in the pre-NMU days, knew him as a whip-cracking bos'n deservedly labeled by the rank-and-file seamen as "no coffee-time Joe." Like Mortimer in the auto industry, Myers was a much loved and respected leader who had helped to build a powerful union from scratch. Both Mortimer and Myers were unparalleled assets to the Communist Party, and yet as disciplined Communists they had to bear the burden of a party line they knew to be wrong. Similarly in the electrical industry, the Communist Party threw its support to James Carey for president of UE at one of the most critical periods in the union's history. However, if in the NMU the party had given power to a man who would later expel all leftists from the waterfront, wreck the union, and abscond with its funds, UE leaders Emspak and Matles refused to follow party policy and blocked the bid for power by Carey and the ACTU over the third largest union in the CIO.[41]

Carey joined the Catholic caucus in 1940, teamed up with the Hillman-Murray-Reuther anti-Left cause, and together with Father Rice of Pittsburgh initiated the anticommunist drive in the electrical industry by sponsoring a Catholic slate of officers to run against the Left in the huge Westinghouse UE Local 601.

On June 22, 1941, when Nazi Germany invaded the Soviet Union, the Communist Party of the United States turned what had been a clandestine policy into public policy by giving all-out support to Roosevelt and the war program.

As the Reuther-devised organizational weapon was thus applied to the UE, so too was its goal: a constitutional clause banning Communists from holding union office. Carey argued that as president of UE, he had the sole authority to determine constitutional provisions of the union. Realizing that the Left would either have to fight or be eliminated, Matles and Emspak led the struggle at the 1941 UE convention to replace Carey as union president with Albert Fitzgerald, former president of Local 201 at the Lynn General Electric plant and head of the New England UE district. The convention voted down Carey's anticommunist clause and elected Fitzgerald, over the opposition of the Communist Party. Emspak, who refused to sacrifice himself and the Left for party interests, a number of years later attempted to account for the Communist Party position:

> The theory behind [Communist Party support for Carey] as well as I can remember, was that now that the Soviet Union was invaded, it was time to get unity in the whole labor movement, to support this new phase of the war. Of course, those of us in the UE who had lived with the situation for the last two years [referring to the Nazi-Soviet nonaggression pact] did not

agree with the Communist position. In part, I think, this explains why the narrowness of the vote on the roll call for president, because of those mixed emotions on it.[42]

In other words, the Communist vote was split between those who represented the ideology of class-conscious unionism and those who followed the party line of begging for cooptation by the Roosevelt regime. Thus, war and the U.S. alliance with the Soviet Union merely deferred the final purge of the Left from the CIO and all other national institutions until such time as history deemed it appropriate. During World War II, the American Communist Party soon forgot that it was living on borrowed time and fostered the illusion that artificial power was the real thing. Without the war the CIO would have split in 1940, but the Left would still have had to face a working class that lacked homogeneity and a common outlook. At the same time, Roosevelt would have found it a great deal more difficult to consolidate the power of the Democratic Party and the state bureaucracy it controlled. With the war as his chief ally, Roosevelt mastered the emergency situation and real power soon resided in the executive branch of the government.

7

War Consolidates the Great Bargain

The struggle by the CIO to establish itself as an independent social force in the nation became a casualty of the war effort. As John T. Flynn put it at the time, "most of the old NRA gang moved back into power, this time under the banner of national defense."[1] The very corporate elite that had consistently fought the New Deal was invited back to Washington to administer war production. As James McGregor Burns argues, Roosevelt was a power broker. "Roosevelt, like Stalin, was a political administrator in the sense that his first concern was power—albeit for very different ends."[2] In the president's own words, "Dr. New Deal" was replaced by "Dr. Win the War." The new goal required new bases of power to achieve it, and Roosevelt once again proved that he was an adroit mediator among interest groups, political leaders, and conflicting ideologies.

From 1935 to 1938 Roosevelt had abandoned the role of broker to lead a "Grand Coalition" of the center and the Left. However, as Burns makes clear, Roosevelt never attempted "to build up a solid, organized mass base for the extended New Deal that he projected in the inaugural speech of 1937. Lacking such a base, he could not establish a rank-and-file majority group in Congress to push through his program."[3] Perhaps this had never been his intention. At any rate, in attempting to maintain his own power as chief executive over a nation divided by class and sectional interests, Roosevelt was required to lurch from Left to Right. The center-Left coalition was weakened after the 1938 elections when Maury Maverick of Texas and other New Deal Progressives lost their seats in Congress. Philip LaFollette was defeated in Wisconsin, Murphy and Earle lost the governorships in Michigan and Pennsylvania, and

Republicans doubled their strength in the House of Representatives from 88 to 170 while adding eight new seats in the Senate. Roosevelt then attempted to appease his still formidable Progressive constituency by supporting the creation of the Temporary National Economic Committee to study corporate concentration in America. He countered this move by restraining Secretary of the Interior Ickes from launching a counterattack on Martin Dies, the reactionary congressman who was head of the House Un-American Activities Committee and spokesman for the congressional coalition against the CIO. Roosevelt told Ickes, "For God's sake don't do it." As a result of this attempt to handle the Right with kid gloves, Dies got a huge new appropriation from Congress in 1939.[4]

Roosevelt kept his foreign policy card up his sleeve, revealing it briefly on October 5, 1937, in his famous "quarantine the aggressor" speech in Chicago. His economic policy was, as Burns argues, "opportunistic in the grand manner," and what he could not achieve domestically, "World War II would achieve as a by-product enabling the Republicans to charge later that the New Deal could end depression only through war."[5] Roosevelt followed world events carefully, as his protracted secret correspondence with Churchill makes clear, and he calculated that he could win a third term in 1940 by turning from domestic to foreign policy. By 1939 the president was already justifying his domestic policies as an aid to national defense and publicly stated that the United States had "passed the period of internal conflict in the launching of our program of social reform."[6] In January 1939, Roosevelt told a group of senators off-the-record that the defense of America "lay on the Rhine."[7]

While the Hillman-Murray-Reuther power grouping utilized its alliance with the state and the Catholic church in an energetic campaign to remove the Left from influence in the CIO, the United Automobile Workers continued to be a major theater for action in the struggle for power between Left and Right. In the period between the 1940 and 1941 UAW national conventions, the last major holdout against unionism in the auto industry, the Ford Motor Company, capitulated to the strongest Communist-led local in the UAW—local 600. "By 1938, 200 Communists worked in the Ford River Rouge plant, and Ford CP members issued a shop paper called the Ford-Dearborn Worker." The Communist Party had a large membership of black and foreign-born workers and "they had a decisive influence on the development of Local 600."[8]

Temporary unity was achieved between the factions in the UAW to unleash this last great offensive against the corporate enemy. Although the Left had lost control over the CIO national office, it was still a formidable force among the workers at the bottom. The true Left in the United States, as elsewhere, was a product of mass struggle, and until that struggle from below was under control it was difficult for Murray, Hillman, and Reuther to consolidate their bargain with the state and the Roosevelt regime. Only a disciplined and coercive national war economy was capable of stilling and taming the mass movement that had created the CIO. In the meantime, the Ford workers carried through a complex and sometimes violent organizing campaign against the last open-shop bastion of the auto industry by utilizing the well-perfected mass-mobilization techniques of industrial unionism in the auto industry. They responded to the company's use of force by mounting an offensive of their own:

> The men, enraged by the years of repression, took things into their own hands. The workers in the rolling mill sat down, demanding the reinstatement of their committeemen (who had been summarily fired by Ford). Other departments followed swiftly and by early evening virtually the entire Rouge was on strike. Bennett [head of Ford's security forces], despite his armed forces, had lost all control and the UAW was taken by surprise.[9]

Mass revolt conquered Ford as it had General Motors and Chrysler. Henry Ford, the personification of American capitalism, surrendered to the union that his publicity office had consistently labeled "Communist influenced and Communist led" by signing the best contract ever won by the UAW to that date. Ford Local 600 emerged as the most radical local in the UAW. Ford later confided to one of his chief executives that he had given in because his wife threatened to divorce him when he decided to close the plant and refuse to sign a contract with the union. If he carried out his threat, she argued, there "would be 'riots and bloodshed,' and she had seen enough of that. And if I did that she would leave me."[10] Ford was never the same man after his defeat by a workforce over whom he had exercised absolute control for many decades.

Ford Local 600 was typical of the many Left strongholds throughout the CIO. The black-dominated key Armour plant in the Chicago packing industry elected Herb Marsh, an avowed Communist, president of the local; New York transport workers elected rank-and-file Communists to leadership positions in the largest transport union in the country; leftists dominated the union organization of the farm-equipment industry, and carried on the historic radical traditions of the western hard-rock miners through the Mine, Mill, and Smelter Workers union. It was the Left in the CIO that pushed Lewis and other national leaders to take up the most advanced and progressive issues of the day, including equal rights for blacks, women workers, and other minorities. The red-baiting attack on the CIO as an institution signaled the response of the corporations and their political allies to the threat posed by the largest Left-led social movement in American history. Fully cognizant of the combined economic and political power of corporate capital, the industrial workers of the thirties set themselves only such historic goals as they could accomplish. Once business was invited back into the Roosevelt coalition to lead the war economy, union goals were confined within the narrow legal framework of collective bargaining.

Left-Led Strikes in the Defense Industry

Just as Lewis had predicted, those CIO leaders who had made an alliance with the state moved rapidly to break strikes in the name of national defense. Hillman, Brophy, Carey, Murray, and Reuther all supported the government in breaking a series of strikes launched by underpaid workers at North American Aviation, Phelps Dodge, and Allis-Chalmers. Wyndham Mortimer, who had contributed so much to the organization of the auto industry, moved to the West Coast in 1939 to organize the aircraft industry for the UAW. There he took on the open shop in the fastest expanding industry in the country by publishing a weekly paper, *The Aircraft Organizer,* and supervising its distribution at Vultee, North American, Lockheed, and Consolidated aviation plants. Despite an intense barrage of red-baiting by the *Los Angeles Times* and the Hearst press, charging that the CIO was a Communist organization, Mortimer won an NLRB election at Vultee and on November 15, 1940, the Vultee aircraft workers struck the plant to force union recognition from the company. When Mortimer called Lewis in Washington to ask for his support for the strike, Lewis agreed and told him: "You must get rid of President Thomas, Wyndham." Lewis often referred to the president of the UAW as a "dunderheaded blabbermouth."[11]

Thomas, of course, wanted to call the strike off, but pressure from Lewis and Addes checked him. The strike effectively halted the production of training planes for the armed forces and the press opened an all-out attack on Mortimer, the UAW, and the CIO for what it called a Communist conspiracy to cripple the aircraft industry. Murray and Hillman demanded that the UAW end the strike and that Mortimer be removed from California. Lewis and Addes threw their weight behind the strike, and in the end, Mortimer and the young strike leaders signed an agreement with the Vultee Corporation that proved to be the best contract yet signed in the low-paying aircraft industry. Thomas then decided to fly into California so that he might be photographed signing the contract. After his success at Vultee, Mortimer moved rapidly to take on the key North American Aviation stronghold.

Despite a massive campaign by the company, the press, and the International Association of Machinists attempting to label Lewis, Mortimer, and Harry Bridges tools of a Communist conspiracy,

Mortimer won a close NLRB election at North American Aviation. However, the company refused to recognize the new union and the workers voted to strike. Thomas then issued an order forbidding Mortimer to have anything to do with the North American Aviation strike. Impatient with the inaction of the UAW national office, the North American aircraft workers struck on their own and set up the largest picket line in the history of California to guarantee that production not be resumed. Frankensteen flew into southern California and demanded that the strike be called off. When his demand was ignored, he went on nationwide radio to denounce both the strike and its leaders as part of a Communist conspiracy to sabotage the national defense effort. Frankensteen then demanded that Mortimer use his influence with the workers to call the strike off. When Mortimer refused, he was fired from the UAW staff. The purge of the radicals who had built the CIO had begun.

A special emergency meeting of the CIO Executive Board was called in Washington to deal with the North American Aviation strike and the CIO's continued participation on the National Defense Advisory Board. North American Aviation strike leaders were called in and taken to task by Murray for supporting a Communist-led strike designed to embarrass Roosevelt's defense program. The strike leaders argued hotly that the strike was called to fight for minimum wages and union recognition and that the so-called war effort was simply being used to smash the union. John L. Lewis walked into the meeting unannounced and directly attacked Roosevelt and Hillman for wanting to shoot down and stab in the back aircraft workers who were simply trying to win a paltry 65¢ an hour wage increase. Murray was quite shaken as Lewis attacked the whole concept of a no-strike pledge, stating that the obligation of labor was to continue organizing and protecting itself and that it should not tie its hands with a no-strike pledge until business and government gave firm commitments to labor.[12]

Sidney Hillman subsequently confirmed the prediction by Lewis that he would carry out Roosevelt's orders to break a strike. With Hillman's approval, Roosevelt called out the army to open the plant:

> On Monday, June 10, over 25,000 troops with fixed bayonets dispersed the picket lines and arrested scores of strikers. This action shocked even those UAW and CIO leaders who had opposed the strike. In what John L. Lewis called "the blackest week in American labor history," the army broke the strike. Mortimer urged a meeting of the local to end the work stoppage, and the demoralized strikers decided to return to their jobs.[13]

Roosevelt and Hillman devised a formula whereby strikes in defense-related industries were outlawed and the disputes between management and labor were turned over to the National Defense Mediation Board and the Office of Production Management (OPM) for settlement. The three key Left-led strikes of the period—North American Aviation, the Allis-Chalmers plant in Milwaukee, and the UE Phelps Dodge strike in New Jersey—were all broken by government fiat and the workers were forced to return to work without a contract. During the Phelps Dodge strike, Carey, who was president of the UE and secretary-treasurer of the CIO, supported the government position that broke the strike.

Pressman argued years afterward that "labor was strong enough at that time that it could have exacted a considerably higher protection than it did in 1939–1940. It didn't. Labor just gave its no-strike pledge and got absolutely no commitment in exchange." He stated that there were no promises from industry to observe the decisions of the National Defense Mediation Board and no promises to observe orders issued by the NLRB.[14] By the summer of 1941, Lewis was openly attacking Roosevelt, Hillman, and John Brophy for utilizing the National Defense Mediation Board to curb the power of labor.

The emergence of a new leadership in the national office of the CIO was hardly an evolutionary process. Roosevelt's campaign to capture the top staff of the CIO was aided by the press, the Catholic church, and the army, all organizational weapons of formidable strength. The outcome was not determined by some natural historical process; in the final analysis, it was determined by a fierce struggle for power in which the state threw in all the resources at its command. Anticommunism, which for many decades had provided the ideology for containing American labor under craft unionism, was once again linked with the ideology of nationalism to contain the radical impulses of industrial unionism. The counterattack against class-conscious industrial unionists proceeded on all fronts after 1940. In Minneapolis, the state came to the aid of Dan Tobin of the Teamsters to break the power of the truckers. In a massive organizing drive, Trotskyist leaders had set up forty-six locals in eleven states under the North Central District Drivers' Council, which had signed an agreement covering 2,000 truck operators and 250,000 men. In 1941 Tobin charged that membership in the Socialist Workers' Party violated the anticommunist clause in the Teamsters' national constitution. The Minneapolis Socialist Workers' Party leaders argued that this clause applied only to Communists, but Tobin had no intention of distinguishing between revolutionary factions, and the SWP members were expelled. The Trotskyist leaders then took their union into the CIO on an offer from John L. Lewis, and labor war between Tobin and the militant truckers of the Northwest broke out.

Tobin immediately called for the aid of the federal government to curb "those disturbers who believe in the policies of foreign, radical governments" during a time when "our country is in a dangerous position."[15] The Department of Justice responded rapidly by securing an indictment under the newly legislated Smith Act against twenty-nine members of the Socialist Workers' Party, including Farrell Dobbs and the Dunne brothers. The Communist Party, much to its discredit, made no protest and, in fact, applauded the jailing of some of the leading radical industrial union leaders in the country. After the war, when the Communist Party itself fell under the axe of the Smith Act, there may have been a few Communists who realized the folly of the party line in the early 1940s.

By its action in imprisoning the Minneapolis Teamster leaders for sedition, the Roosevelt administration delivered the strategic organization built by Dobbs and the Dunne brothers to Jimmy Hoffa. The man who was to become head of the most powerful union in the country had been trained as a young organizer by Dobbs. Hoffa was a nonideological union leader who represented the essence of economism, aligning himself with the professional mob at an early date in his career.

Roosevelt, having helped to deliver the CIO to Hillman and the Teamsters to Hoffa, similarly aided Reuther to capture the UAW. By the 1941 UAW national convention, Hillman, who shared power in the powerful Office of Production Management with William Knudsen, the former president of General Motors, had allied himself with Reuther against the Lewis-Addes faction in the UAW. At issue in the 1941 convention of the United Automobile Workers was another Left-led defense-related strike underway at the Allis-Chalmers Manufacturing Company, located near Milwaukee. Reuther and his Catholic allies in the UAW utilized the strike to launch an all-out attack on George Addes.

The Allis-Chalmers strike involved Local 248, the largest Left-led local union in the UAW region, embracing Wisconsin, Illinois, Iowa, Minnesota, and Colorado, under the determined leadership of Harold Christofel. The long and violent strike at Allis-Chalmers pitted a radical union against what John Steelman, a presidential appointee in charge of labor matters in defense-related industries, termed "one of the most vicious anti-labor organizations in the country."[16] Appeals from both Hillman and Knudsen, acting in their roles as officials of the OPM, and Secretary of the Navy Frank Knox failed to end the strike because the company refused to make any commitments to a settlement and because the UAW local thought it had the strike almost won. Government appeals finally succeeded in persuading some of the workers to break through the picket line and return to work. The strike was finally settled on what Carl Haessler asserts were "fairly reasonable terms." Further bitterness was created when the union by membership vote ordered all the workers who had scabbed to pay a fine before they could be reinstated as union members in good standing.

When the UAW met at the 1941 national convention in Buffalo, the credentials committee controlled by Reuther challenged the ten-man

Allis-Chalmers delegation as being illegally elected. Wrangling went on over this issue for several days, with the result that a committee dominated by the Reuther faction was sent to Milwaukee to take another vote by the Allis-Chalmers local. The committee returned to report that it was impossible to gain the cooperation of Christofel, the head of the union. This report was rejected by the convention, which sent an enlarged committee back to Milwaukee, where another vote of the local was taken and the original Christofel supporters were reelected and seated at the convention. However, the vote was extremely close.

The incident was typical of the Left-Right battles that went on throughout the convention. Tom Doherty, a leader of the Association of Catholic Trade Unionists (ACTU) on the credentials committee, played a key part. Together with the Catholic caucus, he worked closely with priest advisers who helped to plan convention strategy and tactics.

Addes repeatedly attacked the ATU, while Reuther supporters took on those union officials who had supported the North American Aviation strike led by Mortimer and the local West Coast leader, Lew Michner. The two most important issues at the convention concerned strikes in defense-related industries and communism in the UAW. Addes and his faction warded off a resolution that would have severely penalized Lew Michner for his role in the North American Aviation strike, but were unable to protect Mortimer, whose vulnerability as an avowed Communist was manifest. The convention thus voted to uphold the dismissal of the man who had first organized the auto industry and then made the breakthrough in the giant West Coast aircraft industry. Reuther and the Catholic church would harvest the crops Mortimer had sown as the Left was whittled down at each succeeding convention.

Carl Haessler describes the long-range strategy of Reuther and the Catholic church to isolate the Left:

> One of the chores of the Reuther-Catholic caucus was to put brakes on rank and file militancy and to mold the union constitution into the form long ago achieved by old-time AFL international unions: Tightly centralized power at the top, adequate punitive measures to prevent opposition leaders from reaching platforms of influence and public notice within the union by censorship of local newspapers, including the most powerful local union in the UAW, Ford Local 600, and by suppressing opposition papers.[17]

According to Haessler, Walter Reuther proved himself a "master strategist and coalition builder" who maneuvered his Catholic troops with great skill. Both Frankensteen and Leonard, vice-presidents of the UAW, deserted the Unity caucus and went over to the Reuther-Catholic coalition at the 1941 UAW convention. The Reuther-Hillman forces finally succeeded in putting through the issue they had doggedly pursued for more than two years—the insertion of a clause in the UAW constitution banning Communists from office. Addes then defeated Reuther's candidate Leonard for the position of secretary-treasurer by a close vote.

Moscow was thus outlawed as an outside power in the CIO, while Rome was legitimated. Murray, Brophy, and Carey took their places as the major representatives of the Catholic church in the national office of the CIO, while Reuther worked on a long-range program to appoint Catholic vice-presidents, Catholic board members, and Catholic newspaper editors in the UAW. Correspondence from Catholic delegates at UAW conventions to their priest advisers is on deposit in the Association of Catholic Trade Unionists Collection at Wayne State University. One of these letters asks a priest adviser for specific help on research directed toward achieving the inclusion of an anticommunist clause in the UAW constitution:

> I would like to have some factual material and arguments to support this and any other suggestions you may have.
> Reuther is willing to support this proposal, which they didn't do last year. Things look as though a majority may be swung on this issue.
>
> Very sincerely yours,
>
> Tim Daley[18]

Successive amendments to the UAW constitution were made yearly until the centralization of power under Reuther was finally achieved.

The Anti-Fascist War and the U.S. Left

The Nazi invasion of the Soviet Union in the summer of 1941 and the Japanese attack on Pearl Harbor on December 7 of the same year produced a world realignment resulting in the wartime alliance of the United States and the USSR. Thus, an anomaly of history all but ended the independent strategy of the Communist-led Left in the CIO as both Communists and independent leftists rallied behind the war effort. The war gave the Communist Party a new, even if temporary, lease on life, as Roosevelt accepted Communist support for his wartime national unity regime. The president had little to lose by such tolerance, since the Left as an effective force had been eliminated from many key government agencies, no longer influenced top policy formation in the CIO, and had been removed from control of two key national unions—the Teamsters and the UAW. Moreover, Roosevelt was at his best when he had total control of any coalition he had mastered—he was friendly, charming, and witty. Both Julius Emspak and Blackie Myers, although they did not fully trust Roosevelt on union matters, admired his leadership of the

war effort and found they could still win concessions from him on some
manpower issues during the war.

   John L. Lewis, who never followed any party line except his own, was
never enthusiastic about the war, although he was an anti-fascist. He
refused to subordinate the United Mine Workers to the state and struck
the captive mines on September 15, 1941, for what no CIO union
possessed—the union shop. Lewis accused Hillman of attempting to use
the National Defense Mediation Board against the interests of the
miners because of his "vengeful and malignant opposition to the
interests of the United Mine Workers." Lewis ordered the miners to
return to work for thirty days if the employers would match all the
provisions of the contract already won by the commercial miners and
mediate the issue of the union shop. When no agreement was reached,
he threatened to call the miners out again. Roosevelt wrote Lewis a
personal letter stating that uninterrupted production of coal was necessary for making steel, "that basic material of our national defense," and
that he was "asking you and your associated officers of the United Mine
Workers of America, as loyal citizens, to come now to the aid of your
country." Lewis was enraged, and replied:

> Sir:
>
> Your letter at hand.
> I have no wish to betray those whom I represent. There is yet no question of
> patriotism or national security involved in this dispute. . . . This fight is
> only between a labor union and a ruthless corporation—the United States
> Steel Corporation. . . . If you would use the power of the State to restrain
> me, as an agent of labor, then, Sir, I submit that you should use that same
> power to restrain my adversary in this issue, who is an agent of capital. My
> adversary is a rich man named Morgan, who lives in New York.

   Arguing that J. P. Morgan dominated the board of the United States
Steel Corporation, Lewis reminded the president that "Mr. Morgan's
great wealth is increasing from his profits on defense orders." It was not
unreasonable therefore to ask "Mr. Morgan's companies to accept the
wage agreement approved by the National Defense Mediation Board,
and accepted and signed by other captive and commercial coal companies in the nation."[19] On October 27, the miners working the captive
mines shut down the mines once more. Again the president succeeded in
getting them to go back to work pending further mediation by government agencies.

   Lewis understood that labor standards would soon be frozen by
government regulations for the duration of a wartime emergency and as
an aggressive labor leader he intended to take advantage of a crisis period
in the nation's history to utilize government power to get the steel
companies to give up what they had tenaciously preserved for three-

quarters of a century—the open shop. The UMW had won the union shop for 99 percent of the miners where the union held contracts and 95 percent of the workers in the captive mines belonged to the unions. "Because 90 percent of the total annual bituminous production was mined under union-shop agreements, Lewis thought it only logical for the UMW to demand a similar status in the captive mines, where all but 5 percent of eligible employees had joined the union."[20] On October 27, Roosevelt sent another public appeal to the UMW officials urging the miners to go back to work, and in a Navy Day speech the president attacked "selfish leaders," meaning Lewis. The president expressed his anger to Thomas Lamont of U.S. Steel "at Lewis' unwarranted, untrue, and demagogic statement about Jack (Morgan)." He instructed Lamont to tell Morgan "not to concern himself any more about Lewis' attack, for after many years of observation, I have come reluctantly to the conclusion that Lewis' is a psychopathic condition."[21]

Conservative congressmen accused Lewis of treason, and as the climate of war nationalism increased, the press continued to stir up public indignation against Lewis and the mine workers. At the same time, the profits of U.S. Steel were almost one-third higher than those of the previous year. In addition, the Communist Party of the United States, which had turned superpatriotic on June 22, 1941, refused to support the mine workers' strike and publicly attacked Lewis for threatening the national defense effort. On October 30, Lewis called the miners back to work and then set a new strike deadline of November 15, while the UMW waited for a favorable decision on the union-shop issue by the National Defense Mediation Board. The board consisted of four employer representatives, three public representatives, two AFL representatives, and Murray and Kennedy of the United Mine Workers. On November 10 all representatives on the board except Murray and Kennedy voted down the union shop in the captive mines. Murray and Kennedy resigned from the board in protest. President Roosevelt threatened to force passage of anti-strike legislation or to seize the mines and urged both parties to accept arbitration of the issue. On November 17 the miners refused to work once more while Lewis threatened to shut down the entire bituminous coal industry unless the union's demands were met. After a number of maneuvers on both sides, "Roosevelt informed Lewis that the steel industry had agreed to arbitration, and therefore he was appointing Fairless for steel, Lewis for labor, and Dr. John R. Steelman for the public as a board to settle the dispute."[22] Steelman's appointment guaranteed Lewis his victory, for it was well known that the conciliation-service director favored the union's position. After two weeks of determination, Lewis and Steelman granted the union shop to the mine workers while Fairless defended the traditional stance of the steel industry for the open shop. The award was handed down on December 7, 1941, the day the Japanese attacked Pearl Harbor. Lewis, as the representative of a historic social movement, thus won a final victory before resigning himself to the containment of that movement.

In the middle of January 1942, Lewis, acting as chairman of the CIO's standing peace negotiating committee for reconciliation with the AFL, without informing Philip Murray (the president of the CIO), called on Murray of the CIO and William Green of the AFL to resume unity talks. Lewis stated "that if a couplement could be achieved, with unified and competent leadership, the result would be advantageous and in the public interest."[23] Pressing for a merger of the AFL and the CIO, Lewis argued that "if labor is to be mobilized, transported here and there under terms and conditions set by employers and bureaucrats, with its forces divided, there could be but one result—labor will be shortchanged." On January 19, the *New York Times* "carried a front page story by A. H. Raskin describing secret negotiations between Lewis and Daniel Tobin of the AFL teamsters. Together they reportedly had devised a scheme for merging the two organizations that called for Green's retirement, George Meany's promotion to the presidency of the new federation, and Murray's demotion to the position of secretary-treasurer.[24] Murray was deeply hurt by Lewis' failure to consult him and shouted at reporters: "No one has the right to trade me for a job. My manhood requires a little reciprocity—and, by God, despite this feeble frame of mine, I will fight any living man to maintain my manhood." He informed Lewis by letter that all proposals for unity would "have to be initiated through the office of the President of the Congress of Industrial Organizations."[25]

Murray, who had always moved in the shadow of his patron John L. Lewis, first as vice-president of the United Mine Workers and then as president of the CIO, now shifted over entirely to the anti-Lewis camp in the CIO. Dubofsky and Van Tine describe the break between Murray and Lewis as both personal and political:

> The struggle between the Lewis and Hillman wings of the CIO over defense policy further complicated Murray's position. Murray was a man split into two, with old loyalties linking him to one camp and personal convictions pushing him into the other. Into the summer of 1941 he tried to equivocate between the two groups hoping to preserve some semblance of unity within the CIO. With news of the Nazi invasion of Russia and reports of German and Japanese attacks on American vessels, this precarious stalemate collapsed as more and more unionists entered the Hillman camp. Murray, reacting both to international developments and the changing political situation in the CIO, began to shift toward the emerging anti-Lewis majority.[26]

Retreating to his own fiefdom of the UMW, which he controlled with a dictatorial hand, Lewis broke his connection with the great rank-and-file struggle of industrial workers, which had somehow inspired his native fighting capacity. Never a clear political thinker, and not having any consistent philosophy, Lewis drifted back to the conservative world from which he had come.

One of the most significant results of the Lewis-Murray break was the reserved acceptance by Murray of Communist support for the anti-Lewis line of the CIO. The Communists thus became the most ardent supporters of Roosevelt and the war effort; leftists were taken into the Roosevelt coalition as junior partners on probation for good behavior. Lewis subsequently expelled Murray from the UMW. Murray took over the full-time salaried job of president of the United Steelworkers union while retaining his position as president of the CIO. President Roosevelt, realizing that a merger of the AFL and CIO under the patronage of John L. Lewis would weaken his own control over labor, therefore created his own labor council as a part of the state war economy. He set up the Labor Victory Committee to facilitate uninterrupted war production by agreed-on procedures for the peaceful settlement of labor disputes. Organized labor was represented by William Green, Matthew Woll, and George Meany for the AFL, and Murray, Emspak, and Lewis for the CIO. According to Emspak, while serving on this committee he and Lewis led the fight for the closed shop in return for a no-strike pledge, "the creation of joint labor-management councils, equal pay for women, and an accepted number of working hours to make up a working day so that there would be an unquestioned, universal rule on overtime pay."[27]

Once Roosevelt had defeated the Left-syndicalist forces who had attempted to build an independent base for industrial unionism, and once the CIO was safely under the political control of the Democratic Party, the president paid off labor by granting the new industrial unions substantial economic rights. In exchange for the renunciation of independent political power, Roosevelt gave the CIO the union shop. David Brody's summary of CIO gains under wartime conditions is an excellent one.

> By 1941, the economy was becoming fully engaged in defense production. Corporate profits before taxes leaped from 6½ billion dollars in 1939 to 17 billion in 1941. The number of unemployed fell from 8½ million in June 1940 to under 4 million in December 1941. It was this eighteen month period that marked the turning point for the CIO. . . . Above all, collective bargaining after a three-year gap began to produce positive results. On April 14, 1941, U.S. Steel set the pattern for the industry with an increase of ten cents an hour. For manufacturing generally, average hourly earnings from 1940 to 1941 increased over 10 percent and weekly earnings 17 percent; living costs only rose 5 percent.[28]

The federal role in labor-management relations was enlarged and the government entered directly into the collective-bargaining process. "The National War Labor Board largely determined the wartime terms of employment in American industry. This emergency circumstance, temporary although it was, had permanent consequences for mass-production unionism. The wartime experience disposed of the last barriers to viable collective bargaining."[29] Finally, the National War Labor Board granted a maintenance-of-membership clause in all contracts negotiated by unions during the war. As Brody asserts, "The union shop then generally grew from maintenance of membership."[30] Tens of thousands of new members poured into the CIO. Thus, "from the half-decade of war, the industrial unions advanced to their central place in the American economy."[31]

Once more in American history the AFL benefited from a struggle it had opposed. During the consolidation of the great bargain with labor during the war, the AFL gained as much as did the CIO. With the final renunciation of labor independence, the difference between the AFL and the CIO lost its edge. Moreover, the Left-led CIO unions confronted the same laws of the market as those that affected the job-conscious traditional unions; the major differences between unions of the Left and the Right were largely whittled down to a leftist tradition of struggle against employers and for rank-and-file control of the union apparatus. In the long term, the Left-led unions, constrained as they were within the bounds of economism, could not alone affect the tides of history or the return of business unionism as the major form of American unionism. However, the bargain American workers had wrung from capital with their blood and struggle was no small achievement. Left-syndicalists characteristically weighed the results in limited trade union terms. I once asked Blackie Myers whether the building of the CIO had been worth it. He replied in typical working-class and human terms. "Sure it was, fellow worker. We helped a lot of people have a better life." He paused and thought awhile and then added: "And you know what? We had a hell of a lot of fun doing it!" For Myers, Left-syndicalism was a way of life.

There is no doubt that factional struggles within the CIO compromised many of the principles of class-conscious industrial unions. Larger politics of the day were often forgotten during periods of sharp factional infighting. On the other hand, much labor history has been devoted to the tactics of the Left—the come-early-stay-late formula for capturing power in democratic organizations—while dismissing the generally more unscrupulous tactics of the right-wing flag wavers to seize control of the labor movement. The historical record does not grant any distinction to Murray, Hillman, Reuther, and their allies for their devotion to the principles of democratic procedure. The Left, warts and all, produced a better record in this regard. However, during the war, rank-and-file unionists opposed factions of both the Left and the Right for the sacrifice of working conditions to employers whose profits increased under wartime conditions.

This became clear at the 1942 UAW convention, where the main debate was between rank-and-file delegates and a united leadership over the imposition from above of what was called the equality-of-sacrifice principle instituted from April to August in UAW shops. The program called for the surrender of overtime pay for Saturday and Sunday work, retaining overtime only for work over eight hours a day or forty hours a week; the surrender of the right to strike; the commitment of all workers to the increase of war production with no limits; and finally a request to management that executive salaries be limited to $25,000 a year. The last proposal was never instituted and management laughed it to death on the way to the bank. The equality-of-sacrifice program was supported by Communists, Socialists, and the Reuther-Catholic caucus. It was opposed by Ford Local 600 and rank-and-file-workers who were pro-union, anti-employer, and anti-government because they felt that the war was essentially being waged for profit.

After intense debate the convention determined that unless the employers and the government pledged to make equal sacrifices the program would be dropped. When it was realized that the International Association of Machinists (IAM) was persuading workers to vote for the AFL because the IAM had not adopted the equality-of-sacrifice program, the program was shelved by the UAW.[32]

During the decade between 1935 and 1945 the American mass production workers forced capital to a compromise. However, they had not achieved equality through collective bargaining with management. U.S. corporate managers zealously resisted every erosion of management prerogatives. Despite continued militancy from below in the decades following the war, U.S. workers found themselves encased in a complex and formal network of legal rules enforced by management, government, and union officials alike. By the 1980s, when the American manufacturing economy began to disintegrate, U.S. management would demand that the unions give back what they had won during the previous half-century of struggle. The great bargain would come unstuck.

8

A Second Bargain Is Struck

By the end of World War II, the organized industrial working class had fought its way into the American system after a decade of violent and protracted struggle. Having traded political independence for economic rights, a major section of unionized workers in the crafts, construction, and basic industries were incorporated into the advanced capitalist industrial order under a system of collective bargaining. Labor protected its newly won status in 1946 by conducting the greatest strike campaign in American history, when 4.5 million workers stopped production to consolidate and expand their economic rights. After 1946, the war over, the corporations and the government demanded a second bargain from U.S. labor.

The Keynesian Paradox

The Keynesian solution for the ills of capitalism, as is clear to the generation of the eighties, both saved the system and undermined it at the same time. It represented a move toward corporatism, or social bargaining, involving a "system of state control over a predominantly privately-owned economy; a model obviously derived from fascism."[1] It was an economic formula concerned with the short run, a factor made clear by Keynes with his famous quip that "in the long run, we will all be dead." In retrospect, it is evident that the success of this structurally rearranged social system was underwritten by a new era of American imperial expansion. In the years following the war, state and corporate planners believed that the great battle to redistribute the national income would never have to be fought. Rather, the income of all sectors could be increased by enlarging the national income through expansion of overseas markets and thus relative shares would remain the same. This was a happy solution, indeed; the new worldview generated by a reconstructed system of cold war capitalism laid the basis for a broader coalition of politicians, businessmen, professionals, labor unions, and farmers than the country had ever known. To be sure, the economic preconditions for the smooth workings of the new system of advanced capitalism did not depend on foreign expansion alone. Structural and technological changes in American industry fit well with the task of fulfilling the demands of the largest internal market in the world. In 1939 the federal government reached the highest level of state expenditure in American history—$8.5 billion—and yet in 1940 there were still over 8 million people unemployed. During the last year of World War II, the federal government was spending $98 billion and had increased the Gross National Product by 60 percent. In 1945 state expenditures accounted for nearly half of the total national product. Elite consensus across all sectors was achieved in support of a program of federal government maintenance of a high national income, including, in 1945, national full employment. With the reconstitution of the global market system under American leadership at the Bretton Woods International Monetary Conference in 1944, America had replaced Britain as the greatest world advocate of free trade. The Age of Keynes was thus coupled with Pax Americana.[2]

The notion of the expanding pie contained a logic everyone might, with some persuasion, accept. Dean Acheson, who was to become one of the managers of the new world system, explained it all to Congress: "You could probably fix it so that everything produced here would be consumed here, but that would completely change our constitution, our relations to property, human liberty, our very conception of law."[3] In short, imperial expansion and something for everybody was better than fighting over shares.

Labor had already accepted the great trade-off entailing the exchange of political power for money; now it had to be convinced that it must not ask for a larger share of the income pie. Rather, it must be content with incremental shares of the larger pie to come from increased productivity and profits from the foreign market. Thus, a new bargain had to be struck: labor peace based on trade union agreement to demand no wage increases without a matching output in productivity. The patriotism-oriented leadership of the CIO would gain new respectability in the postwar period as junior partners in the new military-industrial coalition once they had struck this second bargain.

National and Global Reconstruction

State-directed capitalism in the postwar period required an up-to-date ideology. Thus, anti-fascism, which guided American society through the war, was transformed at the war's end into anticommunism to provide the framework for a new cold war social order. Patriotism and anticommunism served the dual requirement of creating a strong state at home and economic and military expansion overseas. Since empire-building was to become a major component of national reconstruction, anticommunism emerged as the indispensible instrument capable of integrating both domestic and international strategies. It is noteworthy that the new ideology of global and domestic anticommunism in its liberal guise was first perfected within the CIO and then spread to the rest of the nation.

The official beginning of the cold war is usually dated to March 5, 1946, when Winston Churchill, escorted by President Truman, gave his famous "Iron Curtain" speech at Fulton, Missouri. Churchill's anti-Communist Manifesto called for an Anglo-American alliance directed against the Soviet Union. The domestic red-hunt that followed served to legitimate the permanent role of the American state in a restructured domestic and international system and the CIO National Office adapted rapidly to the new postwar era. Sidney Hillman died only a little more than a year after Roosevelt's death on April 12, 1945. Walter Reuther then quickly took up the reins as the leading social democratic labor leader in the country. Within two weeks after Churchill's Iron Curtain speech, Reuther was elected president of the United Automobile Workers union on an anticommunist platform. Reuther thus became the advance-man for the emerging national current which had been born in Fulton, Missouri. "In his first press conference after assuming office, Reuther announced that he intended to unite 90 percent of the union against the 10 percent with 'outside' loyalties, by which, he said, he meant the Communists."[4] Reuther and his allies then launched a national campaign to purge the Communists from the CIO.

As for the Communist Party of the United States, its vulnerability was increased when, in order to retain a position in the war unity coalition, it proposed a no-strike pledge for the CIO in the postwar period. Some of the most militant left-wing union leaders, including Harry Bridges, found themselves trapped by a party line they did not really have their hearts in. When the party switched back to a policy of struggle in response to a signal from Jacques DuClos of the French Communist Party, anticommunist forces in the United States were able to buttress the charge that the American Left was simply the agent of a foreign power. The ideological force of nationalism, wielded time after time throughout the whole period of American industrialization, swept over

the Left in the postwar years in giant waves. As Engels had predicted in
the 1890s, with the outbreak of another European war "chauvinism
would swamp everything and America would then win out all along the
line."[5] The truth that patriotism is the last refuge of scoundrels had little
effect during the new gilded age of postwar American global supremacy.

Philip Murray, as president of the CIO, was strongly linked to the
ideology and strategy of the prewar New Deal. The inheritor of the
mantle of John L. Lewis was not yet ready to cast off all association with
the social movement that had created the CIO. Murray, therefore,
attempted to take a neutral role when Reuther opened his offensive
against the Left in the CIO. Murray believed that since the anticommunist forces were now in power it might not be necessary to carry
out further purges in the national organization of industrial unions. Furthermore, Murray still needed the Left's troops that could be mobilized
to block the postwar corporate campaign to weaken the CIO. The press
soon noted Murray's role. *Newsweek* joined the *New York Times* in the
count of CIO leaders aligned against the "reds" with an article titled
"Murray's Straddle."[6]

At the same time, business felt itself to be in a stronger position than
at any time in the past decade. Having emerged from the war in a
dominant world position, U.S. corporate leaders saw no reason why
they should not make the same bargain with foreign nations that they
had made with industrial unions at home. In return for world power,
the United States would be willing to grant economic aid. As Cordell
Hull put it at the time, "the political line-up" of the world would follow
"the economic line-up." The bargain in the form of an ultimatum was
first extended to Great Britain. As Richard Freeland points out:

> Dispatched by the British Government immediately following the termina-
> tion of Lend Lease, Keynes arrived in Washington in August 1945 with a
> request for a grant from the United States for six billion dollars to help
> Britain rebuild. He learned very quickly that the British had no chance of
> obtaining a grant and that even a loan would be made available only at the
> price of very considerable concessions by Britain in accordance with
> American multilateral objectives.[7]

Those "very considerable concessions" involved the transfer of the
imperial mantle over the world economic and political system from
Britain to the United States.

Freeland also notes, however, that "while the strategy of linking
cooperation with America's postwar goals to American willingness to
finance economic reconstruction was proving effective in the context of
negotiations between the U.S. and the governments of Britain and
France in late 1945 and early 1946, it did not produce a similar success
in the context of U.S.-Soviet diplomacy."[8] The reason the United States

could not effect the same success with the Soviet Union was that that country emerged out of World War II as the other great world imperialist power, fulfilling the destiny deTocqueville had predicted a hundred years earlier. The United States proved to be dominant only within the capitalist part of the world.

Dealing with the Soviet Union thus required a different strategy—one of containment. Rather than negotiate its differences with the Soviet Union the United States would militarily oppose any extension of Soviet world power and influence; the bi-polar world system was born, and the device to cope with it was the Truman Doctrine.

The Truman Doctrine

The strategic Truman Doctrine was composed of twin pillars, one economic and the other military. It provided the foundation of the military-industrial complex that was to constitute the structure of an advanced capitalist society. At the time the new strategy was being fashioned by Dean Acheson, the problem for the Truman administration was how to get the new strategy accepted, not only by congressional Republicans but by the nation at large. They decided to introduce it piece by piece, winning public opinion gradually, while at once testing the power of opposition of both the Left and the Right.

Washington planners wrestled with the problem of how best to announce the Truman Doctrine. The extension of aid to Greece and Turkey was the first step in unveiling the larger program of massive aid to Europe. But, as Freeland notes, "The American people were not accustomed to thinking . . . in strategic-military terms in time of peace, and too much emphasis upon supplying military aid to Turkey might have been alarming to the point of defeating the proposal."[9] The public had to be convinced that their whole way of life was at stake. Thus, when the president delivered the Truman Doctrine on March 12, 1947, he warned that the basic principles of America's political system were being threatened by "a worldwide campaign of totalitarian aggression composed of communist subversion and Soviet expansion."[10]

Domestic and foreign policy were thereby linked in one tightly knit axiom: anticommunism. Bernard Baruch said that the speech was "tantamount to a declaration of . . . an ideological or religious war."[11]

Since the Republicans were even more passionately anticommunist than the Democrats, the liberal-labor coalition regarded anticommunism as a perfect device for winning support for the cold war and the state-directed economic system they wished to create. Anticommunism, of course, was not a new invention: it was embedded in the American tradition from the great railroad strike of 1877 up to the present time.

But it had always been utilized in a negative sense, to delegitimate the demands of excluded groups that wanted inclusion in the system. In the post-World War II era, anticommunism became an ideology to construct an advanced industrial and global economic system.

The frontal attack on communism, at home and abroad, isolated the Left in the union movement. Having accepted the state-mediated collective bargaining principle, radical industrial unionists had few weapons with which to fight their more conservative trade union colleagues. When Matles, Emspak, and Bridges attempted to fight back against the charge of being agents of Moscow with a counterattack based on the principle of rank-and-file class-conscious unionism, Reuther countered them on purely trade union grounds, arguing that the UE leaders had settled with General Motors in the great 1946 strike before the UAW was ready to settle.

UE may have been a more democratic union, but it was not able to win much more at the bargaining table than the CIO unions under more conservative leaders. By 1947 the Left-led unions in the CIO had come to the end of the road. While Bridges, Emspak and Matles, with a long record of service to their memberships, were able to withstand the worst of the red-baiting gale and maintain their unions intact, they could no longer influence the main direction of American labor. Thus the industrial-union movement drifted back into the main road of business unionism from which it had broken out in the social movement of the thirties.

Congress Pares Down the Great Bargain

But anticommunism hurt more than the Left in the union movement. All of U.S. labor received a serious blow when Congress allied itself with capital and passed the Taft-Hartley Act. This new legislation emasculated the Wagner Act; it banned mass picketing, secondary boycotts, and sympathy strikes, all associated with the tactics of the social movement of industrial unionism identified with the CIO. Elected union officials were required to sign affidavits that they were not members of the Communist Party or lose the use of the National Labor Relations Board. Unions were made legally liable for any strikes by their members in violation of written contracts and the president was given the right to seek injunctions against strikes he deemed against the national interest. "In effect," as David Montgomery points out, "the only union activity which remained legal under Taft-Hartley was that involved in direct bargaining between a certified 'bargaining agent' and the employers of the workers it represented. Both actions of class solidarity and rank-and-file activity outside of the contractual framework were placed beyond the pale of the law."[12]

Harry Truman, in an effort to reduce the strain this wholesale attack on the rights of labor might produce in the state-labor cold war alliance, vetoed the bill. Congress rapidly overrode his veto, and in subsequent years the Landrum-Griffin Act and other congressional legislation, plus right-to-work laws passed by the states, would pare the power of U.S. labor down to a minimum.

Failing to see that by joining the state as junior partners, the labor movement as a movement was pitifully weakened, conservative CIO leaders pointed to the rights of workers and the conditions they were now able to win, which surpassed anything Gompers could have dreamed about. Murray, Reuther, and other CIO leaders were perturbed about Taft-Hartley, but this defeat was soon forgotten in the more important task for which they had been chosen: demonstrating the patriotism of the union movement through support of the administration's foreign policy.

Walter and Victor Reuther, who had emerged from the great struggles of the 1930s as skilled union leaders, would later realize that American labor had been channeled into a cul de sac, but by then it was too late. General Motors and the other great American corporations, as David Brody argues, "defined the terms for dealing with the UAW" and labor in general. Wages were pegged to the cost of living and increases were tied to productivity. "The union was accepted as a permanent presence. Benefits would be forthcoming at regular intervals and in decent increments. The essentials of managerial authority had to be left alone."[13] By the 1980s General Motors would take back what it had given, while at the same time granting large bonuses to its executives. During the great postwar boom the CIO was simply living on borrowed time, and the day would come when the terms of the Faustian bargain had to be paid.

The Purge of the Left from American Labor

At the 1946 CIO convention Murray took up the charges by conservative congressmen that the CIO was a Communist-dominated organization. He sponsored a resolution to answer "all the villainous, slanderous abuses" leveled against the CIO. Murray was determined once and for all to convince the nation that the CIO was "interested in the logical aspirations of all trade unionists in the United States of America." The resolution declared that the "Congress of Industrial Organizations resent and reject efforts of the Communist Party, or other political parties and their adherents, to interfere in the affairs of the CIO. This convention serves notice that we will not tolerate such interference."[14] The resolution was passed without debate.

At both the 1946 and 1947 CIO national conventions James Matles and other radical unionists tried to raise the questions of organizing the unorganized, fighting back against corporate anti-union campaigns, mobilizing the millions of workers who had struck in 1946 to once more confront employers as a united force, and fashioning a resolute CIO response to Taft-Hartley and other reactionary legislation. Unfortunately, this was the agenda of the thirties; Walter Reuther was more in tune with the times. If John L. Lewis had been something of a demagogue, he had been the demagogue of a mass movement; Reuther was a demagogue of the state.

When the 1947 CIO convention convened, the state entered directly into the affairs of the CIO in the person of Secretary of State George C. Marshall, who had come to receive the endorsement of the labor movement for the great plan which bore his name.

In a *Colliers* Magazine article entitled "How to Beat the Communists," Walter Reuther described how the Communists were finally defeated at the 1947 CIO convention. The resolution on foreign policy, he asserted, "was among the most important adopted by the CIO Convention, for it contained a clearly implied endorsement of the Marshall Plan." The issue of foreign policy, Reuther noted, had become the main issue between the Left and the Right in the CIO:

> What Marshall said before the CIO national convention was important, but more significant was the fact that he had been invited to address the CIO. . . . The Stalinists attempted to maneuver convention action on the foreign policy resolution in advance of Secretary Marshall's speech. We blocked such a move. Marshall spoke first and debate followed. The democratic bloc was ready.[15]

CIO leaders thus invited the state to intervene directly in CIO affairs in order to lead the fight against the Left. Murray and Reuther had served public notice that they would not tolerate outside, i.e., Communist Party, interference in CIO affairs, but that did not preclude a direct role for the state and the Catholic church, as the 1948 Convention was to demonstrate.

Reuther exulted in the defeat of the Left: "The Communists were in full retreat." Moreover, he told *Colliers* readers: "The secret battalion had been licked before an international audience. Hundreds of thousands of decent unionists, watching from local union offices throughout the land, had won new heart. They knew now that it could be done; they had just seen it done."[16]

The Communist Party and the Left-syndicalists in the industrial union movement now realized that the political sphere and the economic sphere were inseparably linked and moved together in one last desperate effort to block the countercoup of the new center-Right alliance by mobilizing the campaign of Henry Wallace for president in 1948. The American Left, which had been born in the great 1877 national railroad rebellion, went down with Henry Wallace. After Truman's narrow victory over Dewey in 1948, the *New York Times* reported that Truman told a friend on the day after the election, "Labor did it." And the *CIO News* declared: "Frankly, we don't intend to be a bit modest about the part organized labor played in the Democratic victory."[17]

The CIO was now fully incorporated into a reconstructed political economy on terms dictated by the state. All CIO leaders signed the non-Communist Taft-Hartley affidavits. John L. Lewis, who retained his old fighting independence, refused to sign; thus the United Mine Workers and the rank-and-file unionists of the Left who had built the CIO from the ground up were cast out of the mainstream of organized American labor. A year later, at the 1949 CIO convention, in an atmosphere of national anticommunist hysteria, eleven "Communist-dominated" unions were expelled from the CIO; the state and the Catholic church filled the ideological vacuum this action created. Class-conscious and radical trade unionists were thus expunged from the history they had written.

Established labor, having dutifully expelled the Communists and other militants, was soon guaranteed a share in what was to become an expanding national pie baked by military expenditures, productivity increases, and foreign markets. The AFL-CIO merger in the mid-fifties officially symbolized the return of American labor to the principles of business unionism. U.S. labor was given a stake in the international labor network as a part of the cold war coalition and AFL-CIO officials dutifully carried out U.S. foreign policy objectives by fulfilling their assignment of splitting the labor movement in Europe, Asia, and Latin America. The end of an era of labor revolt ended as it had begun, with the jailing and blacklisting of labor militants. Economic gains for millions of workers would improve significantly for two decades and then drift downward in the seventies and eighties in what appeared to be a secular decline.

World Strategy and National Consensus

The tasks of building "American security" and "safeguarding freedom" required that the United States build up a military-industrial-political economy that could protect "free peoples against communist aggression and subversion." America had cleansed itself; now it would cleanse the world. The material underpinning for the new doctrine was provided by the combination of American economic strength and the monopoly of nuclear weapons. The Marshall Plan as promulgated by Walter Reuther was simply an economic aid plan, designed to help rebuild the war-exhausted nations of Europe. On the surface, it did not appear to be a military plot, as the Left had charged. However, within a few years the ascendancy of the military side of American policy was clear: "The United States' view of the altered scale of priorities now giving first place to the military components of the power balance, was made explicit to recipients of Marshall Plan assistance. . . . By 1951, the European Economic Recovery program was formally subordinated to 'security' considerations under the omnibus Mutual Security Act."[18]

National Security Council Study No. 68 established the major premises and long-range policy for what was to become the U.S. military blueprint for the cold war.[19] The 1950 policy directive provided the links for the new structure of military-state-corporate power and the dovetailing of American foreign and domestic programs. Keynesian economics was thus integrated with a military definition of global power. Most significantly, the plan argued that the United States could afford to devote as much as 20 percent of the nation's GNP for national security as compared with the 5 percent devoted to national defense in 1950. In terms of the federal budget the plan advocated an expenditure of $60 billion annually compared to the $15 billion programmed in 1949.

There was some hesitancy in governmental circles over the adoption of such a far-reaching and revolutionary reordering of national priorities, but the Korean war conveniently appeared to win over even the most hesitant. The plan was quickly accepted and put into effect. Massive military budgets thus became a permanent feature of the American political economy.

The synthesis of a military build-up with the liberal Keynesian philosophy based on an expanding world market system was possible only in a country with great national wealth and resources. This was the corporate, political, and military structure of power first described by C. Wright Mills: a functional system designed to organize the world for American interests. It was on this analytic foundation that the theory of corporate liberalism was erected. It was an accurate description, not a theory, of the American social order during the fifties. Some social scientists viewed the industrial order of advanced capitalism as a perfectly balanced machine which had achieved a functional equilibrium. New Left theorists, while accepting the stability of the whole edifice, deplored the pathology of a historical development for which there seemed no solution. The problem with corporate liberal theory was that while making a more or less accurate analysis of the present it was unable either to explain the past or predict the future.

Business Unionism Comes to the End of the Road

An extensive literature describes the bourgeoisification of American workers as the reunited AFL-CIO led its members to the achievement of middle-class status. There is some truth in this description. Engels recognized the phenomenon in Britain as early as 1858 when he wrote to Marx that "the English proletariat is actually becoming more and more bourgeois, so that this most bourgeois of all nations is apparently aiming ultimately at the possession of a bourgeois aristocracy and a bourgeois proletariat alongside the bourgeoisie. For a nation which exploits the whole world this is of course to a certain extent justifiable."[20] Some years later he again called attention to the corruption of those English workers who "gaily share the feast of England's monopoly of the world market and the colonies."[21] However, England lost that monopoly in the long run, and the American imperial phase was to last a mere twenty years, from 1950 to 1970.

A relative social harmony had been achieved during the cold war era, when military strategies and power appeared to fit the dual requirements of national security and economic prosperity. In the late sixties, when state power served neither and, in fact, threatened both, the national corporate-military-political consensus began to unravel. The Vietnam war led to the collapse of the domestic great bargain that had sought to buy off competing sectors of American society; by 1971 the economic component of the postwar Keynesian system was in serious crisis.

According to *Business Week*, the "beginning of the end of Pax Americana occurred in 1971, when two decades of international deficits and a worsening of the U.S position in world trends forced the dollar off the gold standard. Then, as 40 years earlier when Britain's pound was knocked off the gold standard, floating exchange rates were chosen simply because there was no alternative."[22] The Bretton Woods monetary system, on which the whole Amerian military-economic structure had been constructed, simply collapsed. *Business Week* summed up the end of an era:

> The postwar period of U.S. leadership and central bank coordination is now over. The international monetary system is sliding once again into economic competition and financial anarchy. Just as Britain faded from its central role as stabilizer for the West following the erosion of her industrial supremacy, the U.S. is now fading as the pivot for the global economy following the decline of its economic lead. The huge expense of Vietnam and the Great Society programs started the inflationary syndrome that is stripping the dollar of its central role as the universal central currency.[23]

The crisis in the labor movement, like the crisis in other American institutions, was masked by the economic boom of the sixties. Labor union membership has been declining in absolute numbers since 1974, when it peaked at 22.5 million. Unions are doing even worse when membership is measured as a percentage of the workforce. By that measurement, the peak year was 1945, when 35.5 percent of American workers belonged to unions; today only 23.8 percent belong to unions. Organizing on any extensive scale ended when the CIO was transformed from a social movement to a bureaucratic business service institution. The AFL-CIO supported few, if any, of the progressive struggles of the sixties and seventies. It was largely absent from the struggle for black rights, women's rights, and the greatest social movement of the period—the national anti-Vietnam war revolt. During the 1930s there was no great social issue with which the CIO was not identified. Thus, bureaucratic unionism has lost the social respect once given an industrial working-class movement regarded as a great moral force.[24]

By the 1980s the real income of all American workers was on the decline. The high-wage industries which contained the very workers who had pioneered the collective bargaining system were disintegrating. Structural changes caused by American integration into a global manufacturing system had produced what has been called the de-industrialization of the American economy. Massive layoffs and redundancy now face unionized workers in the auto, steel, rubber, maritime, and electrical industries. New technology and the restructuring of the global economy guaranteed that the old soldiers of the class wars of the thirties would simply fade away.

As Emma Rothschild reveals, the much-vaunted service sector of the economy has turned the American labor force into an army of fast food attendants and bellhops. Since 1973 the increase in employment in eating and drinking places is greater than the total employment in the auto and steel industries combined. Total employment in three industries—restaurants, health services, and business services—is greater than the total employment in an entire range of basic productive industries, including construction, all machinery, all electric and electronic equipment, motor vehicles, aircraft, ship-building, all chemicals and products, and all scientific and other instruments.[25] Thus high-wage industries which made up the old CIO are being replaced with low-wage service shops. Xerox machine operators, nurses aides, and waiters have neither the income nor the working conditions carved out by the auto and steel unions in the basic industries. The United States now faces both de-industrialization and de-unionization at an accelerated pace.

From 1950 to 1970 the greatest boom in world capitalist history had produced what appeared to be an affluent society. That boom was based on the automobile, the suburban economy and its concomitant highway construction, and the new miracles of technology, including television and computers. The consumer society created in the fifties was fleshed out by a fortuitous combination of cheap food, cheap energy, government subsidized agriculture and housing, and enormous amounts of credit. By the 1980s that ensemble of growth no longer exists. Its demise was inherent in the nature of the consumer society itself. What in fact had been produced was a dual society. One sector of the workforce, benefiting from the great bargain worked out among capital, labor, and the state, had been granted the entitlements of high wages, paid vacations, seniority protections, dental and medical insurance, and the spurious status of middle-class citizenship. However, a larger sector was left out; these workers had no seniority, no high wages, no health insurance, and no possibility of being absorbed into a primary labor sector which was already shrinking. The trade union structure of the nation was similarly split into rich unions and poor unions. White male union members earned more than women workers doing comparable work, and workers belonging to ethnic and racial minorities were assigned the lowest slots in the occupational pyramid. Members of the construction trades who were still employed prospered while garment and textile workers eked out a living.

Labor force demands in the 1980s are being met by one of the greatest waves of immigration in American history, second only to the great migratory surge of 1910. High-wage, unionized industries are seeking the solution to production costs by instituting a massive program of union give-backs, total automation (including robots and computerized production) of factories and offices, and the movement of entire sections of the production process (if not the industry itself) to low-wage areas. At the same time, nonunionized, low-wage industries are filling the slots at the bottom with immigrants from Asia and Latin America. The wage structure of the unionized industries is now threatened by the huge reserve army of unemployed. What is left of the business union structure in the country has turned supplicant, willing to exchange wages and working conditions for short-term job security.

This time, however, the way out of a systemic crisis eludes militarists, business leaders, and politicians alike. Historical options are limited. War equals total destruction, increased budgets mean more inflation, and wage cuts demand a return to class struggle. Military Keynesianism is a poor substitute for the original panacea that promised something for everybody. It is, perhaps, significant to recall that when the business society of the 1920s collapsed, the American people in general remained in a state of shock for the first years of the 1930s as they hoped for a miracle to turn things around. When no miracle occurred in 1934 the industrial working class took things into its own hands and created history on its own. In a similar fashion the year 1982 surprised the American power holders by producing a mass protest against nuclear war. Hopefully, 1984 may produce, rather than an Orwellian future, a new movement of historically aware Americans armed with a great deal of information and geared to an advanced political struggle which eluded the great industrial working-class movement of the thirties. With the failure of business unionism and the collapse of the affluent society it is not impossible that the present generation of workers might take up the old working-class slogan: "The rich have their money, and the poor have their politics."

Notes

Introduction

1. Mike Davis, "Why the US Working Class Is Different," *New Left Review*, September–October 1980, p. 7.
2. The "corporate liberalism" thesis was developed by the Wisconsin school of New Left and revisionist historians who were the students of William Appleman Williams. In this view, twentieth-century American history simply becomes the product of Big Business. See, for example, James Weinstein, *The Corporate Ideal in the Liberal State, 1900–1918* (Boston: Beacon Press, 1968) and Ronald Radosh, "The Corporate Ideology of American Labor Leaders from Gompers to Hillman," reprinted in James Weinstein and David Eakins, eds., *For a New America: Essays in History and Politics from 'Studies on the Left' 1959–1967* (New York: Random House, 1970).
3. Robert H. Wiebe, *Businessmen and Reform: A Study of the Progressive Movement* (Chicago: Quadrangle Books, 1968), p. 212.
4. Ibid., p. 217.
5. See Edwin M. Epstein, *The Corporation in American Politics* (Englewood Cliffs, N.J.: Prentice Hall, 1969), p. 99.
6. See "A Pervasive Government and 'Voluntary' Regulation," *Business Week*, 50th anniversary issue, September 3, 1979. The magazine of business suggests that, "eventually, 'voluntary' compliance will shake down into a kind of internalized mechanism in which the regulated do their own enforcement while the government hovers overhead as a regulator of last resort in case anyone gets out of line." In short, "business itself will enforce federal rules," as the headline on p. 203 declares.
7. Daniel Bell, quoted in *Newsweek*, December 5, 1975, p. 37.
8. Karl Marx, *Poverty of Philosophy* (1847), quoted by Hal Draper, *Karl Marx's Theory of Revolution*, vol. 2 (New York: Monthly Review Press, 1978), pp. 86–87.
9. Karl Marx, from an article in the *New York Tribune*, 1853, quoted by Draper, *Karl Marx's Theory of Revolution*, vol. 2, p. 96.
10. Richard Hyman, *Marxism and the Sociology of Trade Unionism* (London: Pluto Press, 1971). This is one of the most thorough and scholarly essays I have seen on the theory of trade unionism, and I am much indebted to it.
11. Ibid., p. 38.

12. Such class trade-offs have many historical precedents. Marx, for example, discussing German developments in the nineteenth century, noted that the German bourgeoisie bowed to the political rule of the Prussian aristocracy by exchanging the right to rule for the right to make money. This was the famous alliance of Iron and Rye.

13. Frederick Engels letters to Sorge, December 7, 1889, and February 8, 1890, in *Karl Marx and Frederick Engels: Selected Correspondence,* 2nd ed. (Moscow: Progress Publishers, 1965), pp. 224–25.

14. Ibid. Engels was closely observing the emergence of the Dockworkers' Union in England. Hal Draper, in his discussion of the "New Unionism," writes: "The Dockworkers' Union was the next and decisive step; and a new era of unionism opened up. (It may be compared to the later rise of the CIO in the United States.)" (*Karl Marx's Theory of Revolution,* vol. 2, p. 111). This is exactly the argument I am making in this book.

15. Quoted in Robert V. Bruce, *1877: A Year of Violence* (New York: Bobbs-Merrill, 1959), p. 276.

16. Philip S. Foner, *History of the Labor Movement of the United States,* vol. 2 (New York: International Publishers, 1955), p. 103.

17. For an account of the defeat at Homestead, see Foner, *History of the Labor Movement,* vol. 2, pp. 207–17; for the victory in the Coeur d'Alene, pp. 230–34. The most valuable sources on the Pullman Strike are Senate Executive Document No. 7, 53rd Cong., 2nd sess. (Washington, D.C.: Government Printing Office, 1895) and Almont Lindsey, *The Pullman Strike: The Story of a Unique Experiment and of a Great Labor Upheaval* (Chicago: University of Chicago Press, 1942). *The Railway Times,* the official paper of the industrial-type American Railway Union (ARU) led by Eugene Debs, summed up the lessons of the historic Pullman Strike, which was smashed by federal troops and court injunctions under the direction of President Grover Cleveland: "No it was not a defeat—this ending of the most momentous strike of modern times. It could not be, when we are so near a century that is surely to see the rights of the masses take that place in the policies of nations which is now basely devoted to the privileges of classes." Debs stated during the strike: "Government ownership of railroads is decidely better for the people than railroad ownership of the government." (Quoted by Lindsey, p. 352).

18. Statistics from Foner, *History of the Labor Movement,* vol. 3, pp. 27–29.

19. Milton Derber, "Growth and Expansion," in Milton Derber and Edwin Young, eds., *Labor and the New Deal* (New York: DaCapo Press, 1957), p. 8.

20. Quoted by Foner, *History of the Labor Movement,* vol. 3, p. 210.

21. Ibid.

22. Ibid., p. 211.

23. Allan Nevins and Henry Steele Commager, *A Short History of the United States* (New York: Modern Library, 1945), p. 458.

24. David Brody, *Labor in Crisis: The Steel Strike of 1919* (New York: J. B. Lippincott, 1965), pp. 43–47. See also *Report on the Steel Strike of 1919* by the Commission of Inquiry, the Interchurch World Movement (New York: Harcourt, Brace & Howe, 1920).

25. Brody, *Labor in Crisis,* pp. 113–14.

26. Quoted in ibid. p. 158.

27. Quoted in ibid. pp. 130–33.

28. Ibid.

29. Alfred D. Chandler, Jr., *The Visible Hand: The Managerial Revolution in American Business* (Cambridge: Harvard University Press, 1977), pp. 493–94.

30. Allan J. Lichtman, "Do Americans Really Want 'Coolidge Prosperity' Again?" *Christian Science Monitor,* August 19, 1981. Lichtman is a professor of history at the American University, Washington, D.C.

31. Karl Polanyi, *The Great Transformation: The Political and Economic Origins of Our Time* (Boston: Beacon Press, 1957), pp. 3, 244.
32. Frederick Lewis Allen, *The Lords of Creation* (Chicago: Quadrangle Books, 1966), p. 418.

1. Revolt from Below

1. Data taken from U.S Department of Commerce, Bureau of the Census, *Long Term Economic Growth, 1860–1965: A Statistical Compendium*, ES-4, no. 1 (Washington, D.C.: Government Printing Office, 1970), pp. 191 ff.
2. Herbert Hoover, State of the Union Message, December 6, 1932.
3. Franklin D. Roosevelt, quoted by Irving Bernstein in *Turbulent Years: A History of the American Worker 1933–1941* (Boston: Houghton Mifflin, 1971), pp. 1–2. Bernstein quotes Raymond Moley as stating: "We were agreed that the heart of the recovery program was and must be domestic."
4. Elliot A. Rosen, *Hoover, Roosevelt and the Brains Trust: From Depression to New Deal* (New York: Columbia University Press, 1977), p. 41.
5. Frances Perkins, *The Roosevelt I Knew* (New York: Harper Colophon Books, 1946), p. 183.
6. R. G. Tugwell, *The Brains Trust* (New York: Viking Press, 1969), p. 519.
7. Arthur M. Schlesinger, Jr., *The Age of Roosevelt: The Politics of Upheaval* (Boston: Houghton Mifflin, 1960), pp. 441–42.
8. Bernstein, *Turbulent Years*, p. 3.
9. "The American Federation of Labor," *Fortune* Magazine, December 1933, p. 8.
10. Bernard Karsh and Phillips L. Garman, "The Impact of the Political Left," in Milton Derber and Edwin Young, eds., *Labor and the New Deal* (New York: Da Capo Press, 1957), pp. 83–84.
11. Irving Bernstein, *The Lean Years: A History of the American Worker 1920–1933* (Boston: Houghton Mifflin, 1972), p. 343.
12. See ibid., pp. 432–34; Bert Cochran, *Labor and Communism: The Conflict That Shaped American Unions* (Princeton, N.J.: Princeton University Press, 1977), pp. 63–64; and Frances Fox Piven and Richard A. Cloward, *Poor People's Movements: Why They Succeed, How They Fail* (New York: Pantheon, 1977), p. 59.
13. Cochran, *Labor and Communism*, p. 33.
14. Interview with Robert Wohlforth and Matthew Josephson by Jerold Auerbach, November 6, 1963, Columbia University Oral History Collection.
15. Cochran, *Labor and Communism*, p. 30.
16. John Brooks, *The Great Leap: The Past Twenty-Five Years in America* (New York: Viking, 1966), p. 18.
17. *Fortune* Magazine, June 1937.
18. Cochran, *Labor and Communism*, p. 33.
19. Ibid., p. 42.
20. Melvyn Dubofsky and Warren Van Tine, *John L. Lewis: A Biography* (New York: Quadrangle/The New York Times Book Co., 1977), p. 183.
21. Andrew Shonfield, *Modern Capitalism: The Changing Balance of Public and Private Power* (New York: Oxford University Press, 1965), p. 231.
22. Dubofsky and Van Tine, *John L. Lewis*, p. 184.
23. William E. Leuchtenburg, *Franklin D. Roosevelt and the New Deal 1932–1940* (New York: Harper Colophon Books, 1963), p. 107.
24. Derber and Young, eds., *Labor and the New Deal*, p. 8.
25. Quoted by Dubofsky and Van Tine, *John L. Lewis*, p. 185.

26. See Henry Kraus Papers, File on Auto Workers Union, Archives of Labor History and Urban Affairs, Wayne State University, Detroit, Michigan.
27. Bernstein, *Turbulent Years,* pp. 174–75.
28. Quoted by Dubofsky and Van Tine, *John L. Lewis,* p. 191.
29. Ibid., p. 188.
30. Ibid., p. 190.
31. Ibid.
32. Quoted in ibid., p. 191.
33. Ibid., p. 186.
34. Franklin D. Roosevelt Papers, Roosevelt Library, Hyde Park, New York, Official Files 175.
35. Dubofsky and Van Tine, *John L. Lewis,* p. 192.
36. Bernstein, *Turbulent Years,* p. 175. Bernstein quotes a letter from Roosevelt to Frankfurter on December 22, saying strikes "are so extraordinarily few that I am almost worried by their scarcity. Bob Wagner's Board has done a wonderful job." The quote reveals the intuition of a master politician who understands that executive policy is dependent on the support of social forces. At the very time this letter was written, Ernest T. Weir of Weirton Steel Company and the Budd Manufacturing Company, in Bernstein's words, "openly defied the NLB and brought the agency to it knees" (p. 177).
37. Ibid.
38. Ibid., p. 182. Roosevelt's ruling, in effect, rejected the Reading Formula of majority rule and exclusive representation and substituted for it a system of plural unionism and proportional representation. Company unions were given equal rights with bona fide unions.
39. Ibid., p. 185.
40. "Some Notes on Documentation of Steel Organizing Movement in 1934," Heber Blankenhorn Collection, File 12, Archives of Labor History and Urban Affairs, Wayne State University, Detroit, Michigan.
41. Ibid.
42. Ibid.

2. The General Strike Wave

1. Irving Bernstein in *Turbulent Years: A History of the American Worker 1933–1941* (Boston: Houghton Mifflin, 1971), cites 1,856 work stoppages in 1934 involving 1,470,000 workers (p. 217).
2. Ibid., p. 223.
3. Ibid., p. 224.
4. Ibid., p. 226.
5. For description of the early organization days of what became the International Longshoremen's and Warehousemen's Union (ILWU) see the account by Harry Bridges in the Official Report of Proceedings Before the Immigration and Naturalization Service of the Department of Labor, Docket No. 55073/217. In the Matter of Harry Bridges. Deportation Hearing.
6. Mike Quin, *The Big Strike* (Olema, Calif.: Olema Publishing, 1949), p. 41.
7. Ibid., pp. 43–44. I have relied on Quin as the single best source on the 1934 General Strike in San Francisco. Not only are his facts accurate, but as an eyewitness and sympathetic observer of the events described he is able to reproduce the atmosphere of the period. Unless otherwise cited, basic description and quotations are taken from Quin.
8. Quoted in ibid., p. 53.
9. Ibid.

10. Ibid., p. 55. See also the oral history interview by Roger Lapham, giving his view that the strike was a Communist plot (transcript in the University of California at Berkeley Library).
11. Quin, *The Big Strike*, p. 53.
12. Ibid., p. 59.
13. See ibid., pp. 77–79, for text of Maillard statement and reply by Forbes.
14. Excerpts from Governor Meriam statement, ibid., p. 80.
15. San Francisco Industrial Association telegram to Roosevelt, excerpts quoted in ibid., p. 87.
16. The offer of a bribe to Bridges is well known within union circles on the waterfront, but it has also been confirmed by Randolph Sevier in a 1963 San Francisco interview with Charles Larrowe. Sevier told Larrowe, "Oh, we tried to bribe him all right. The money was put up by an officer of this company" (see Charles P. Larrowe, *Harry Bridges: The Rise and Fall of Radical Labor in the U.S.* [New York: Lawrence Hill, 1972], p. 57).
17. Quoted in Quin, *The Big Strike*, p. 115.
18. Paul Eliel, *The Waterfront and General Strikes* (San Francisco: Industrial Association, 1934), p. 57. Eliel describes the waterfront employers' 1934 strike strategy in this work.
19. Ibid., p. 59.
20. See Official File 407-B for communications to Roosevelt on the 1934 General Strike in San Francisco, and Presidential Press Conference No. 141, Roosevelt Library, Hyde Park, New York.
21. Ibid.
22. Quin, *The Big Strike*, pp. 147–48.
23. Ibid.
24. Quoted in ibid., p. 177.
25. Charles Rumford Walker, *American City* (New York: Farrar & Rinehart, 1937), p. 87.
26. Farrell Dobbs, *Teamster Rebellion* (New York: Monad Press, 1972), p. 56.
27. Ibid., p. 42.
28. Ibid., p. 43.
29. Ibid., p. 61.
30. Ibid., p. 63.
31. Ibid., p. 65.
32. Walker, *American City*, p. 94.
33. Bernstein, *Turbulent Years*, p. 234.
34. Ibid.
35. Ibid.
36. Dobbs, *Teamster Rebellion*, p. 71.
37. Ibid., p. 75.
38. Quoted in Walker, *American City*, pp. 107–08.
39. Dobbs, *Teamster Rebellion*, p. 96.
40. Ibid., p. 102.
41. Walker, *American City*, p. 157.
42. See ibid., chap. 10, "The Civil War in July."
43. Ibid. For testimony on police-employer collusion in the Minneapolis truck strike see "Violations of Free Speech and Assembly and Interference with Rights of Labor," Hearings Before a Subcommittee of the Committee on Education and Labor, United States Senate, 74th Cong., 2nd sess., on Senate Resolution 266, p. 44.
44. Ibid.
45. Dobbs, *Teamster Rebellion*, p. 127.
46. Walker, *American City*, p. 209.

47. Ibid.
48. Bernstein, *Turbulent Years*, p. 248.
49. Ibid., pp. 248–49.
50. Ibid., p. 250.
51. Ibid., p. 251.
52. I have relied on Bernstein, *Turbulent Years*, pp. 298–317, for an account of the great 1934 textile strike. Unless cited otherwise, all quotations are taken from Bernstein. Martha Gellhorn's reports to Harry Hopkins are in the Hopkins manuscript collection at the Roosevelt Library, Hyde Park, New York.
53. Bernstein, *Turbulent Years*, p. 301.
54. Ibid., p. 305.
55. Cited by Bernstein, *Turbulent Years*, p. 309. See Robert R. Brooks, "The United Textile Workers of America" (Ph.D. diss., Yale University, New Haven, Connecticut), chap. 10.
56. Ibid., p. 311.
57. Ibid., p. 315.
58. Henry Kraus Papers, File on Auto Workers Union—Membership 1934, Archives of Labor History and Urban Affairs, Wayne State University, Detroit, Michigan.
59. Wyndham Mortimer, *Organize: My Life as a Union Man* (Boston: Beacon Press, 1971), p. 71.
60. Ibid.
61. See Walter Galenson, *The CIO Challenge to the AFL: A History of the American Labor Movement* (Cambridge: Harvard University Press, 1960), chap. 5, "The Electrical and Radio Manufacturing Industries."
62. Matthew Josephson, *Sidney Hillman: Statesman of American Labor* (New York: Harcourt, Brace, 1952), p. 362.

3. The CIO: Organization of a Social Movement

1. Melvyn Dubofsky and Warren Van Tine, *John L. Lewis: A Biography* (New York: Quadrangle/The New York Times Book Co., 1968), p. 208.
2. Ibid., p. 209.
3. Irving Bernstein, *Turbulent Years: A History of the American Worker* (Boston: Houghton Mifflin, 1971), p. 353.
4. Ibid., p. 355.
5. Ibid., p. 356.
6. See Dubofsky and Van Tine, *John L. Lewis*, p. 211.
7. See Minutes of the Executive Council, AFL, January 29–February 14, 1935, pp. 56–59. Quoted in Dubofsky and Van Tine, *John L. Lewis*, p. 212.
8. Ibid., p. 213.
9. Ibid., p. 214.
10. Ibid., p. 215.
11. Ibid., pp. 215–16.
12. See James MacGregor Burns, *Roosevelt: The Lion and the Fox* (New York: Harcourt, Brace & World, 1956), pp. 218–19; John L. Lewis quoted by Heber Blankenhorn, Blankenhorn Collection, Box 1, 1935–1936, Archives of Labor History and Urban Affairs, Wayne State University, Detroit, Michigan.
13. Dubofsky and Van Tine, *John L. Lewis*, p. 216.
14. Ibid., pp. 216–17.
15. See Proceedings, 1935 Convention, A. F. of L.; Bernstein, *Turbulent Years*, p. 387.
16. Wyndham Mortimer, *Organize: My Life as a Union Man* (Boston: Beacon Press, 1971), p. 91.

17. Quoted in Bernstein, *Turbulent Years,* p. 397, from Edward Levinson, *Labor on the March* (New York: Harper, 1938), pp. 99–117.
18. Dubofsky and Van Tine, *John L. Lewis,* p. 223.
19. Heber Blankenhorn, "Memorandum January 21, 1936, to Mr. Madden, Mr. Carmody, Mr. Smith: From H. Blankenhorn, Subject, Present Status of Lewis Movement," Blankenhorn Collection, Box 1, Archives of Labor History and Urban Affairs, Wayne State University, Detroit, Michigan.
20. Bernstein, *Turbulent Years,* p. 401.
21. Lee Pressman, Oral History Transcript, Columbia University Oral History Collection, vol. 1, p. 92.
22. Bert Cochran, *Labor and Communism: The Conflict That Shaped American Unions* (Princeton, N.J.: Princeton University Press, 1977), pp. 98–99.
23. Harold S. Roberts, *The Rubber Workers: Labor Organization and Collective Bargaining in the Rubber Industry* (New York: Harper and Bros., 1944), p. 64.
24. Ibid., p. 130.
25. Ibid.
26. Ruth Mckenney, *Industrial Valley* (New York: Harcourt, Brace, 1939), p. 250.
27. Roberts, *The Rubber Workers,* p. 145.
28. Mortimer, *Organize,* p. 99.
29. Dubofsky and Van Tine, *John L. Lewis,* p. 230.
30. Roger Keeran, *The Communist Party and the Auto Workers Unions* (Bloomington: Indiana University Press, 1980), p. 142.
31. Sidney Fine, *Sit-Down: The General Motors Strike, 1936–1937* (Ann Arbor: University of Michigan Press, 1969), p. 64.
32. Ibid.
33. See Walter Galenson, *The CIO Challenge to the AFL: A History of the American Labor Movement* (Cambridge: Harvard University Press, 1960), chap. 5, "The Electrical and Radio Manufacturing Industries."
34. Bernstein, *Turbulent Years,* p. 611.
35. Ibid., p. 603.
36. Julius Emspak, Oral History Transcript, Columbia University Oral History Collection, p. 361.
37. Quoted in Bernstein, *Turbulent Years,* p. 613.
38. James J. Matles and James Higgins, *Them and Us: Struggles of a Rank and File Union* (Boston: Beacon Press, 1974), p. 71.
39. Ibid., p. 77.
40. Ibid., p. 79–80.

4. The Roosevelt-CIO Coalition

1. William E. Leuchtenburg, *Franklin D. Roosevelt and the New Deal* (New York: Harper Colophon Books, 1963), p. 231. For a popular account of Roosevelt's battle with the Supreme Court see Joseph Alsop and Turner Catledge, *The 168 Days* (Garden City, N.Y.: Doubleday, 1938).
2. Arthur M. Schlesinger, Jr., *The Politics of Upheaval* (Boston: Houghton Mifflin, 1960), p. 443.
3. *Wall Street Journal,* September 20, 1979, p. 1.
4. Quoted in Schlesinger, *Politics of Upheaval,* p. 634.
5. *Fortune* Magazine, October 1936.
6. *New York Times,* July 26, 1936, p. 2.
7. Melvyn Dubofsky and Warren Van Tine, *John L. Lewis: A Biography* (New York:

Quadrangle/The New York Times Book Co., 1968), p. 251. Text in *United Mine Workers Journal,* August 15, 1936.

8. Ibid.
9. Ibid., p. 252.
10. Quoted in ibid., p. 253.
11. Sidney Fine, *Sit-Down: The General Motors Strike 1936–1937* (Ann Arbor: University of Michigan Press, 1969), p. 140.
12. Quoted in ibid., pp. 182–83.
13. Irving Bernstein, *Turbulent Years: A History of the American Worker 1933–1941* (Boston: Houghton Mifflin, 1971), p. 525.
14. Fine, *Sit-Down,* pp. 187–91.
15. Ibid., p. 201. Sidney Fine's report of the Flint sit-downers relies on the first-hand account by Henry Kraus, *The Many and the Few: A Chronicle of the Dynamic Auto Workers* (Los Angeles: Plantin Press, 1947).
16. Dubofsky and Van Tine, *John L. Lewis,* p. 259.
17. *New York Times,* January 22, p. 1.
18. Fine, *Sit-Down,* p. 259.
19. Bernstein, *Turbulent Years,* pp. 538–39.
20. Wyndham Mortimer, *Organize: My Life as a Union Man* (Boston: Beacon Press, 1971), p. 132. Mortimer reveals that when he replaced Martin at the negotiating table, on the first day that the GM officials actually sat down at the table with the union negotiators Knudsen leaned over the table and said to him, "This is a hell of a committee. It is all lawyers and coal miners and only two auto workers."
21. Quoted in ibid., p. 134.
22. Ibid., p. 135.
23. Ibid. Mortimer says that Governor Murphy showed the UAW negotiating committee the telegram from the AFL and Lewis told him: "I would suggest Governor, that you summon Bill Green to Detroit, and see if he can get these men back to work."
24. Settlement of General Motors Strike, February 10, Heber Blankenhorn Papers, Series 1, Box 1, File 1-37, Archives of Labor History and Urban Affairs, Wayne State University, Detroit, Michigan. Blankenhorn quotes a Lewis version of his conversation with Governor Murphy.
25. Ibid.
26. Mortimer, *Organize,* p. 139.
27. Fine, *Sit-Down,* p. 303.
28. Kraus, *The Many and the Few,* p. 287.
29. Mortimer, *Organize,* p. 143.
30. Bernstein, *Turbulent Years,* p. 551.
31. Quoted in ibid., 554.
32. Lee Pressman, Oral History Transcript, Columbia University Oral History Collection, vol. 1, p. 55.
33. Dubofsky and Van Tine, *John L. Lewis,* p. 273.
34. Matthew Josephson, Oral History Transcript, Interview with Robert Wohlforth and Matthew Josephson by Jerold Auerbach, November 6, 1963, p. 36, Columbia University Oral History Collection.
35. Dubofsky and Van Tine, *John L. Lewis,* p. 276.
36. Bernstein, *Turbulent Years,* p. 471.
37. Ibid.
38. Quoted by Dubofsky and Van Tine, *John L. Lewis,* p. 278.

5. The Limits of Industrial Unionism Under the New Deal

1. Lenin often argued that there were four major bulwarks blocking the road to

revolutionary change in Europe: the Prussian General Staff, the Roman Catholic church, the English House of Lords, and the French Academy.

2. Quoted by Irving Bernstein, *Turbulent Years: A History of the American Worker 1933–1941* (Boston: Houghton Mifflin, 1971), p. 483.

3. See LaFollette Civil Liberties Committee Report, "The Chicago Memorial Day Incident," July 22, 1937.

4. Quoted in Bernstein, *Turbulent Years,* p. 481.

5. Most facts on the Little Steel Strike are taken from Bernstein, *Turbulent Years,* pp. 478–98.

6. Quoted by Melvyn Dubofsky and Warren Van Tine, *John L. Lewis: A Biography* (New York: Quadrangle/The New York Times Book Co., 1968), p. 314.

7. See Franklin D. Roosevelt Press Conferences, Transcripts, vol. 9, p. 467, Roosevelt Library, Hyde Park, New York.

8. Bernstein, *Turbulent Years,* p. 497.

9. Lee Pressman, Oral History Transcript, Columbia University Oral History Collection, p. 194. Pressman reveals that the majority of local organizers and rank-and-file steelworkers associated with SWOC favored a strike against the Little Steel Companies. Murray was thus pushed into a strike he was not prepared for.

10. Bernstein, *Turbulent Years,* pp. 620–21.

11. Quoted in James L. Matles and James Higgins, *Them and Us: Struggles of a Rank and File Union* (Boston: Beacon Press, 1974), p. 98.

12. Pressman, Oral History Transcript, p. 207.

13. Ibid., p. 210.

14. Ibid., p. 215.

15. Ibid.

16. William E. Leuchtenburg, *Franklin D. Roosevelt and the New Deal* (New York: Harper Colophon Books, 1963), p. 273.

17. Interview with Robert Wohlforth and Matthew Josephson by Jerold Auerbach, Columbia University Oral History Collection, pp. 73–74.

18. Carl Haessler, Oral History Transcript, Archives of Labor History and Urban Affairs, Wayne State University, Detroit, Michigan, p. 19.

19. Jerold S. Auerbach, *Labor and Liberty: The LaFollette Committee and the New Deal* (New York: Bobbs-Merrill, 1966), p. 55.

20. Ibid., p. 60.

21. Ibid., p. 65.

22. Robert Wohlforth, Oral History Transcript, p. 17. In answer to the question, "How sympathetic was the administration to the investigation? What kind of help did you get?" Wohlforth replied, "Actually a green light. . . . We got all sorts of help."

23. Pressman, Oral History Transcript, p. 210.

24. Gardner Jackson, Oral History Transcript, Columbia University Oral History Collection, p. 13.

25. Dubofsky and Van Tine record a press interview held by Lewis in Chicago on August 27: "Millions of Americans, he asserted, now desired a third party, and if the two old parties failed to act decisively to reorder national priorities, farmers and workers would know what to do" (*John L. Lewis,* p. 327). The *New York Times* carried the interview on the front page August 28, 1937.

26. *New York Times,* September 4, 1937, p. 1. According to John Brophy, Sidney Hillman scolded Brophy and Pressman for not restraining the "Big Boy" from criticizing Roosevelt publicly (see Dubofsky and Van Tine, *John L. Lewis,* p. 327).

27. Ibid.

28. Letter from Rex Tugwell to Roosevelt, December 14, 1937, President's Personal File 564, Franklin D. Roosevelt Papers, Roosevelt Library, Hyde Park, New York.

29. James T. Patterson, *Congressional Conservatism and the New Deal: The Growth of*

the Conservative Coalition in Congress 1933–1939 (Lexington: University of Kentucky Press, 1967), p. 136.

30. Ibid., p. 189.
31. Quoted in ibid., p. 198.
32. Ibid., p. 213.
33. Leuchtenburg, *Franklin Roosevelt and the New Deal*, p. 248.
34. Bernstein, *Turbulent Years*, p. 687.
35. Pressman, Oral History Transcript, p. 210.
36. Bernstein, *Turbulent Years*, p. 346.
37. Auerbach, *Labor and Liberty*, p. 152.
38. Ibid., p. 164.
39. Ibid., pp. 164–66.
40. Ibid., p. 166.
41. Bernstein, *Turbulent Years*, p. 667.

6. Roosevelt Captures the CIO

1. George Q. Flynn, *American Catholics and the Roosevelt Presidency 1932–1936* (Lexington: University of Kentucky Press, 1968). This and David J. O'Brien, *American Catholics and Social Reform: The New Deal Years* (New York: Oxford University Press, 1968) are excellent sources for the relationship of Roosevelt to the Catholic church.
2. See Association of Catholic Trade Unionists Collection, Archives of Labor History and Urban Affairs, Wayne State University, Detroit, Michigan. This is probably the most extensive collection of materials on Catholic involvement in the American Labor Movement.
3. Carl Haessler, Oral History Transcript, Archives of Labor, History and Urban Affairs, Wayne State University, p. 41. Russell Porter of the *New York Times,* who covered the UAW in Detroit during the 1930s, refers to Haessler as "an honest reporter."
4. Wyndham Mortimer, *Organize: My Life as a Union Man* (Boston: Beacon Press, 1971). Murray attacked Mortimer, Addes, and Hall as reds at the 1939 UAW convention. Mortimer comments, "Now George Addes could by no stretch of the imagination be labeled a Communist. He was the most devout Catholic I ever knew in my life. And Ed Hall was a thirty-second degree Mason" (p. 162).
5. Roger Keeran, *The Communist Party and the Auto Workers Unions* (Bloomington: Indiana University Press, 1980), p. 142.
6. Ibid., p. 143.
7. Ibid., pp. 186–87.
8. Ibid., p. 194.
9. Ibid., p. 125.
10. Ibid., p. 195.
11. Ibid., p. 196.
12. Ibid., p. 203.
13. Ibid., p. 198.
14. Bernstein, *Turbulent Years: A History of the American Worker 1933–1941* (Boston: Houghton Mifflin, 1971), p. 566.
15. Ibid., p. 569.
16. Mortimer, *Organize,* p. 163. Both Lee Pressman in his Oral History and Roger Keeran support Mortimer's assertion that Addes and Mortimer had a substantial majority at the 1939 UAW convention. John Williamson, a leading Communist Party official who was deported to England during the witchhunts after World War II, says in his autobiography: "In my opinion the left-progressive majority made a

mistake in capitulating to the pressure of Murray and Hillman." However, the Left capitulated to Browder, not Hillman.

17. Ibid., p. 162.
18. Ibid. Looking back on the whole affair, Mortimer adds that he thought "we made a tremendous mistake in not just overriding Hillman and Murray. Were it not for the interference of Murray and Hillman at the Cleveland convention a far different CIO would probably exist today [1971]. George Addes or I would unquestionably become President of the UAW, and the union would have played a more militant and decisive role in the years that followed" (p. 162).
19. Bernstein, *Turbulent Years*, p. 557. Mortimer was representative of many loyal Communist worker-militants whose devotion to the cause of the auto workers was greater than it was to narrow party interests. George Addes, on the other hand, was distrusted and hated by the Catholic faction in the UAW for the same reason the Communist Party distrusted Mortimer; Addes could not be controlled by the church and gave his first loyalty to an industrial-union movement he had helped to create in the great 1934 Toledo general strike.
20. Mortimer, *Organize*, p. 163.
21. Keeran, *The Communist Party and the Auto Workers Unions*, p. 200.
22. Melvyn Dubofsky and Warren Van Tine, *John L. Lewis: A Biography* (New York: Quadrangle/The New York Times Book Co., 1968), p. 321.
23. Mortimer, *Organize*, p. 165.
24. *San Francisco Chronicle*, October 11, 1939.
25. Matthew Josephson, *Sidney Hillman: Statesman of American Labor* (New York: Doubleday & Co., 1952), p. 469.
26. Ibid., p. 470.
27. Dubofsky and Van Tine, *John L. Lewis*, p. 330.
28. Ibid.
29. Ibid.
30. Haessler, Oral History Transcript, pp. 58–60.
31. Ibid., p. 67.
32. Ibid., p. 41.
33. Ibid., p. 69.
34. See United Mine Workers of America, District 6 Papers, Ohio University Archives, 1940, p. 103.
35. Saul Alinsky, *John L. Lewis: An Unauthorized Biography* (New York: G. P. Putnam's Sons, 1949), pp. 183–84.
36. Josephson, *Sidney Hillman*, p. 484.
37. Ibid., p. 485.
38. See CIO Convention Proceedings, Archives of Labor History and Urban Affairs, Wayne State University, 1940, for texts of the Lewis-Hillman debate.
39. I once asked Blackie Myers for his opinion on Hillman and he replied: "Sidney was a professional. He knew what he wanted and went after it. If you had power he would deal with you."
40. Josephson, *Sidney Hillman*, pp. 582–83.
41. I was an active member of the National Maritime Union, CIO, from 1942 to 1948 when Myers ran for president of the union in a hotly contested and violent contest against Joseph Curran. Myers lost in a close vote, which many believed to have been a stolen election. Curran then united with the shipowners and the government to expel all leftists from the waterfront. I maintained a close friendship with Myers until he died as a result of an accident suffered on the San Francisco docks. Myers was no different during the period he was a nationally known CIO leader than he was in the years he resumed his life as an ordinary worker and member of the International Longshoremen's and Warehousemen's Union on the West Coast. He was truly representative of the worker-militants who built the CIO, fearless and totally

incorruptible. I was a member of the UE from 1949 to 1953, served as a chief shop steward in a St. Louis local, and was elected a delegate to the 1952 UE national convention.

42. Julius Emspak, Oral History, Columbia University Oral History Collection, p. 272.

7. War Consolidates the Great Bargain

1. Quoted by Ellis Hawley, *The New Deal and the Problem of Monopoly: A Study in Economic Ambivalence* (Princeton: Princeton University Press, 1966), p. 442.
2. James McGregor Burns, *Roosevelt: The Lion and the Fox, 1882–1940* (New York: Harcourt, Brace & World, 1956), p. 373.
3. Ibid., p. 376.
4. Ibid., p. 369.
5. Ibid., p. 336.
6. Ibid., p. 367. On May 16, 1940, Roosevelt appeared before a cheering Congress to ask for almost $1 billion in increased defense spending and set a goal for the production of 50,000 planes a year.
7. Ibid., p. 389.
8. Roger Keeran, *The Communist Party and the Auto Workers Unions* (Bloomington: Indiana University Press, 1980), p. 218.
9. Irving Bernstein, *Turbulent Years: A History of the American Worker 1933–1941* (Boston: Houghton Mifflin, 1971), p. 743.
10. Ibid., p. 751.
11. Wyndham Mortimer, *Organize: My Life as a Union Man* (Boston: Beacon Press, 1971), p. 170.
12. Lee Pressman, Oral History Transcript, Columbia University Oral History Collection, p. 320.
13. Keeran, *The Communist Party*, p. 218. According to Haessler, Mortimer was actually made the scapegoat for Frankensteen, who had sanctioned the strike at North American and bore responsibility. Frankensteen had actually incited the strike before he realized its consequences. Thomas, the president of the UAW, later admitted that there was no way to control wildcat strikes in the defense industry: "When the men are on strike, what can you do? If you don't authorize it, they'll go out anyway."
14. Pressman, Oral History Transcript, pp. 325 and 348.
15. Bernstein, *Turbulent Years*, p. 743.
16. Carl Haessler, Oral History Transcript, Archives of Labor History and Urban Affairs, Wayne State University, Detroit, Michigan, p. 80.
17. Ibid., p. 264.
18. See Association of Catholic Trade Unionist Collection, Archives of Labor History and Urban Affairs, Wayne State University, Detroit, Michigan.
19. Bernstein, *Turbulent Years*, pp. 758–59.
20. Melvyn Dubofsky and Warren Van Tine, *John L. Lewis: A Biography* (New York: Quadrangle/The New York Times Book Co., 1977), p. 397.
21. Ibid., p. 401.
22. Ibid., p. 404.
23. Ibid., p. 405.
24. Ibid., pp. 405–6.
25. Ibid.
26. Ibid., p. 408.
27. Julius Emspak, Oral History Transcript, p. 272.
28. David Brody, *Workers in Industrial America: Essays on the 20th Century Stuggle* (New York: Oxford University Press, 1980), p. 112.

29. Ibid., p. 113.
30. Ibid., p. 114.
31. Ibid., p. 116.
32. Haessler, Oral History Transcript, p. 117. According to Haessler, Walter Reuther, who was classified 1A in the draft, was reclassified when Thomas and Murray intervened with the government to plead that Reuther was essential to the war production program.

8. A Second Bargain Is Struck

1. Robert Skidelsky, ed., *The End of the Keynesian Era* (New York: Holmes & Meier, 1977), Introduction, p. xi.
2. Ibid., p. x.
3. Richard M. Freeland, *The Truman Doctrine and the Origins of McCarthyism: Foreign Policy, Domestic Politics, and Internal Security 1946–1948* (New York: Alfred A. Knopf, 1972), p. 17.
4. Roger Keeran, *The Communist Party and the Auto Workers Unions* (Bloomington: Indiana University Press, 1980), p. 256.
5. Engels letter to Sorge, January 7, 1888, *Karl Marx and Frederick Engels, Letters to Americans 1848–1895,* (New York: International Publishers, 1953), p. 194.
6. *Newsweek,* May 27, 1946. Also see "Reuther Moves Against Communists," *New York Times,* March 31, 1946, and the editorial on the communist issue, May 16, 1946.
7. Freeland, *The Truman Doctrine and the Origins of McCarthyism,* p. 47.
8. Ibid., p. 51.
9. Ibid., p. 99. Senator Vandenberg told President Truman that he would have "to scare hell out of the country" to win approval for his program.
10. Ibid., pp. 99–100.
11. Ibid., p. 100.
12. David Montgomery, *Workers Control in America: Studies in the History of Work, Technology, and Labor Struggle* (London: Cambridge University Press, 1979), p. 166.
13. David Brody, *Workers in Industrial America: Essays on the 20th Century Struggle* (New York: Oxford University Press, 1980), p. 185. There was little, if any, difference in bargaining tactics between unions of the Left and Right. "Pork chops" was the key issue for all unionists who had accepted the bargain to confine their activities to economic and not control issues. In the UE "wage increases had become the chief goal of the union movement in the electrical industry." See Ronald Schatz, "American Electrical Workers: Work, Struggles, Aspirations, 1930–1950" (Ph.D. diss., University of Pittsburgh, 1977), quoted by Brody, p. 191.
14. See CIO Convention Proceedings, 1946.
15. Walter Reuther, "How to Beat the Communists," *Colliers,* February 28, 1948, reprinted in Henry M. Christman, ed., *Walter P. Reuther: Selected Papers* (New York: Macmillan, 1961), p. 32.
16. Ibid.
17. *New York Times,* November 4, 1948, p. 1. *CIO News* quoted by Arthur F. McClure, *The Truman Administration and the Problems of Postwar Labor, 1945–1948* (Cranbury, N.J.: Fairleigh Dickinson University Press, 1969), p. 234.
18. Seyom Brown, *The Faces of Power: Constancy and Change in United States Foreign Policy from Truman to Johnson* (New York: Columbia University Press, 1968), p. 58.
19. For summary of NSC/68, see ibid., pp. 51–54.
20. Engels letter to Marx, October 7, 1958, *Marx and Engels: Selected Correspondence* (Moscow: Progress Publishers, 1955), p. 110.
21. Engels letter to Kautsky, September 12, 1882, in ibid., p. 351.

22. "The Postwar Era of Monetary Leadership by the U.S. Is Now Over," *Business Week,* September 3, 1979.

23. Ibid. Chancellor Helmut Schmidt of West Germany was reported by the press to have confided to friends that in the recent world economic crisis he felt an at a loss in the face of a situation for which economists no longer have any solutions. Nobody, he said, even thinks he knows what to do. Financial leaders on Wall Street were saying the same kind of thing in 1932.

24. See for example, "Labor Day 1977—Can an Aging Leadership Deal With a Troubled Movement?" *New York Times* Magazine, September 4, 1977.

25. Emma Rothschild, "Reagan and the Real America," *New York Review of Books,* February 5, 1981.

Index